Rodolfo Lanciani

Pagan and Christian Rome

Rodolfo Lanciani

Pagan and Christian Rome

ISBN/EAN: 9783744784672

Printed in Europe, USA, Canada, Australia, Japan

Cover: Foto ©Lupo / pixelio.de

More available books at **www.hansebooks.com**

Title: Pagan and Christian Rome

Author: Rodolfo Lanciani

Release Date: July 26, 2007 [EBook #22153]

Language: English

Character set encoding: ISO-8859-1

Transcriber's Notes

1. Footnotes have been moved to the end of the text.
2. Greek transliterations can be found by hovering the mouse over the
   greek text.
3. Typographical errors have been corrected, this is indicated in the
   html like this, hover with the mouse over the word for an
   explanation.

BATTLE BETWEEN CONSTANTINE AND MAXENTIUS

(From a painting by Giulio Romano, Francesco Penni and Raffaellino del Colle)

PAGAN AND CHRISTIAN ROME

BY

RODOLFO LANCIANI

AUTHOR OF "ANCIENT ROME IN THE LIGHT OF RECENT DISCOVERIES"

PROFUSELY ILLUSTRATED

BOSTON AND NEW YORK

HOUGHTON, MIFFLIN AND COMPANY

The Riverside Press, Cambridge

1893

Copyright, 1892,

BY HOUGHTON, MIFFLIN & CO.

All rights reserved.

The Riverside Press, Cambridge, Mass., U.S.A.

Electrotyped and Printed by H.O. Houghton & Co.

CONTENTS

LIST OF ILLUSTRATIONS

FULL-PAGE PLATES

vi

ILLUSTRATIONS IN THE TEXT

vii

The drawings in this volume, with a few exceptions, are by Harold B. Warren, of Boston, who also made the drawings for "Ancient Rome in the Light of Recent Discoveries."

PAGAN AND CHRISTIAN ROME.

CHAPTER I.

THE TRANSFORMATION OF ROME FROM A PAGAN INTO A CHRISTIAN CITY.[1]

The early adoption of Christianity not confined to the poorer classes.—
Instances of Roman nobles who were Christians.—The family of the Acilii
Glabriones.—Manius Acilius the consul.—Put to death because of his religion.
—Description of his tomb, recently discovered.—Other Christian patricians.—
How was it possible for men in public office to serve both Christ and Cæsar?
—The usual liberality of the emperors towards the new religion.—Nevertheless
an open profession of faith hazardous and frequently avoided.—Marriages
between Christians and pagans.—Apostasy resulting from these.—Curious
discovery illustrating the attitude of Seneca's family towards Christianity.—
Christians in the army.—The gradual nature of the transformation of Rome.—
The significance of the inscription on the Arch of Constantine.—The readiness
of the early Church to adopt pagan customs and even myths.—The curious
mixture of pagan and Christian conceptions which grew out of this.—Churches
became repositories for classical works of art, for which new interpretations
were invented.—The desire of the early Christians to make their churches as
beautiful as possible.—The substitution of Christian shrines for the old pagan
altars at street corners.—Examples of both.—The bathing accommodations of
the pagan temples adopted by the Church.—Also the custom of providing
public standards of weights and measures.—These set up in the basilicas.—
How their significance became perverted in the Dark Ages.—The adoption of
funerary banquets and their degeneration.—The public store-houses of the
emperors and those of the popes.—Pagan rose-festivals and their conversion
into a Christian institution.

It has been contended, and many still believe, that in ancient Rome the doctrines of Christ
found no proselytes, except among the lower and poorer classes of citizens. That is certainly
a noble picture which represents the new faith as searching among the haunts of poverty and
slavery, seeking to inspire faith, hope, and charity in their occupants; to transform them from
things into human beings; to make them believe in the happiness of a future life; to alleviate
their present sufferings; to redeem their children from shame and servitude; to proclaim them
equal to their masters. But the gospel found its way also to the mansions of the masters, nay,
even to the palace of the Cæsars. The discoveries lately made on this subject are startling,
and constitute a new chapter in the history of imperial Rome. We have been used to consider
early Christian history and primitive Christian art as matters of secondary importance, and
hardly worthy the attention of the classical student. Thus, none of the four or five hundred

volumes on the topography of ancient Rome speaks of the basilicas raised by Constantine; of the church of S. Maria Antiqua, built side by side with the Temple of Vesta, the two worships dwelling together as it were, for nearly a century; of the Christian burial-grounds; of the imperial mausoleum near S. Peter's; of the porticoes, several miles in length, which led from the centre of the city to the churches of S. Peter, S. Paul, and S. Lorenzo; of the palace of the Cæsars transformed into the residence of the Popes. Why should these constructions of monumental and historical character be expelled from the list of classical buildings? and why should we overlook the fact that many great names in the annals of the empire are those of members of the Church, especially when the knowledge of their conversion enables us to explain events that had been, up to the latest discoveries, shrouded in mystery?

It is a remarkable fact that the record of some of these events should be found, not in church annals, calendars, or itineraries, but in passages in the writings of pagan annalists and historians. Thus, in ecclesiastical documents no mention is made of the conversion of the two Domitillæ, or Flavius Clemens, or Petronilla, all of whom were relatives of the Flavian emperors; and of the Acilii Glabriones, the noblest among the noble, as Herodianus calls them (2, 3). Their fortunes and death are described only by the Roman historians and biographers of the time of Domitian. It seems that when the official *feriale*, or calendar, was resumed, after the end of the persecutions, preference was given to names of those confessors and martyrs whose deeds were still fresh in the memory of the living, and of necessity little attention was paid to those of the first and second centuries, whose acts either had not been written down, or had been lost during the persecutions.

As the crypt of the Acilii Glabriones on the Via Salaria has become one of the chief places of attraction, since its re-discovery in 1888, I cannot begin this volume under better auspices than by giving an account of this important event.[2]

In exploring that portion of the Catacombs of Priscilla which lies under the Monte delle Gioie, near the entrance from the Via Salaria, de Rossi observed that the labyrinth of the galleries converged towards an original crypt, shaped like a Greek Γ (Gamma), and decorated with frescoes. The desire of finding the name and the history of the first occupants of this noble tomb, whose memory seems to have been so dear to the faithful, led the explorers to carefully sift the earth which filled the place; and their pains were rewarded by the discovery of a fragment of a marble coffin, inscribed with the letters: ACILIO GLABRIONI FILIO.

Tablet of Acilius Glabrio.

Did this fragment really belong to the Γ crypt, or had it been thrown there by mere chance? And in case of its belonging to the crypt, was it an isolated record, or did it belong to a group of graves of the Acilii Glabriones? The queries were fully answered by later discoveries; four inscriptions, naming Manius Acilius ... and his wife Priscilla, Acilius Rufinus, Acilius Quintianus, and Claudius Acilius Valerius were found among the débris, so that there is no doubt as to the ownership of the crypt, and of the chapel which opens at the end of the longer arm of the Γ.

The Manii Acilii Glabriones attained celebrity in the sixth century of Rome, when Acilius Glabrio, consul in 563 (B. C. 191), conquered the Macedonians at the battle of Thermopylae. We have in Rome two records of his career: the Temple of Piety, erected by him on the west side of the Forum Olitorium, now transformed into the church of S. Nicola in Carcere; and the pedestal of the equestrian statue, of gilt bronze, offered to him by his son, the first of its kind ever seen in Italy, which was discovered by Valadier in 1808, at the foot of the steps of the temple, and buried again. Towards the end of the republic we find them established on the Pincian Hill, where they had built a palace and laid out gardens which extended at least from the convent of the Trinità dei Monti to the Villa Borghese.[3] The family had grown so rapidly to honor, splendor, and wealth, that Pertinax, in the memorable sitting of the Senate in which he was elected emperor, proclaimed them the noblest race in the world.

The Glabrio best known in the history of the first century is Manius Acilius, who was consul with Trajan, A. D. 91. He was put to death by Domitian in the year 95, as related by Suetonius (*Domit.* 10): "He caused several senators and ex-consuls to be executed on the charge of their conspiring against the empire,—*quasi molitores rerum novarum*,—among them Civica Cerealis, governor of Asia, Salvidienus Orfitus, and Acilius Glabrio, who had previously been banished from Rome."

The expression *molitores rerum novarum* has a political meaning in the case of Cerealis and Orfitus, both staunch pagans, and a religious and political one in the case of Glabrio, a convert to the Christian faith, called *nova superstitio* by Suetonius and Tacitus. Other details of Glabrio's fate are given by Dion Cassius, Juvenal, and Fronto. We are told by these authors that during his consulship, A. D. 91, and before his banishment, he was compelled by Domitian to fight against a lion and two bears in the amphitheatre adjoining the emperor's villa at Albanum. The event created such an impression in Rome, and its memory lasted so long that, half a century later, we find it given by Fronto as a subject for a rhetorical composition to his pupil Marcus Aurelius. The amphitheatre is still in existence, and was excavated in 1887. Like the one at Tusculum, it is partly hollowed out of the rocky side of the mountain, partly built of stone and rubble work. It well deserves a visit from the student and the tourist, on account of its historical associations, and of the admirable view which its ruins command of the vine-clad slopes of Albano and Castel Savello, the wooded plains of Ardea and Lavinium, the coast of the Tyrrhenian, and the islands of Pontia and Pandataria.

Xiphilinus states that, in the year 95, some members of the imperial family were condemned by Domitian on the charge of atheism, together with other leading personages who had embraced "the customs and persuasion of the Jews," that is, the Christian faith. Manius Acilius Glabrio, the ex-consul, was implicated in the same trial, and condemned on the same indictment with the others. Among these the historian mentions Clemens and Domitilla, who were manifestly Christians. One particular of the case, related by Juvenal, confirms the account of Xiphilinus. He says that in order to mitigate the wrath of the emperor and avoid a catastrophe, Acilius Glabrio, after fighting the wild beasts at Albanum, assumed an air of stupidity. In this alleged stupidity it is easy to recognize the prejudice so common among the pagans, to whom the Christians' retirement from the joys of the world, their contempt of public honors, and their modest behavior appeared as *contemptissima inertia*, most despicable laziness. This is the very phrase used by Suetonius in speaking of Flavius Clemens, who was murdered by Domitian *ex tenuissima suspicione*, on a very slight suspicion of his faith.

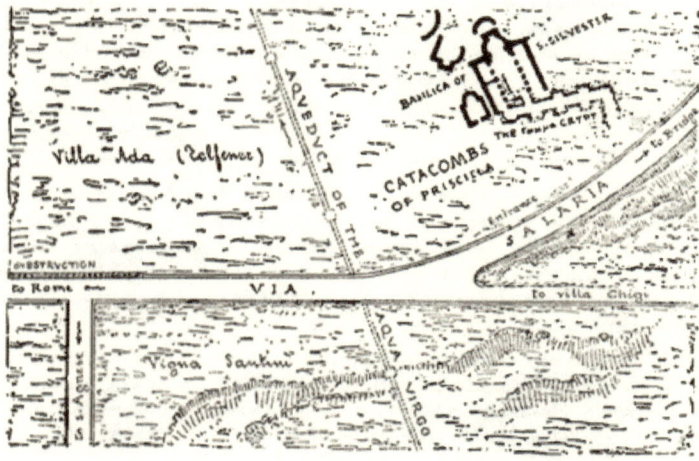

Map of the Via Salaria.

Glabrio was put to death in his place of exile, the name of which is not known. His end helped, no doubt, the propagation of the gospel among his relatives and descendants, as well as among the servants and freedmen of the house, as shown by the noble sarcophagi and the humbler loculi found in such numbers in the crypt of the Catacombs of Priscilla. The small oratory at the southern end of the crypt seems to have been consecrated exclusively to the memory of its first occupant, the ex-consul. The date and the circumstances connected with the translation of his relics from the place of banishment to Rome are not known.

Both the chapel and the crypt were found in a state of devastation hardly credible, as though the plunderers had taken pleasure in satisfying their vandalic instincts to the utmost. Each of the sarcophagi was broken into a hundred pieces; the mosaics of the walls and ceiling had been wrenched from their sockets, cube by cube, the marble incrustations torn off, the altar dismantled, the bones dispersed.

When did this wholesale destruction take place? In times much nearer ours than the reader may imagine. I have been able to ascertain the date, with the help of an anecdote related by Pietro Sante Bartoli in § 144 of his archæological memoirs: "Excavations were made under Innocent X. (1634-1655), and Clement IX. (1667-1670), in the Monte delle Gioie, on the Via Salaria, with the hope of discovering a certain hidden treasure. The hope was frustrated;

but, deep in the bowels of the mound, some crypts were found, encrusted with white stucco, and remarkable for their neatness and preservation. I have heard from trustworthy men that the place is haunted by spirits, as is proved by what happened to them not many months ago. While assembled on the Monte delle Gioie for a picnic, the conversation turned upon the ghosts who haunted the crypt below, when suddenly the carriage which had brought them there, pushed by invisible hands, began to roll down the slope of the hill, and was ultimately precipitated into the river Anio at its base. Several oxen had to be used to haul the vehicle out of the stream. This happened to Tabarrino, butcher at S. Eustachio, and to his brothers living in the Via Due Macelli, whose faces still bear marks of the great terror experienced that day."

9

There is no doubt that the anecdote refers to the tomb of the Acilii Glabriones, which is cut under the Monte delle Gioie, and is the only one in the Catacombs of Priscilla remarkable for a coating of white stucco. Its destruction, therefore, took place under Clement IX., and was the work of treasure-hunters. And the very nature of clandestine excavations, which are the work of malicious, ignorant, and suspicious persons, explains the reason why no mention of the discovery was made to contemporary archæologists, and the pleasure of re-discovering the secret of the Acilii Glabriones was reserved for us.

These are by no means the only patricians of high standing whose names have come to light from the depths of the catacombs. Tacitus (*Annal.* xiii. 32) tells how Pomponia Græcina, wife of Plautius, the conqueror of Britain, was accused of "foreign superstition," tried by her husband, and acquitted. These words long since gave rise to a conjecture that Pomponia Græcina was a Christian, and recent discoveries put it beyond doubt. An inscription bearing the name of ΠΟΜΠΟΝΙΟC ΓΡΗΚΕΓΝΟC has been found in the Cemetery of Callixtus, together with other records of the Pomponii Attici and Bassi. Some scholars think that Græcina, the wife of the conqueror of Britain, is no other than Lucina, the Christian matron who interred her brethren in Christ in her own property, at the second milestone of the Appian Way.

Other evidence of the conquests made by the gospel among the patricians is given by an inscription discovered in March, 1866, in the Catacombs of Prætextatus, near the monument of Quirinus the martyr. It is a memorial raised to the memory of his departed wife by Posturnius Quietus, consul A. D. 272. Here also was found the name of Urania, daughter of Herodes Atticus, by his second wife, Vibullia Alcia,[4] while on the other side of the road, near S. Sebastiano, a mausoleum has been found, on the architrave of which the name URANIOR[UM] is engraved.

10

In chapter vii. I shall have occasion to refer to many Christian relatives of the emperors Vespasian and Domitian. Eusebius, in speaking of these Flavians, and particularly of Domitilla the younger, niece of Domitian, quotes the authority of the historian Bruttius. He evidently means Bruttius Præsens, the illustrious friend of Pliny the younger, and the grandfather of Crispina, the empress of Commodus. In 1854, near the entrance to the crypt of the Flavians, at Torre Marancia (Via Ardeatina), a fragment of a sarcophagus was found, with the name of Bruttius Crispinus. If, therefore, the history of Domitilla's martyrdom was written by the grandfather of Bruttia Crispina, the empress, it seems probable that the two families were united not only by the close proximity of their villas and tombs, and by friendship, but especially by community of religion.

I may also cite the names of several Cornelii, Cæcilii, and Æmilii, the flower of Roman nobility, grouped near the graves of S. Cæcilia and Pope Cornelius; of Liberalis, a *consul suffectus*,[5] and a martyr, whose remains were buried in the Via Salaria; of Jallia Clementina, a relative of Jallius Bassus, consul before A. D. 161; of Catia Clementina, daughter or relative of Catius, consul A. D. 230, not to speak of personages of equestrian rank, whose names have been collected in hundreds.

A difficulty may arise in the mind of the reader: how was it possible for these magistrates, generals, consuls, officers, senators, and governors of provinces, to attend to their duties without performing acts of idolatry? In chapter xxxvii. of the Apology, Tertullian says: "We are but of yesterday, yet we fill every place that belongs to you, cities, islands, outposts; we fill your assemblies, camps, tribes and decuries; the imperial palace, the Senate, the forum; we only leave to you your temples." But here lies the difficulty; how could they fill these places, and leave the temples?

First of all, the Roman emperors gave plenty of liberty to the new religion from time to time; and some of them, moved by a sort of religious syncretism, even tried to ally it with the official worship of the empire, and to place Christ and Jupiter on the steps of the same *lararium*. The first attempt of the kind is attributed to Tiberius; he is alleged to have sent a message to the Senate requesting that Christ should be included among the gods, on the strength of the official report written by Pontius Pilatus of the passion and death of our Lord. Malala says that Nero made honest inquiries about the new religion, and that, at first, he showed himself rather favorable towards it; a fact not altogether improbable, if we take into consideration the circumstances of Paul's appeal, his absolution, and his relations with Seneca, and with the converts *de domo Cæsaris*, "of the house of Cæsar." Lampridius, speaking of the religious sentiments of Alexander Severus, says: "He was determined to raise a temple to Christ, and enlisted him among the gods; a project attributed also to Hadrian. There is no doubt that Hadrian ordered temples to be erected in every city to an unknown god; and because they have no statue we still call them temples of Hadrian. He is said to have prepared them for Christ; but to have been deterred from carrying his plan into execution by the consideration that the temples of the old gods would become deserted, and the whole population turn Christian, *omnes christianos futuros*."[6]

The freedom enjoyed by the Church under Caracalla is proved by the *graffiti* of the Domus Gelotiana, described in my "Ancient Rome."[7] The one caricaturing the crucifixion, which is reproduced on p. 122 of that volume, stands by no means alone in certifying to the spreading of the faith in the imperial palace. The name of Alexamenos, "the faithful," is repeated thrice. There is also a name, LIBANUS, under which another hand has written EPISCOPUS, and, lower down, LIBANUS EPI[SCOPUS]. It is very likely a joke on Libanus, a Christian page like Alexamenos, whom his fellow-disciples had nicknamed "the bishop." It is true that the title is not necessarily Christian, having been used sometimes to denote a municipal officer;[8] but this can hardly be the case in an assembly of youths, like the one of the Domus Gelotiana; and the connection between the *graffiti* of Libanus and those of Alexamenos seems evident. In reading these *graffiti*, now very much injured by dampness, exposure, and the unscrupulous hands of tourists, we are really witnessing household quarrels between pagan and Christian dwellers in the imperial palace, in one of which Caracalla, when still young, saw one of his playmates struck and punished on account of his Christian origin and persuasion.

Septimius Severus and Caracalla issued a constitution,[9] which opened to the Jews the way to the highest honors, making the performance of such ceremonies as were in opposition to the principles of their faith optional with them. What was granted to the Jews by the law of the empire may have been permitted also to the Christians by the personal benevolence of the emperors.

Portrait Bust of Philip the Younger.

When Elagabalus collected, or tried to collect, in his own private chapel the gods and the holiest relics of the universe, he did not forget Christ and his doctrine.[10] Alexander Severus, the best of Roman rulers, gave full freedom to the Church; and once, the Christians having taken possession of a public place on which the *popinarii*, or tavern-keepers, claimed rights, Alexander gave judgment in favor of the former, saying it was preferable that the *place* should serve for divine worship, rather than for the sale of drinks.[11]

There can scarcely be any doubt that the emperor Philip the Arab (Marcus Julius Philippus, A. D. 244), his wife Otacilia Severa, and his son Philip the younger were Christians, and friends of S. Hippolytus. Still, in spite of these periods of peace and freedom of the Church, we cannot be blind to the fact that for a Christian nobleman wishing to make a career, the position was extremely hazardous. Hence we frequently see baptism deferred until mature or old age, and strange situations and even acts of decided apostasy created by mixed marriages.

The wavering between public honors and Christian retirement is illustrated by some incidents in the life of Licentius, a disciple of S. Augustine. Licentius was the son of Romanianus, a friend and countryman of Augustine; and when the latter retired to the villa of Verecundus, after his conversion, in the year 386, Licentius, who had attended his lectures on eloquence at Milan, followed him to his retreat. He appears as one of the speakers in the academic disputes which took place in the villa.[12] In 396, Licentius, who had followed his master to Africa, seduced by the hopes of a brilliant career, determined to settle in Rome. Augustine, deeply grieved at losing his beloved pupil, wrote to call him back, and entreated him to turn his face from the failing promises of the world. The appeal had no effect, and no more had the epistles, in prose and verse, addressed to him for the same purpose by Paulinus of Nola. Licentius, after finishing the course of philosophy, being scarcely a catechumen, and a very unsteady one at that, entered a career for public honors. Paulinus of Nola describes him as aiming not only at a consulship, but also at a pagan pontificate, and reproaches and pities him for his behavior. After this, we lose sight of Licentius in history, but a discovery made at S. Lorenzo fuori le Mura in December, 1862, tells us the end of the tale. A marble sarcophagus was found, containing his body, and his epitaph. This shows that Licentius died in Rome in 406, after having reached the end of his desires, a place in the Senate; and that he died a Christian, and was buried near the tomb of S. Lorenzo. This sarcophagus, hardly noticed by visitors in spite of its great historical associations, is preserved in the vestibule of the Capitoline Museum.

Inscription found near the Porta del Popolo, 1877.

As regards mixed marriages, a discovery made in 1877, near the Porta del Popolo, has revealed a curious state of things. In demolishing one of the towers by which Sixtus IV. had flanked that gate, we found a fragment of an inscription of the second century, containing these strange and enigmatic words: "If any one dare to do injury to this structure, or to otherwise disturb the peace of her who is buried inside, because she, my daughter, has been [or has appeared to be] a pagan among the pagans, and a Christian among the Christians" ... Here followed the specification of the penalties which the violator of the tomb would incur. It was thought at first that the phrase *quod inter fedeles fidelis fuit, inter alienos pagana fuit* had been dictated by the father as a jocose hint of the religious inconsistency of the girl; but such an explanation can hardly be accepted. A passage of Tertullian in connection with mixed marriages leads us to the true understanding of the epitaph. In the second book Ad Uxorem, Tertullian describes the state of habitual apostasy to which Christian girls marrying gentiles willingly exposed or submitted themselves, especially when the husband was kept in ignorance of the religion of the bride. He mentions the risks they would incur of betraying their conscience by accompanying their husbands to state or civil ceremonies, thus sanctioning acts of idolatry by the mere fact of their presence. In the book De Corona, he concludes his argument with the words: "These are the reasons why we do not marry infidels, because such marriages lead us back to idolatry and superstition." The girl buried on the Via Flaminia, by the modern Porta del Popolo, must have been born of a Christian mother and a good-natured pagan father; still, it seems hardly consistent with the respect which the ancients had for tombs that he should be allowed to write such extraordinary words on that of his own daughter.

We must not believe, however, that gentiles and Christians lived always at swords' points. Italians in general, and Romans in particular, are noted for their great tolerance in matters of religion, which sometimes degenerates into apathy and indifference. Whether it be a sign of feebleness of character, or of common sense, the fact is, that religious feuds have never been allowed to prevail among us. In no part of the world have the Jews enjoyed more freedom and tolerance than in the Roman Ghetto. The same feelings prevailed in imperial Rome, except for occasional outbursts of passion, fomented by the official persecutors.

D . M

M . ANNEO
PAVLO . PETRO
M . ANNEVS . PAVLVS
FILIO . CARISIMO

Inscription in a tomb of the
Via Severiana at Ostia.

An inscription was discovered at Ostia, in January, 1867, in a tomb of the Via Severiana, of which I append an accurate copy.

The tomb and the inscription are purely pagan, as shown by the invocation to the infernal gods, Diis Manibus. This being the case, how can we account for the names of Paul and Peter, which, taken separately, give great probability, and taken together give almost absolute certainty, of having been adopted in remembrance of the two apostles? One circumstance may help us to explain the case: the preference shown for the name of Paul over that of Peter; the former was borne by both father and son, the latter appears only as a surname given to the son. This fact is not without importance, if we recollect that the two men who show such partiality for the name of Paul belong to the family of Anneus Seneca, the philosopher, whose friendship with the apostle has been made famous by a tradition dating at least from the beginning of the fourth century. The tradition rests on a foundation of truth. The apostle was tried and judged in Corinth by the proconsul Marcus Anneus Gallio, brother of Seneca; in Rome he was handed over to Afranius Burro, prefect of the prætorium, and an intimate friend of Seneca. We know, also, that the presence of the prisoner, and his wonderful eloquence in preaching the new faith, created a profound sensation among the members of the prætorium and of the imperial household. His case must have been inquired into by the philosopher himself, who happened to be *consul suffectus* at the time. The modest tombstone, discovered by accident among the ruins of Ostia, gives us the evidence of the bond of sympathy and esteem established, in consequence of these events, between the Annei and the founders of the Church in Rome.

Its resemblance to the name of the Annei reminds me of another remarkable discovery connected with the same city, and with the same question. There lived at Ostia, towards the

17

middle of the second century, a manufacturer of pottery and terracottas, named Annius Ser......, whose lamps were exported to many provinces of the empire. These lamps are generally ornamented with the image of the Good Shepherd; but they show also types which are decidedly pagan, such as the labors of Hercules, Diana the huntress, etc. It has been surmised that Annius Ser...... was converted to the gospel, and that the adoption of the symbolic figure of the Redeemer on his lamps was a result of his change of religion; but to explain the case it is not necessary to accept this theory. I believe he was a pagan, and that the lamps with the Good Shepherd were produced by him to order, and from a design supplied to him by a member of the local congregation.

Lamp of Annius Ser......, with figure of the Good Shepherd.

Another question concerning the behavior of early Christians has reference to their military service under the imperial eagles, and to the cases of conscience which may have arisen from it. On this I may refer the reader to the works of Mamachi, Lami, Baumgarten, Le Blant, and de Rossi,[13] who have discussed the subject thoroughly. Speaking from the point of view of material evidence, I have to record several discoveries which prove that officers and men of the *cohortes prætoriæ* and *urbanæ* could serve with equal loyalty their God and their sovereign.

In November, 1885, I was present at the discovery of a marble sarcophagus in the military burial-grounds of the Via Salaria, opposite the gate of the Villa Albani. It bore two inscriptions, one on the lid, the other on the body. The first defies interpretation,[14] the second mentions the name of a little girl, Publia Ælia Proba, who was the daughter of a captain of the ninth battalion of the prætorians, and a lady named Clodia Plautia. They were all Christians; but for a reason unknown to us, they avoided making a show of their persuasion, and were buried among the gentiles.

Another stray Christian military tomb, erected by a captain of the sixth battalion, named Claudius Ingenuus, was found, in 1868, in the Vigna Grandi, near S. Sebastiano. Here also we find the intention of avoiding an open profession of faith. A regular cemetery of Christian prætorians was found in the spring of the same year by Marchese Francesco Patrizi, in his villa adjoining the prætorian camp. It is neither large nor interesting, and it seems to prove that the gospel must have made but few proselytes in the imperial barracks.

We must not believe that the transformation of Rome from a pagan into a Christian city was a sudden and unexpected event, which took the world by surprise. It was the natural result of the work of three centuries, brought to maturity under Constantine by an inevitable reaction against the violence of Diocletian's rule. It was not a revolution or a conversion in the true sense of these words; it was the official recognition of a state of things which had long ceased to be a secret. The moral superiority of the new doctrines over the old religions was so evident, so overpowering, that the result of the struggle had been a foregone conclusion since the age of the first apologists. The revolution was an exceedingly mild one, the transformation almost imperceptible. No violence was resorted to, and the tolerance and mutual benevolence so characteristic of the Italian race was adopted as the fundamental policy of State and Church.

The transformation may be followed stage by stage in both its moral and material aspect. There is not a ruin of ancient Rome that does not bear evidence of the great change. Many institutions and customs still flourishing in our days are of classical origin, and were adopted, or tolerated, because they were not in opposition to Christian principles. Beginning with the material side of the question, the first monument to which I have to refer is the Arch of Constantine, raised in 315 at the foot of the Palatine, where the Via Triumphalis diverges from the Sacra Via.

ARCH OF CONSTANTINE

The importance of this arch, from the point of view of the question treated in this chapter, rests not on its sculptured panels and medallions,—spoils taken at random from older structures, from which the arch has received the nickname of Æsop's crow (*la cornacchia di Esopo*),—but on the inscription engraved on each side of the attic. "The S. P. Q. R. have dedicated this triumphal arch to Constantine, because *instinctu divinitatis* (by the will of God), and by his own virtue, etc., he has liberated the country from the tyrant [Maxentius] and his faction." The opinion long prevailed among archæologists that the words *instinctu divinitatis* were not original, but added after Constantine's conversion. Cardinal Mai thought that the original formula was *diis faventibus*, "by the help of the gods," while Henzen suggested *nutu Iovis optimi maximi*, "by the will of Jupiter." Cavedoni was the first to declare that the inscription had never been altered, and that the two memorable words—the first proclaiming officially the name of the true God in the face of imperial Rome—belonged to the original text, sanctioned by the Senate. The controversy was settled in 1863, when Napoleon III. obtained from the Pope the permission to make a plaster cast of the arch. With the help of the scaffolding, the scholars of the time examined the inscription, the shape of each letter, the holes of the bolts by which the gilt-bronze letters were fastened, the joints of the marble blocks, the color and quality of the marble, and decided unanimously that the inscription had never been tampered with, and that none of its letters had been changed.

The arch was raised in 315. Was Constantine openly professing his faith at that time? Opinions are divided. Some think he must have waited until the defeat of Licinius in 323; others suggest the year 311 as a more probable date of his profession. The supporters of the first theory quote in its favor the fact that the pagan symbols and images of gods appear on coins struck by Constantine and his sons; but this fact is easily explained, when we consider that the coinage of bronze was a privilege of the Senate, and that the Senate was pagan by a large majority. Many of Constantine's constitutions and official letters speak in favor of an early declaration of faith. When the Donatists appealed to him from the verdict of the councils of Arles and Rome, he wrote to the bishops: *Meum judicium postulant, qui ipse judicium Christi expecto*: "They appeal to me, when I myself must be judged by Christ." The verdict of the council of Rome against the sectarians was rendered on October 2, 313, in the "palace of Fausta in the Lateran;" the imperial palace of the Lateran, therefore, had already been handed over to the bishop of Rome, and a portion of it turned into a place of worship. The basilica of the Lateran still retains its title of "Mother and head of all churches of Rome, and of the world," ranking above those of S. Peter and S. Paul in respect to age.

Such being the state of affairs when the triumphal arch was erected, nothing prevents us from believing those two words to be original, and to express the relations then existing between the first Christian emperor and the old pagan Senate. At all events, nothing is more uncompromising than these two words, because the titles of *Deus summus, Deus altissimus, magnus, æternus*, are constantly found on monuments pertaining to the worship of Atys and Mithras. "These words," concludes de Rossi, "far from being a profession of Christianity engraved on the arch at a later period, are simply a 'moyen terme,' a compromise, between the feelings of the Senate and those of the emperor."[15]

Many facts related by contemporary documents prove that the change of religion was, at the beginning, a personal affair with the emperor, and not a question of state; the emperor was a Christian, but the old rules of the empire were not interfered with. In dealing with his pagan subjects Constantine showed so much tact and impartiality as to cast doubts upon the sincerity of his conversion. He has been accused of having accepted from the people of Hispellum (Spello, in Umbria), the honor of a temple, and from the inhabitants of Roman Africa that of a priesthood for the worship of his own family (*sacerdotium Flaviæ gentis*). The exculpation is given by Constantine himself in his address of thanks to the Hispellates:

"We are pleased and grateful for your determination to raise a temple in honor of our family and of ourselves; and we accept it, provided you do not contaminate it with superstitious practices." The honor of a temple and of a priesthood, therefore, was offered and accepted as a political demonstration, as an act of loyalty, and as an occasion for public festivities, both inaugural and anniversary.

Picture of Orpheus found in the Catacombs of Priscilla.

In accepting rites and customs which were not offensive to her principles and morality, the Church showed equal tact and foresight, and contributed to the peaceful accomplishment of the transformation. These rites and customs, borrowed from classical times, are nowhere so conspicuous as in Rome. Giovanni Marangoni, a scholar of the last century, wrote a book on this subject which is full of valuable information.[16] The subject is so comprehensive, and in a certain sense so well known, that I must satisfy myself by mentioning only a few particulars connected with recent discoveries. First, as to symbolic images allowed in churches and cemeteries. Of Orpheus playing on the lyre, while watching his flock, as a substitute for the Good Shepherd, there have been found in the catacombs four paintings, two reliefs on sarcophagi, one engraving on a gem. Here is the latest representation discovered, from the Catacombs of Priscilla (1888).

The Four Seasons, from the Imperial Palace, Ostia.

The belief that the sibyls had prophesied the advent of Christ made their images popular. The church of the Aracœli is particularly associated with them, because tradition refers the origin of its name to an altar—ARA PRIMOGENITI DEI—raised to the son of God by the emperor Augustus, who had been warned of his advent by the sibylline books. For this reason the figures of Augustus and of the Tiburtine sibyl are painted on either side of the arch above the high altar. They have actually been given the place of honor in this church; and formerly, when at Christmas time the *Presepio* was exhibited in the second chapel on the left, they occupied the front row, the sibyl pointing out to Augustus the Virgin and the Bambino who appeared in the sky in a halo of light. The two figures, carved in wood, have now disappeared; they were given away or sold thirty years ago, when a new set of images was offered to the *Presepio* by prince Alexander Torlonia. Prophets and sibyls appear also in Renaissance monuments; they were modelled by della Porta in the Santa Casa at Loretto, painted by Michelangelo in the Sistine chapel, by Raphael in S. Maria della Pace, by Pinturicchio in the Borgia apartments, engraved by Baccio Baldini, a contemporary of Sandro Botticelli, and "graffite" by Matteo di Giovanni in the pavement of the Duomo at Siena.

The images of the Four Seasons are not uncommon on Christian sarcophagi. The latest addition to this class of subjects is to be found in the church of S. Paolo alle Tre Fontane. Four medallions of polychrome mosaic, representing the *Hiems*, *Ver*, *Æstas*, and *Autumnus*, discovered in the so-called imperial palace at Ostia, were inserted in the pavement of this church by order of Pius IX. Galenus and Hippokrates, manipulating medicines and cordials, were painted in the lower basilica at Anagni, Hermes Trismegistos was represented in mosaic in the Duomo di Siena, the labors of Hercules were carved in ivory in the cathedra of S. Peter's. Montfaucon describes the tomb of the poet Sannazzaro in the church of the Olivetans, Naples, as ornamented with the statues of Apollo and Minerva, and with groups of satyrs. In the eighteenth century the ecclesiastical authorities tried to give a less profane aspect to the composition, by engraving the name of David under the Apollo, and of Judith under the Minerva. Another mixture of sacred and profane conceptions is to be found in the names of some of our Roman churches,—as S. Maria in Minerva, S. Stefano del Cacco (Kynokephalos), S. Lorenzo in Matuta, S. Salvatore in Tellure, all conspicuous landmarks in the history of the transformation of Rome.

I shall mention one more instance. The portrait bust of S. Paul, of silver gilt, from the chapel of the Sancta Sanctorum, was loaded with gems and intaglios of Greek or Græco-Roman workmanship, among which was a magnificent cameo with the portrait-head of Nero, which had been worn, most probably, by the very murderer of the apostle.[17]

Ancient Candelabrum in the church of SS. Nereo ed Achilleo.

In the next chapter I shall speak of ancient temples as museums of statuary, galleries of pictures, and cabinets of precious objects. I need not describe the acceptance and development of this tradition by the Church. To it we are indebted for the inexhaustible wealth in works of art of every kind, of which Italy is so proud. But in the period which elapsed between the fall of the empire and the foundation of the Cosmati school, the Christians were compelled, by the want of contemporary productions, to borrow works of art and decorative fragments from temples, palaces, and tombs. The gallery of the Candelabra, in the Vatican museum, has been formed mostly of specimens formerly set up in churches. The accompanying cut represents the candelabrum still existing in the church of SS. Nereo ed Achilleo, one of the most exquisite and delicate works of the kind. The Biga, or two-horse chariot, in the Vatican, was used for centuries as an episcopal throne in the choir of S. Mark's. In the church of the Aracœli there was an altar dedicated to Isis by some one who had returned safely from a perilous journey. This bore the conventional emblem of two footprints, which were believed by the Christians to be the footprints of the angel seen by Gregory the Great on the summit of Hadrian's tomb. Philip de Winghe describes them as those of a *puer quinquennis*, a boy five years old.[18] This curious relic has been removed to the Capitoline Museum.

The indifference with which these profane and sometimes offensive works were admitted within sacred edifices is astonishing. The high altar in the church of S. Teodoro was supported, until 1703, by a round *ara*, on the rim of which the following words are now engraved: "On this marble of the gentiles incense was offered to the gods." Another altar, in the church of S. Michele in Borgo, was covered with bas-reliefs and legends belonging to the superstition of Cybele and Atys; a third, in the church of the Araceli, had been dedicated to the goddess Annona by an importer of wheat. The pavement of the basilica of S. Paul was patched with nine hundred and thirty-one miscellaneous inscriptions; and so were those of S. Martino ai Monti, S. Maria in Trastevere, SS. Giovanni e Paolo, etc. We have one specimen left of these inscribed pavements in the church of SS. Quattro Coronati on the Cælian, which may be called an epigraphic museum.

The Templum Sacræ Urbis (SS. Cosma e Damiano).

In the third chapter I shall have occasion to describe the transformation of nearly all the great public buildings of imperial Rome into places of Christian worship, but it falls within the scope of this chapter to remark that, in many instances, the pagan decorations of those buildings were not affected by the change. When Felix IV. took possession of the *templum sacræ urbis*, and dedicated it to SS. Cosma and Damianus, the walls of the building were covered with incrustations of the time of Septimius Severus representing the wolf and other profane emblems. Pope Felix not only accepted them as an ornament to his church, but tried to copy them in the apse which he rebuilt. The same process was followed by Pope Simplicius (A. D. 468-483), in transforming the basilica of Junius Bassus on the Esquiline into the church of S. Andrea.[19] The faithful, raising their eyes towards the tribune, could see the figures of Christ and his apostles in mosaic; turning to the side walls, they could see Nero, Galba, and six other Roman emperors, Diana hunting the stag, Hylas stolen by the nymphs, Cybele on the chariot drawn by lions, a lion attacking a centaur, the chariot of Apollo, figures performing mysterious Egyptian rites, and other such profanities, represented in *opus sectile marmoreum*, a sort of Florentine mosaic. This unique set of intarsios was destroyed in the sixteenth century by the French Antonian monks for a reason worth relating. They believed that the glutinous substance by which the layer of marble or mother-of-pearl was kept fast was an excellent remedy against the ague; hence every time one of them was attacked by fever, a portion of those marvellous works was sacrificed. Fever must have raged quite fiercely among the French monks, because when this wanton practice was stopped, only four pictures were left. Two are now preserved in the church of S. Antonio, in the chapel of the saint; two in the Palazzo Albani del Drago alle Quattro Fontane, on the landing of the stairs.[20]

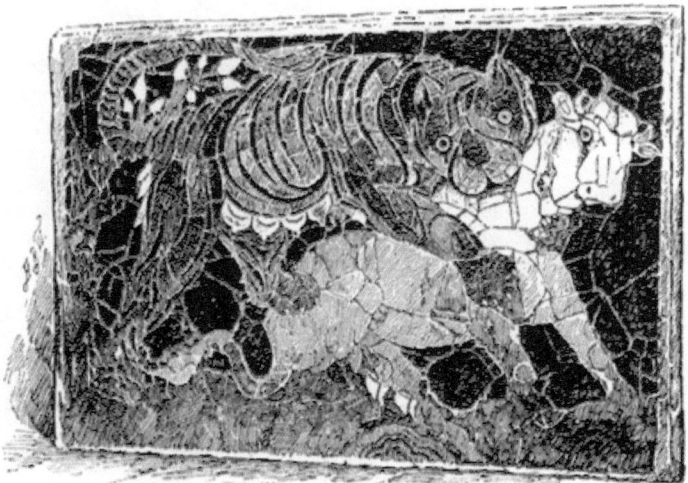

Mosaic from the church of S. Andrea.

Intarsios of the same kind have been seen and described in the basilica of S. Croce in Gerusalemme, in the church of S. Stefano Rotondo, in that of S. Adriano, etc. When the offices adjoining the Senate Hall were transformed into the church of S. Martina, the side walls were adorned with the bas-reliefs of the triumphal arch of M. Aurelius, now in the Palazzo dei Conservatori (first landing, nos. 42, 43, 44). One of them, representing the emperor sacrificing before the Temple of Jupiter, is given opposite page 90.

The decoration of the churches, like that of the temples, was mostly done by private contributions and gifts of works of art. The laying out of the pavement, for instance, or the painting of the walls was apportioned to voluntary subscribers, each of whom was entitled to inscribe his name on his section of the work. The pavement of the lower basilica of Parenzo, in Dalmatia, is divided into mosaic panels of various sizes, representing vases, wreaths, fish, and animals; and to each panel is appended the name of the contributor:—

"Lupicinus and Pascasia made one hundred [square] feet.

"Clamosus and Successa, one hundred feet.

"Felicissimus and his relatives, one hundred feet.

"Fausta, the patrician, and her relatives, sixty feet.

"Claudia, devout woman, and her niece Honoria, made one hundred and ten feet, in fulfilment of a vow."[21]

Theseus killing the Minotaur in the labyrinth of Crete, and labyrinths in general, were favorite subjects for church pavements, especially among the Gauls. The custom is very ancient, a labyrinth having been represented in the church of S. Vitale at Ravenna as early as the sixth century. Those of the cathedral at Lucca, of S. Michele Maggiore at Pavia, of S. Savino at Piacenza, of S. Maria in Trastevere at Rome (destroyed in the restoration of 1867), are of a later date. The image of Theseus is accompanied by a legend in the "leonine" rhythm:—

Theseus intravit, monstrumque biforme necavit.

The symbolism of the subject is explained thus: The labyrinth, so easy of access, but from which no one can escape, is symbolical of human life. At the time of the Crusades, church labyrinths began to be used for a practical purpose. The faithful were wont to go over the meandering paths on their knees, murmuring prayers in memory of the passion of the Lord. Under the influence of this practice the classic and Carolingian name—labyrinth—was forgotten; and the new one of *rues de Jerusalem*, or *leagues*, adopted. The *rues de Jerusalem* in the cathedral at Chartres, designed in blue marble, were 666 feet long; and it took an hour to finish the pilgrimage. Later the labyrinths lost their religious meaning, and became a pastime for idlers and children. The one in the church at Saint-Omer has been destroyed, because the celebration of the office was often disturbed by irreverent visitors trying the sport.[22]

In Rome we have several instances of these private artistic contributions in the service of churches. The pavement of S. Maria in Cosmedin is the joint offering of many parishioners; and so were those of S. Lorenzo fuori le Mura and S. Maria Maggiore before their modern restoration. The names of Beno de Rapiza, his wife Maria Macellaria, and his children Clement and Attilia are attached to the frescoes of the lower church of S. Clemente; and that of Beno alone to the paintings of S. Urbano alla Caffarella. In the apse of S. Sebastiano in Pallara, on the Palatine, and in that of S. Saba on the Aventine, we read the names of a

Benedictus and of a Saba, at whose expense the apses were decorated.

We cannot help following with emotion the development of this artistic feeling even among the lowest classes of mediæval Rome.[23] We read of an Ægidius, son of Hippolytus, a shoemaker of the Via Arenula, leaving his substance to the church of S. Maria de Porticù, with the request that it should be devoted to the building of a chapel, "handsome and handsomely painted, so that everybody should take delight in looking at it." Such feelings, exceptional in many Italian provinces, were common throughout Tuscany. When the triptych of Duccio Buoninsegna, now in the "Casa dell' opera" at Siena, was carried from his studio to the Duomo, June 9, 1310, the whole population followed in a triumphant procession. Renzo di Maitano, another Sienese artist of fame, had the soul of a poet. He was the first to advocate the erection of a church, "grand, beautiful, magnificent, whose just proportions in height, breadth, and length should so harmonize with the details of the decoration as to make it decorous and solemn, and worthy of the worship of Christ in hymns and canticles, for the protection and glory of the city of Siena." So spoke the artists of that age, and their language was understood and felt by the multitudes. Their lives were made bright and cheerful in spite of the troubles and misfortunes which weighed upon their countries. Think of such sentiments in our age!

33

THE TRANSLATION OF S. CYRIL'S REMAINS
(Fresco in S. Clemente, done at the order of Maria Macellaria)

But I am digressing from my subject. Another step of the religious and material transformation of the city is marked by the substitution of chapels and shrines for the old *aræ compitales*, at the crossings of the main thoroughfares. The institution of altars in honor of the *Lares*, or guardian genii of each ward or quarter, is ancient, and can be traced to prehistoric times.

When Servius Tullius enclosed the city with his walls, there were twenty-four such altars, called *sacraria Argeorum*. Two facts speak in favor of their remote antiquity. The priestess of Jupiter was not allowed to sacrifice on them, unless in a savage attire, with hair unkempt and untrimmed. On the 17th of May, the Vestals used to throw into the Tiber, from the Sublician bridge, manikins of wickerwork, in commemoration of the human sacrifices once performed on the same altars.

When Augustus reorganized the capital and its wards, in the year 7 B. C., the number of street-shrines had grown to more than two hundred. Two hundred and sixty-five were registered, A. D. 73, in the census of Vespasian; three hundred and twenty-four at the time of Constantine. A man of much leisure, and evidently of no occupation, the cavaliere Alessandro Rufini, numbered and described the shrines and images which lined the streets of Rome in the year 1853. As modern civilization and indifference will soon obliterate this historical feature of the city, I quote some results of Rufini's investigations.[24] There were 1,421 images of the Madonna, 1,318 images of saints, ornamented with 1,928 precious objects, and 110 ex-votos; 1,067 lamps were kept burning day and night before them,—a most useful institution in a city whose streets have not been regularly lighted until recent years.

The Shrine and Altar of Mercurius Sobrius.

As prototypes of a classical and Christian street-shrine, respectively, we may take the *ædicula compitalis* of Mercurius Sobrius, discovered in April, 1888, near S. Martino ai Monti, and the *immagine di Ponte*, at the corner of the Via dei Coronari and the Vicolo del Micio. The shrine of Mercury near S. Martino was dedicated by Augustus, in the year 10 B. C. The inscription engraved on the front of the altar says: "The emperor Augustus dedicated this shrine to Mercury in the year of the City, 744, from money received as a new-year's gift, during his absence from Rome."

Suetonius (Chapter 57) says that every year, on January 1, all classes of citizens climbed the Capitol and offered *strenæ calendariæ* to Augustus, when he was absent; and that the emperor, with his usual generosity, appropriated the money to the purchase of *pretiosissima deorum simulacra*, "the most valuable statues of gods," to be set up at the crossings of thoroughfares. Four pedestals of these statues have already been found: one near the Arch of Titus, at the beginning of the sixteenth century; one, in 1548, near the Senate House; one, in the same year, by the Arch of Septimius Severus. The fourth pedestal, that recently discovered near S. Martino ai Monti, was raised at the crossing of two important streets, the *clivus suburanus* (Via di S. Lucia in Selci), and the *vicus sobrius* (Via dei Quattro Cantoni), from which the statue was nicknamed *Mercurius Sobrius*, "Mercury the teetotaller."

The *immagine di Ponte*, in the Via dei Coronari, the prototype of modern shrines, contains an image of the Virgin in a graceful niche built, or re-built, in 1523, by Alberto Serra of Monferrato, from designs by Antonio da Sangallo. Its name is derived from that of the lane leading to the Ponte S. Angelo (Canale di Ponte). The house to which it belongs is No. 113 Via dei Coronari, and No. 5 Vicolo del Micio.

Monumental crosses were sometimes erected instead of shrines. Count Giovanni Gozzadini has called the attention of archæologists to this subject in a memoir "Sulle croci monumentali che erano nelle vie di Bologna del secolo XIII." He proves from the texts of historians, Fathers, and councils that the practice of erecting crosses at the junction of the main streets is very ancient, and belongs to the first century of the freedom of the Church, when the faithful withdrew the emblem of Christ from the catacombs, and raised it in opposition to the street shrines of the gentiles. Bologna has the privilege of possessing the oldest of these crosses. One bears the legend "In the name of God; this cross, erected long since by Barbatus, was renewed under the bishopric of Vitalis (789-814)." This class of monuments abounds in Rome, although it belongs to a comparatively recent age. Such are the crosses before the churches of SS. Sebastiano, Cesareo, Nereo ed Achilleo, Pancrazio, Lorenzo, Francesco a Ripa, and others. 36

The most curious and interesting is perhaps the column of Henry IV. of France, which was erected under Clement VIII. in front of S. Antonio all' Esquilino, and which the modern generation has concealed in a recess on the east side of S. Maria Maggiore. It is in the form of a culverin—a long slender cannon of the period—standing upright. From the muzzle rises a marble cross supporting the figure of Christ on one side, and that of the Virgin on the other. It was erected by Charles d'Anisson, prior of the French Antonians, to commemorate the absolution given by Clement VIII. to Henry IV. of France and Navarre, on September 17 of the year 1595. The monument has a remarkable history. Although apparently erected by private enterprise, the kings of France regarded it as an insult of the Curia, an official boast of their submission to the Pope; and they lost no opportunity of showing their dissatisfaction in consequence. Louis XIV. found an occasion for revenge. The gendarmes who had escorted his ambassador, the duc de Crequi, to Rome, had a street brawl with the Pope's Corsican body-guards; and although it was doubtful which side was to blame, Louis obliged Pope Alexander VII. to raise a pyramid on the spot where the affray had taken place, with the following humiliating inscription:—

"In denunciation of the murderous attack committed by the Corsican soldiers against his Excellency the duc de Crequi, Pope Alexander VII. declares their nation deprived forever of the privilege of serving under the flag of the Church. This monument was erected May 21, 1664, according to the agreement made at Pisa."

The revenge could not have been more complete; so bitter was it that Alexander VII. drew a violent protest against it, to be read and published only after his death. His successor, 37

Clement IX., a favorite with Louis XIV., obtained leave that the pyramid should be demolished, which was done in June, 1668, with the consent of the French ambassador, the duc de Chaulnes. Whether by stipulation or by the good will of the Pope, the inscription of the column of Henry IV. was made to disappear at the same time. We have found it concealed in a remote corner of the convent of S. Antonio.[25] The column itself, and the canopy which sheltered it, fell to the ground on Thursday, February 15, 1744; and when Benedict XIV. restored the monument in the following year, he severed forever its connection with these remarkable historical events, by dedicating it DEIPARÆ VIRGINI. Having been dismantled in 1875, during the construction of the Esquiline quarter, it was reërected in 1880, not far from its original place, on the east side of S. Maria Maggiore,—not without opposition, because there are always men who think they can obliterate history by suppressing monuments which bear testimony to it.

One of the characteristics of ancient sanctuaries, by which the weary pilgrim was provided with bathing accommodations, is also to be found in the old churches of Rome. We are told in the "Liber Pontificalis" that Pope Symmachus (498-514), while building the basilica of S. Pancrazio, on the Via Aurelia, *fecit in eadem balneum*, "provided it with a bath." Another was erected by the same Pope near the apse of S. Paolo fuori le Mura, the supply of water of which was originally derived from a spring; later from wheels, or noriahs, established on the banks of the Tiber. Notices were written on the walls of these bathing apartments, warning laymen and priests to observe the strictest rules of modesty. One of these inscriptions, from the baths annexed to the churches of SS. Sylvester and Martin, is preserved in section II. of the Christian epigraphic museum of the Lateran. It ends with the distich:— 38

NON NOSTRIS NOCET OFFICIIS NEC CULPA LABACRI
QUOD SIBIMET GENERAT LUBRICA VITA MALUM EST,—

"There is no harm in seeking strength and purity of body in baths; it is not water but our own bad actions that make us sin." These verses are not so good as their moral; but inscriptions like this prove that the abandonment of such useful institutions must be attributed not to the undue severity of Christian morality, but to the ruin of the aqueducts by which fountains and baths were fed. However, even in the darkest period of the Middle Ages we find the traditional "kantharos," or basin, in the centre of the quadri-porticoes or courts by which the basilicas were entered. Such is the vase in the court of S. Cæcilia, represented on the next page, and that in front of S. Cosimato in Trastevere; and such is the famous *calix marmoreus*, which formerly stood near the church of SS. Apostoli, mentioned in the Bull of John III. (A. D. 570), by which the boundary line of that parish was determined. This historical monument, a prominent landmark in the topography of mediæval Rome, was removed to the Baths of Diocletian at the beginning of last year.

In many of our churches visitors may have noticed one or more round black stones, weighing from ten to a hundred pounds, which, according to tradition, were tied to the necks of martyrs when they were thrown into wells, lakes, or rivers. To the student these stones tell a different tale. They prove that the classic institution of the *ponderaria* (sets of weights and 39 measures) migrated from temples to churches, after the closing of the former, A. D. 393.

Kantharos in the Court of St. Cæcilia.

As the *amphora* was the standard measure of capacity for wine, the *metreta* for oil, the *modius* for grain, so the *libra* was the standard measure of weight.[26] To insure honesty in trade they were examined periodically by order of the ædiles; those found *iniquæ* (short) were broken, and their owners sentenced to banishment in remote islands. In A. D. 167, Junius Rusticus, prefect of the city, ordered a general inspection to be made in Rome and in the provinces; weights and measures found to be legal were marked or stamped with the legend "[Verified] by the authority of Q. Junius Rusticus, prefect of the city." These weights of Rusticus are discovered in hundreds in Roman excavations.[27]

The original standards were kept in the Temple of Jupiter on the Capitol, and used only on extraordinary occasions. Official duplicates were deposited in other temples, like those of Castor and Pollux, Mars Ultor, Ops, and others, and kept at the disposal of the public, whence their name of *pondera publica*. Barracks and market-places were also furnished with them. The most important discovery connected with this branch of Roman administration was made at Tivoli in 1883, when three *mensæ ponderariæ*, almost perfect, were found in the portico or peribolos of the Temple of Hercules, adjoining the cathedral of S. Lorenzo. This wing of the portico is divided into compartments by means of projecting pilasters, and each recess is occupied by a marble table resting on "trapezophoroi" richly ornamented with symbols of Hercules and Bacchus, like the club and the thyrsus. Along the edge of two of the tables runs the inscription, "Made at the expense of Marcus Varenus Diphilus, president of the college of Hercules," while the third was erected at the expense of his wife Varena. The tables are perforated by holes of conical shape, varying in diameter from 200 to 380 millimetres. Brass measures of capacity were fastened into each hole, for use by buyers and sellers. They were used in a very ingenious way, both as dry and liquid measures. The person who had bought, for instance, half a modius of beans, or twenty-four *sextarii* of wine, and wanted to ascertain whether he had been cheated in his bargain, would fill the receptacle to the proper line, then open the valve or spicket below, and transfer the tested contents again to his sack or flask.

41

The institution was accepted by the Church, and *ponderaria* were set up in the principal basilicas. The best set which has come down to us is that of S. Maria in Trastevere, but there is hardly a church without a "stone" weighing from five or ten to a hundred pounds. The popular superstition by which these practical objects were transformed into relics of martyrdoms is very old. Topographers and pilgrims of the seventh century speak of a stone exhibited in the chapel of SS. Abundius and Irenæus, under the portico of S. Lorenzo fuori le Mura, "which, in their ignorance, pilgrims touch and lift." They mention also another weight, exhibited in the church of S. Stephen, near S. Paul's, which they believed to be one of the stones with which the martyr was killed.

In 1864 a *schola* (a memorial and banqueting hall) was discovered in the burial grounds adjoining the prætorian camp, which had been used by members of a corporation called the *sodalium serrensium*, that is, of the citizens of Serræ, a city of Samothrake, I believe. Among the objects pertaining to the hall and its customers were two measures for wine, a *sextarium*, and a *hemina*, marked with the monogram of Christ and the name of the donor.[28] They are now exhibited in the *sala dei bronzi* of the Capitoline museum.

42

The hall of the citizens of Serræ, discovered in 1864, belongs to a class of monuments very common in the suburbs of Rome. They were called *cellæ, memoriæ, exedræ*, and *scholæ*, and were used by relatives and friends of the persons buried under or near them, in the performance of expiatory ceremonies or for commemorative banquets, for which purpose all the necessaries, from the table-service to the festal garments, were kept on the spot, in cabinets entrusted to the care of a watchman. This practice—save the expiatory offerings—was adopted by the Christians. The *agapai*, or love-feasts, before degenerating into those excesses and superstitions so strongly denounced by the Fathers of the Church, were celebrated over or near the tombs of martyrs and confessors, the treasury of the local congregation supplying food and drink, as well as the banqueting robes. In the inventory of the property confiscated during the persecution of Diocletian, in a house at Cirta

(Constantine, Algeria), which was used by the faithful as a church, we find registered, chalices of gold and silver, lamps and candelabras, eighty-two female tunics, sixteen male tunics, thirteen pairs of men's boots, forty-seven pairs of women's shoes, and so on.[29] A remarkable discovery, illustrating the subject, has been lately made in the Catacombs of Priscilla; that of a *graffito* containing this sentence: "February 5, 375, we, Florentinus, Fortunatus, and Felix, came here AD CALICE[M] (for the cup)." To understand the meaning of this sentence, we must compare it with others engraved on pagan tombs. In one, No. 25,861 of the "Corpus," the deceased says to the passer-by: "Come on, bring with you a flask of wine, a glass, and all that is needed for a libation!" In another, No. 19,007, the same invitation is worded: "Oh, friends (*convivæ*), drink now to my memory, and wish that the earth may be light on me." We are told by S. Augustine[30] that when his mother, Monica, visited Milan in 384, the practice of eating and drinking in honor of the martyrs had been stopped by S. Ambrose, although it was still flourishing in other regions, where crowds of pilgrims were still going from tomb to tomb with baskets of provisions and flasks of wine, drinking heavily at each station. Paulinus of Nola and Augustine himself strongly stigmatized the abuse. The faithful were advised either to distribute their provisions to the poor, who crowded the entrances to the crypts, or to leave them on the tombs, that the local clergy might give them to the needy. There is no doubt that the record *ad calicem venimus*, scratched by Florentinus, Fortunatus, and Felix on the walls of the Cemetery of Priscilla, refers to these deplorable libations.

Many drinking-cups used on these occasions have been found in Rome, in my time. They are generally works of the fourth century of our era, cut in glass by unskillful hands, and they show the portrait-heads of SS. Peter and Paul, in preference to other subjects of the kind. This fact is due not only to the special veneration which the Romans professed for the founders of their church, but also

Sample of a Drinking-cup.

to the habit of celebrating their anniversary, June 29, with public or domestic *agapai*. S. Peter's day was to the Romans of the fourth century what Christmas is to us, as regards joviality and sumptuous banquets. On one of these occasions S. Jerome received from his friend Eustochio fruit and sweets in the shape of doves. In acknowledging the kind remembrance, S. Jerome recommends sobriety on that day more than on any other: "We must celebrate the birthday of Peter rather with exaltation of spirit, than with abundance of food. It is absurd to glorify with the satisfaction of our appetites the memory of men who pleased God by mortifying theirs." The poorer classes of citizens were fed under the porticoes of the Vatican basilica. The gatherings degenerated into the display of such excesses of drunkenness that Augustine could not resist writing to the Romans: "First you persecuted the martyrs with stones and other instruments of torture and death; and now you persecute their memory with your intoxicating cups."

The institution of public granaries (*horrea publica*) for the maintenance of the lower classes was also accepted and favored by Christian Rome. On page 250 of my "Ancient Rome," I have spoken of the warehouses for the storage of wheat, built by Sulpicius Galba on the plains of Testaccio, near the Porta S. Paolo, named for him *horrea galbana*, even after their purchase by the state. These public granaries originated at the time of Caius Gracchus and his grain laws. Their scheme was developed, in course of time, by Clodius, Pompey, Seianus, and the emperors, to such an extent that, in 312 A. D., there were registered in Rome alone two hundred and ninety granaries. They may be divided into three classes: In the first, and by far the most important, a plentiful supply of breadstuffs was kept at the expense of the state, to meet emergencies of scarcity or famine, and the wants of a population one third of which was fed gratuitously by the sovereign. The second was intended especially for the storage of paper (*horrea chartaria*), candles (*horrea candelaria*), spices (*horrea piperataria*), and other such commodities. The third class consisted of buildings in which the citizens might deposit their goods, money, plate, securities, and other valuables for which they had no place of safety in their own houses. There were also private *horrea*, built on speculation, to be let as strong-rooms like our modern vaults, storage-warehouses, and "pantechnicons."

45

The building of the new quarter of the Testaccio, the region of *horrea* par excellence, has given us the chance of studying the institution in its minutest details. I shall mention only one discovery. We found, in 1885, the official advertisement for leasing a *horrea*, under the empire of Hadrian. It is thus worded:—

"To be let from to-day, and hereafter annually (beginning on December 13): These warehouses, belonging to the Emperor Hadrian, together with their granaries, wine-cellars, strong-boxes, and repositories.

"The care and protection of the official watchmen is included in the lease.

"Regulations: I. Any one who rents rooms, vaults, or strong-boxes in this establishment is expected to pay the rent and vacate the place before December 13.

"II. Whoever disobeys regulation No. I., and omits to arrange with the *horrearius* (or keeper-in-chief) for the renewal of his lease, shall be considered as liable for another year, the rent to be determined by the average price paid by others for the same room, vault, or strong-box. This regulation to be enforced in case the *horrearius* has not had an opportunity to rent the said room, vault, or strong-box to other people.

"III. Sub-letting is not allowed. The administration will withdraw the watch and the guarantee from rooms, vaults, or strong-boxes which have been sub-let in violation of the existing rules.

46

"IV. Merchandise or valuables stored in these warehouses are held by the administration as security for payment of rental.

"V. The tenant will not be reimbursed by the administration for improvements, additions, and other such work which he has undertaken on his own account.

"VI. The tenant must give an assignment of his goods to the keeper-in-chief, who shall not be held responsible for the safe-keeping of merchandise or valuables which have not been duly declared. The tenant must claim a receipt for the said assignment and for the payment of his rental."[31]

The granaries of the Church were intended only for the storage of corn. The landed estates which the Church owned in Africa and Sicily were administered by deputies, whose special duty it was to ship the produce of the harvest to Rome. During the first siege of Totila, in 546, Pope Vigilius, then on his way to Constantinople, despatched from the coast of Sicily a fleet of grain-laden vessels, under the care of Valentine, bishop of Silva Candida. The attempt to relieve the city of the famine proved useless, and the vessels were seized by the besiegers on their landing at Porto. In 589 an inundation of the Tiber, described by Gregoire de Tours, carried away several thousand bushels of grain, which had been stored in the *horrea ecclesiæ*, and the granaries themselves were totally destroyed.

The "Liber Pontificalis," vol. i. p. 315, describes the calamities which befell the city of Rome in the year 605; King Agilulf trying to enter the city by violence; heavy frosts killing the vines; rats destroying the harvest, etc. However, as soon as the barbarians were induced to retire by an offer of twelve thousand *solidi*, Pope Sabinianus, who was then the head of the Church, *iussit aperiri horrea ecclesiæ* (threw open the granaries), and offered their contents at auction, at a valuation of one *solidus* for thirty *modii*.

A Granary of Ostia.

The grain was not intended to be sold, but to be distributed among the needy; the act of Sabinianus was, therefore, strongly censured, as being in strong contrast to the generosity of Gregory the Great. A legend on this subject is related by Paulus Diaconus in chapter xxix. of the Life of Gregory. He says that Gregory appeared thrice to Sabinianus, in a vision, entreating him to be more generous; and having failed to move him by friendly advice, he struck him dead. The price of one *solidus* for thirty *modii* is almost exorbitant; grain cost exactly one half this at the time of Theodoric.

The institution has outlived all the vicissitudes of the Middle Ages. Gregory XIII., in 1566, Paul V., in 1609, Clement XI., in 1705, re-opened the *horrea ecclesiæ* in the ruined halls of the Baths of Diocletian; and Clement XIII. added a wing to them, for the storage of oil. These buildings are still in existence around the Piazza di Termini, although devoted to other purposes.

It would be impossible to follow in all its manifestations the material and moral transformation of Rome from the third to the sixth centuries, without going beyond the limits of a single chapter.

The customs and practices of the classical age were so deeply rooted among the citizens that even now, after a lapse of sixteen centuries, they are noticeable to a great extent. When we read, for instance, of Popes elected by the people assembled at the Rostra,[32] such as Stephen III., in 768, we must regard the circumstance as caused by a remembrance of past ages. Under the pontificate of Innocent II. (1130), of Eugenius III. (1145-1150), and of Lucius III. (1181-1185) the senators, or municipal magistrates, used to sit and administer justice in S. Martina and S. Adriano, that is, in the classic Roman Curia. Many other details will be incidentally described in the following chapters. I close the present one by referring to a graceful custom, borrowed likewise from the classic world,—the use of roses in church or funeral ceremonies and in social life.

The ancients celebrated, in the month of May, a feast called *rosaria*, in which sepulchres were profusely decorated with the favorite flower of the season. Roses were also used on occasions of public rejoicing. A Greek inscription, discovered by Fränkel at Pergamon, mentions, among the honors shown to the emperor Hadrian, the *Rhodismos*, which is interpreted as a scattering of roses. Traces of the custom are found in more recent times. In the Illyrian peninsula, and on the banks of the Danube, the country people, still feeling the influence of Roman civilization, celebrated feasts of flowers in spring and summer, under the name of *rousalia*. In the sixth century, when the Slavs were vacillating between the influence of the past and the present, the celebration of the Pentecost was mixed up with that of the half-pagan, half-barbarous *rousalia*. Southern Russians believe in supernatural female beings, called *Rusalky*, who bring prosperity to the fields and forests, which they have inhabited as flowers.

The early Christians decorated the sepulchres of martyrs and confessors, on the anniversary of their interment, with roses, violets, amaranths, and evergreens; and they celebrated the *rosationes* on the name-days of churches and sanctuaries. Wreaths and crowns of roses are often engraved on tombstones, hanging from the bills of mystic doves. The symbol refers more to the joys of the just in the future life than to the fleeting pleasures of the earth. The Acts of Perpetua relate a legend on this subject; that Saturus had a vision in the dungeon in which he was awaiting his martyrdom, in which he saw himself transported with Perpetua to a heavenly garden, fragrant with roses, and turning to his fair companion, he exclaimed: "Here we are in possession of that which our Lord promised!"

Roses and other flowers are painted on the walls of historical cubiculi. In a fresco of the crypts of Lucina, in the Catacombs of Callixtus, are painted birds, symbolizing souls who have been separated from their bodies, and are playing in fields of roses around the Tree of Life. As the word *Paradeisos* signifies a garden, so its mystic representation always takes the form of a delightful field of flowers and fruit. Dante gives to the seat of the blessed the shape of a fair rose, inside of which a crowd of angels with golden wings descend and return to the Lord:—

> "Nel gran fior discendeva, che s'adorna
> Di tante foglie: e quindi risaliva,
> Là dove lo suo amor sempre soggiorna."[33]
>
> *Paradiso*, xxxi. 10-12.

Possibly it is from this allegory of paradise that the rite of the "golden rose" which the Pope blesses on Quadragesima Sunday is derived. The ceremony is very ancient, although the first mention of it appears only in the life of Leo IX. (1049-1055); and I may mention, as a curious coincidence, that the kings and queens of Navarre, their sons, and the dukes and peers of the realm, were bound to offer roses to the Parliament at the return of spring.

Roses played such an important part in church ceremonies that we find a *fundus rosarius* given as a present by Constantine to Pope Mark. The *rosaria* outlived the suppression of pagan superstitions, and by and by assumed its Christian form in the feast of Pentecost, which falls in the month of May. In that day roses were thrown from the roofs of churches on the worshipers below. The Pentecost is still called by the Italians *Pasqua rosa*.

50

51

CHAPTER II.

PAGAN SHRINES AND TEMPLES.

Ancient temples as galleries of art.—The adornment of statues with jewelry, etc.—Offerings and sacrifices by individuals.—Stores of ex-votos found in the *favissæ* or vaults of temples.—Instances of these brought to light within recent

Ancient guide-books of Rome, published in the middle of the fourth century,[34] mention four hundred and twenty-four temples, three hundred and four shrines, eighty statues of gods, of precious metal, sixty-four of ivory, and three thousand seven hundred and eighty-five miscellaneous bronze statues. The number of marble statues is not given. It has been said, however, that Rome had two populations of equal size, one alive, and one of marble.

I have had the opportunity of witnessing or conducting the discovery of several temples, altars, shrines, and bronze statues. The number of marble statues and busts discovered in the last twenty-five years, either in Rome or the Campagna, may be stated at one thousand.

Before beginning the description of these beautiful monuments, I must allude to some details concerning the management and organization of ancient places of worship, upon which recent discoveries have thrown a considerable, and in some cases, unexpected light.

Roman temples, like the churches of the present day, were used not only as places of worship, but as galleries of pictures, museums of statuary, and "cabinets" of precious objects. In chapter v. of "Ancient Rome," I have given the catalogue of the works of art displayed in the temple of Apollo on the Palatine. The list includes: The Apollo and Artemis driving a quadriga, by Lysias; fifty statues of the Danaids; fifty of the sons of Egypt; the Herakles of Lysippos; Augustus with the attributes of Apollo (a bronze statue fifty feet high); the pediment of the temple, by Bupalos and Anthermos; statues of Apollo, by Skopas; Leto, by Kephisodotos, son of Praxiteles; Artemis, by Timotheos; and the nine Muses; also a chandelier, formerly dedicated by Alexander the Great at Kyme; medallions of eminent men; a collection of gold plate; another of gems and intaglios; ivory carvings; specimens of palæography; and two libraries.

Entablature of the Temple of Concord.

The Temple of Apollo was by no means the only sacred museum of ancient Rome; there were scores of them, beginning with the Temple of Concord, so emphatically praised by Pliny. This temple, built by Camillus, at the foot of the Capitol, and restored by Tiberius and Septimius Severus, was still standing at the time of Pope Hadrian I. (772-795), when the inscription on its front was copied for the last time by the *Einsiedlensis*. It was razed to the ground towards 1450. "When I made my first visit to Rome," says Poggio Bracciolini, "I saw the Temple of Concord almost intact (*ædem fere integram*), built of white marble. Since then the Romans have demolished it, and turned the structure into a lime-kiln." The platform of the temple and a few fragments of its architectural decorations were discovered in 1817. The reader may appreciate the grace of these decorations, from a fragment of the entablature now in the portico of the Tabularium, and one of the capitals of the cella, now in the Palazzo dei Conservatori. The cella contained one central and ten side niches, in which eleven masterpieces of Greek chisels were placed, namely, the Apollo and Hera, by Baton; Leto nursing Apollo and Artemis, by Euphranor; Asklepios and Hygieia, by Nikeratos; Ares and Hermes, by Piston; and Zeus, Athena, and Demeter, by Sthennis. The name of the sculptor of the Concordia in the apse is not known. Pliny speaks also of a picture by Theodoros, representing Cassandra; of four elephants, cut in obsidian, a miracle of skill and labor, and of a collection of precious stones, among which was the sardonyx set in the legendary ring of Polykrates of Samos. Most of these treasures had been offered to the goddess by Augustus, moved by the liberality which Julius Cæsar had shown towards his ancestral goddess, Venus Genetrix. We know from Pliny, xxxv. 9, that Cæsar was the first to give due honor to paintings, by exhibiting them in his Forum Julium. He gave about $72,000 (eighty talents), for two works of Timomachos, representing Medea and Ajax. At the base of the Temple of Venus Genetrix he placed his own equestrian statue, the horse of which, modelled by

Lysippos, had once supported the figure of Alexander the Great. The statue of Venus was the work of Arkesilaos, and her breast was covered with strings of British pearls. Pliny (xxxvii. 5), after mentioning the collection of gems made by Scaurus, and another made by Mithradates, which Pompey the Great had offered to Jupiter Capitolinus, adds: "These examples were surpassed by Cæsar the dictator, who offered to Venus Genetrix six collections of cameos and intaglios."

A descriptive catalogue of these valuables and works of art was kept in each temple, and sometimes engraved on marble. The inventories included also the furniture and properties of the sacristy. In 1871 the following remarkable document was discovered in the Temple of Diana Nemorensis. The inventory, engraved on a marble pillar three feet high, is now preserved in the Orsini Castle at Nemi. It has been published by Henzen in "Hermes," vol. vi. p. 8, and reads as follows, in translation:—

Objects offered to [or belonging to] both temples [the temple of Isis and that of Bubastis]:— Seventeen statues; one head of the Sun; four silver images; one medallion; two bronze altars; one tripod (in the shape of one at Delphi); a cup for libations; a patera; a diadem [for the statue of the goddess] studded with gems; a sistrum of gilded silver; a gilt cup; a patera ornamented with ears of corn; a necklace studded with beryls; two bracelets with gems; seven necklaces with gems; nine ear-rings with gems; two nauplia [rare shells from the Propontis]; a crown with twenty-one topazes and eighty carbuncles; a railing of brass supported by eight *hermulæ*; a linen costume comprising a tunica, a pallium, a belt, and a stola, all trimmed with silver; a like costume without trimming.

[Objects offered] to Bubastis:—A costume of purple silk; another of turquoise color; a marble vase with pedestal; a water jug; a linen costume with gold trimmings and a golden girdle; another of plain white linen.

The objects described in this catalogue did not belong to the Temple of Diana itself, one of the wealthiest in central Italy; but to two small shrines, of Isis and Bubastis, built by a devotee within the sacred enclosure, on the north side of the square.

The ancients displayed remarkably bad taste in loading the statues of their gods with precious ornaments, and in spoiling the beauty of their temples with hangings of every hue and description. A document published by Muratori[35] speaks of a statue of Isis which was dedicated by a lady named Fabia Fabiana as a memorial to her deceased granddaughter Avita. The statue, cast in silver, weighed one hundred and twelve and a half pounds, and was muffled in ornaments and jewelry beyond conception. The goddess wore a diadem in which were set six pearls, two emeralds, seven beryls, one carbuncle, one *hyacinthus*, and two flint arrow-heads; also earrings with emeralds and pearls, a necklace composed of thirty-six pearls and eighteen emeralds, two clasps, two rings on the little finger, one on the third, one on the middle finger; and many other gems on the shoes, ankles, and wrists. Another inscription discovered at Constantine, Algeria, describes a statue of Jupiter dedicated in the Capitol of that city. The devotees had placed on his head an oak-wreath of silver, with thirty leaves and fifteen acorns; they had loaded his right hand with a silver disk, a Victory waving a palm-leaf, and a crown of forty leaves; and in the other had fastened a silver rod and other emblems.

The hangings and tinsel not only disfigured the interior of temples, but were a source of danger from their combustibility. When we hear of fires destroying the Pantheon in A. D. 110, the Temple of Apollo in 363, that of Venus and Rome in 307, and that of Peace in 191, we may assume that they were started and fed by the inflammable materials with which the interiors were filled. There is no other explanation to be given, inasmuch as the structures were fire-proof, with the exception of the roof. As for the disfiguration of sacred buildings with all sorts of hangings, it is enough to quote the words of Livy (xl. 51). "In the year of Rome, 574, the censors M. Fulvius Nobilior and M. Æmilius Lepidus restored the temple of Jupiter on the Capitol. On this occasion they removed from the columns all the tablets, medallions, and military flags *omnis generis* which had been hung against them."

The right of performing sacrifices was sometimes granted to civilians, on payment of a fee. An 57 inscription discovered among the ruins of the Temple of Malakbelos, outside the Porta Portese, on the site of the new railway station, relates how an importer of wine, Quintus Octavius Daphnicus, having built at his own expense a banqueting hall within the sacred enclosure, was rewarded with the *immunitas sacrum faciendi*, that is, the right of performing sacrifices without the assistance of priests. The performances were regulated by tariffs, which specified a price for every item; and one of these has actually survived to our day.[36]

D....

For the blood of —— (perhaps a bull)	——
And for its hide	——
If the victim be entirely burnt	xxv asses.
For the blood and skin of a lamb	iv asses.
If the lamb be entirely burnt	vi½ asses.

For a cock (entirely burnt)	ii½ asses.
For blood alone	xiii asses.
For a wreath	iv asses.
For hot water (per head)	ii asses.

The meaning of this tariff will be easily understood if we recall the details of a Græco-Roman sacrifice, in regard to the apportionment of the victim's flesh. The parts which were the perquisite of the priests differ in different worships; sometimes we hear of legs and skin, sometimes of tongue and shoulder. In the case of private sacrifices the rest of the animal was taken home by the sacrificer, to be used for a meal or sent as a present to friends. This was, of course, impossible in the case of "holocausts," in which the victim was burnt whole on the altar. In the Roman ritual, hides and skins were always the property of the temple.[37] In the above tariff two prices are charged: a smaller one for ordinary sacrifices, when only the intestines were burnt, and the rest of the flesh was taken home by the sacrificer; a larger one for "holocausts," which required a much longer use of the altar, spit, gridiron, and other sacrificial instruments. Four asses are charged for each crown or wreath of flowers, half that amount for hot water.

The site of a sanctuary can be determined not only from its actual ruins, but, in many cases, from the contents of its *favissæ*, or vaults, which are sometimes collected in a group, sometimes spread over a considerable space of ground. The origin of these deposits of terra-cotta or bronze votive objects is as follows:—

Each leading sanctuary or place of pilgrimage was furnished with one or more rooms for the exhibition and safe-keeping of ex-votos. The walls of these rooms were studded with nails on which ex-voto heads and figures were hung in rows by means of a hole on the back. There were also horizontal spaces, little steps like those of a *lararium*, or shelves, on which were placed those objects that could stand upright. When both surfaces were filled, and no room was left for the daily influx of votive offerings, the priests removed the rubbish of the collection, that is, the terra-cottas, and buried them either in the vaults (*favissæ*) of the temple, or in trenches dug for the purpose within or near the sacred enclosure.

During these last years I have been present at the discovery of five deposits of ex-votos, each marking the site of a place of pilgrimage. The first was found in March, 1876, on the site of a temple of Hercules, outside the Porta S. Lorenzo; the second in the spring of 1885, on the site of the Temple of Diana Nemorensis; the third in 1886, near the Island of Æsculapius (now of S. Bartolomeo); the fourth in 1887, near the shrine of Minerva Medica; the last in 1889, on the site of the Temple of Juno at Veii.

The existence of a temple of Hercules, outside the Porta S. Lorenzo, within the enclosure of the modern cemetery, was first made known in 1862, in consequence of the discovery of an altar raised to him by Marcus Minucius, the "master of the horse" or lieutenant-general of Q. Fabius Maximus (217 b. c.). This altar is now exhibited in the Capitoline Museum.[38] Fourteen years later, in 1876, the *favissæ* of the temple were found in the section of the cemetery called the Pincio. There were about two hundred pieces of terra-cotta, vases of

Etruscan and Italo-Greek manufacture; several statuettes of bronze, and pieces of *æs rude*, and *æs grave librale*, one of them from the town of Luceria. This deposit seems to have been buried at the beginning of the sixth century of Rome.

Nemi and the site of the Temple of Diana.
A Platform of the Temple of Diana. *B* Village of Nemi and Castle of the Orsinis.

The excavation of the temple of Diana Nemorensis was undertaken in 1885, by Sir John Savile Lumley, now Lord Savile of Rufford, the English ambassador at Rome, with the kind consent of the Italian government. It seems that this *Artemisium Nemorense* was not only a place of worship and devotion, but also a hydro-therapeutic establishment. The waters employed for the cure were those which spring from the lava rocks at Nemi, and which, until a few years ago, fell in graceful cascades into the lake, at a place called "Le Mole." They now supply the city of Albano, which has long suffered from water-famine. I can vouch for their therapeutic efficiency from personal experience; in fact I could honestly put up my votive offering to the long-forgotten goddess, having recovered health and strength by following the old cure. Diana, however, was chiefly worshipped in this

60

Portrait Bust of Person cured at Nemi.

place as Diana Lucina. I need not enter into particulars on this subject. The ex-votos collected in large quantity by Lord Savile, representing young mothers nursing their first-born, and other offerings of the same nature, testify to the skill of the priests. Perhaps they practised

61

other branches of surgery, because, among the curiosities brought to light in 1885, are several figures with large openings on the front, through which the intestines are seen. Professor Tommasi-Crudeli, who has made a study of this class of curiosities, says that they cannot be considered as real anatomical models, because the work is too rough and primitive to enable us to distinguish one intestine from the other. The number of objects collected by Lord Savile may be estimated at three thousand.

The stem of the ship of the Island of the Tiber.

Characteristic objects of a like nature—breasts cut open and showing the anatomy—have been found in large numbers in and near the island of the Tiber, where the Temple of Æsculapius stood, at the stern of the marble ship. It seems that the street leading from the Campus Martius to the Pons Fabricius, and across it to the temple, was lined with shops and booths for the sale of ex-votos, as is the case now with the approaches to the sanctuaries of Einsiedeln, Lourdes, Mariahilf, and S. Jago. In the foundations of the new quays of the Tiber, above and below the bridge, the ex-votos have been found in regular strata along the line of the banks, whereas in the island itself they have come to light in much smaller quantities. As the votive objects deposited in this sanctuary, from the year 292 before Christ to the fall of the Empire, may be counted not by thousands, but by millions of specimens, I believe that the bed of the Tiber must have been used as a *favissa*.

The name of Minerva Medica is familiar to students and visitors of old Rome;[39] but the monument which bears it, a nymphæum of the gardens of the Licinii, near the Porta Maggiore, has no connection whatever with the goddess of wisdom. Minerva Medica was the name of a street on the Esquiline, so called from a shrine which stood at the crossing, or near the crossing, with the Via Merulana, not far from the church of SS. Pietro e Marcellino. Its foundations and its deposit of ex-votos were discovered in 1887.

Fragment of a Lamp inscribed with the name of Minerva.

The shape and nature of the offerings bear witness to numberless cases of recovery performed by the merciful goddess, the Athena Hygieia or Paionia of the Greeks. There is a fragment of a lamp inscribed with her name, which leaves no doubt as to the identity of the deposit. There is also a votive head, not cast from the mould, but modelled *a stecco*, which alludes to Minerva as a restorer of hair. The scalp is covered with thick hair in front and on the top, while the sides are bald, or showing only an incipient growth. It is evident, therefore, that the woman whose portrait-head we have found had lost her curls in the course of some malady, and having regained them through the intercession of Minerva, as she piously believed, offered her this curious token of gratitude. This, at least, is Visconti's opinion. Another testimonial of Minerva's efficiency in restoring hair has been found at Piacenza, a votive tablet put up MINERVÆ MEMORI by a lady named Tullia Superiana, RESTITUTIONE SIBI FACTA CAPILLORUM (for having restored her hair).

Votive Head.

As regards the multitude of ex-votos, no other temple or deposit discovered in my time can be compared with the *favissæ* of the Temple of Juno at Veii. In Roman traditions this temple was regarded as the place where Camillus emerged from the *cuniculus*, or mine, on the day of the capture of the city. The story runs that Camillus, having carried his *cuniculus* under the Temple of Juno within the citadel, overheard the Etruscan *aruspex* declare to the king of Veii that victory would rest with him who completed the sacrifice. Upon this, the Roman soldiers burst through the floor, seized the entrails of the victims, and bore them to Camillus, who offered them to the goddess with his own hand, while his followers were gaining possession of the city. The account is certainly more or less fabricated; but, as Livy remarks, "it is not worth while to prove or disprove these things." We are content to know that within the citadel of Veii, the "Piazza d' Armi" of the present day, there was a temple of great veneration and antiquity, and that it was dedicated to Juno. Both points have been proved and illustrated by modern discoveries.

The Cliffs under the Citadel of Veii (now called Piazza d' Armi).

The ex-votos of the Latin sanctuaries were, as I have just remarked, buried in the *favissæ*; but at Veii, because of the danger and the difficulty of excavating them within the citadel, and in solid rock, the ex-votos were carted away and thrown from the edge of the cliff into the valley below. The place selected was the north side of the rocky ridge connecting the citadel with the city, which ridge towers one hundred and ninety-eight feet above the cañon of the Cremera. The mass of objects thrown over here in the course of centuries has produced a slope which reaches nearly to the top of the cliff. The reader will appreciate the importance of the deposit from the fact that the mine has been exploited ever since the time of Alexander

65

VII. (1655-1667); and in the spring of 1889, when the most recent excavations were made, by the late empress Theresa of Brazil, the mass of terra-cottas brought to the surface was such that work had to be given up after a few days, because there was no more space in the farmhouse for the storage of the booty. Pietro Sante Bartoli left an account of the excavations made on the same spot by cardinal Chigi, during the pontificate of Alexander VII. Modern topographers do not seem to be aware of this fact; it is not mentioned by Dennis, or Gell, or Nibby, although it is the only evidence left of the discovery of the famous sanctuary. "Not far from the Isola Farnese a hill [the Piazza d' Armi], rises from the valley of the Cremera, on the plateau of which cardinal Chigi has discovered a beautiful temple with fluted columns of the Ionic order. The frieze is carved with trophies and panoplies of various kinds; the reliefs of the pediment represent the emperor Antoninus[?] sacrificing a ram and a sow, and although the panels lie scattered around the temple, and the figures are broken, apparently no important piece is missing. There is also an altar four feet high, with figures of Etruscan type, which was removed to the Palazzo Chigi [now Odescalchi]. The columns and marbles of the temple were bought by cardinal Falconieri to build and ornament a chapel in the church of S. Giovanni de' Fiorentini.... Not far from the temple a stratum of ex-votos has been found, so rich that the whole of Rome is now overrun with terra-cottas. Every part of the human body is represented,—heads, hands, feet, fingers, eyes, noses, mouths, tongues, entrails, lungs, symbols of fecundity, whole figures of men and women, horses, oxen, sheep, pigs,—in such quantities as to make several hundred cartloads. There were also bronze statuettes, sacred utensils, and mirror-cases, which were all stolen or destroyed. I have known of one workman breaking marvellous objects (*cose insigni*) into small fragments to melt them into handles for knives."

When the farms of Isola Farnese and Vaccareccia, in which the remains of Veii and of its extensive cemeteries are situated, were sold, a few years ago, by the empress of Brazil to the marchese Ferraioli, the parties concerned agreed that the right of excavating and the objects discovered should belong to her, for a limited number of years, up to 1891, I believe. The first campaign, opened January 2, 1889, and closed in June, must be considered as one of the most valuable contributions to the study of Etruscan civilization which have been supplied of late to students, either by chance or by design. Had the empress been able to carry out her plans for two or three years more, the whole city and necropolis would have been explored, surveyed, and illustrated, in the most strictly scientific manner. Political events and the death of this noble woman brought the enterprise to a close. To come back, however, to the bed of votive objects in terra-cotta and bronze, I was able to make a rough estimate of its dimensions, which are two hundred and fifty feet in length, fifty feet in width, and from three to four in depth; nearly forty-four thousand cubic feet. The objects collected in two weeks number four thousand; the fragments buried again as worthless, double that number. The heads of veiled goddesses alone amount to four hundred and forty-seven, of which three hundred and seventy are full-faced, the rest in profile. The vein contains fifty-two varieties of types; to Bartoli's list, we must add busts, masks, arms, breasts, wombs, spines, bowels, lungs, toes, figures cut open across the breast and showing the anatomy, figures approximately human, or male and female embryos ending like the trunk of a tree with stumps corresponding to the feet, figures of hermaphrodites, human torsos modelled purposely without heads, arms without hands, legs without feet, hands holding apples or jewel-caskets, figurines of mothers nursing twins, beautiful life-sized statues of draped women, with movable hands and feet, rats, wild boars, sucking pigs, cows, rams, apples and other fruits, and "marbles."

The first structures dedicated to the gods in Rome were called *aræ*, and had the shape of a cube of masonry, in the centre of a square platform. They were modelled, in a measure, on the pattern of the Pelasgic *hierones*, in which the territory of Tibur and Signia is especially abundant. The *aræ* best known in Roman history and topography are six in number, namely, the *ara maxima Herculis*; the *Roma quadrata*; the *ara Aii Locutii*; the *ara Ditis et Proserpinæ*; the *ara pacis Augustæ*; and the *ara incendii Neroniani*. The oldest of these were built of rough stones; those of later periods took the characteristic shape of the altar of Verminus, represented on page 52 of my "Ancient Rome," and of the altar raised to Vedjovis by the members of the Julian family, at Bovillæ, their birthplace, where it was found by the Colonnas in 1823. It is now in the villa of that family on the Quirinal.[40] In imperial times the conventional shape was preserved, with the addition of two *pulvini*, or volutes, on the opposite edges of the cornice, as represented in the illustration on page 35 of "Ancient Rome" (a marble altar found at Ostia).

A Pelasgic hieron, or platform of altar, at Segni.

THE ARA MAXIMA HERCULIS. This altar, the oldest in Rome, was raised in memory of the visit of Hercules to our country. Tacitus and Pliny attribute its construction to Evander the Arcadian, forgetting that in prehistoric times the tract of land on which the altar stood, between the Forum Boarium and the Circus Maximus, was submerged by the waters of the Velabrum. It was at all events a very ancient structure, held in great veneration. Its rough shape and appearance were never changed, as shown by a precious—yet unpublished—sketch by Baldassarre Peruzzi which I found among his autographs in Florence. A round temple was built near the altar, in later times, of which we know two particulars: first, that it had a mysterious

Round Temple of Hercules in the Forum Boarium.

power of repulsion for dogs and flies;[41] second, that it contained, among other works of art, a picture by the poet Pacuvius, next in antiquity and value to the one painted by Fabius Pictor, in the Temple of Health, in 303 B. C.[42] The Temple of Hercules, the Ara Maxima, and the bronze statue of the hero-god were discovered, in a good state of preservation, during the pontificate of Sixtus IV., between the apse of S. Maria in Cosmedin (the Temple of Ceres), and the Circus Maximus. We have a description of the discovery by Pomponio Leto, Albertini, and Fra Giocondo da Verona; and excellent drawings by Baldassarre Peruzzi.[43]

Except the bronze statue, and a few votive inscriptions, which were removed to the Capitoline Museum, everything—temple, altar, and platform—was levelled to the ground by the illustrious Vandals of the Renaissance.

THE ROMA QUADRATA. According to the ancient ritual, the founder of a city, after tracing the *sulcus primigenius* or furrow which marked its limits, buried the plough, the instruments of sacrifice, and other votive offerings, in a round hole, excavated in the centre of the marked space. The round hole was called *mundus*, and its location was indicated by a heap of stones, which in course of time took the shape of a square altar. The *mundus* of ancient Rome was located in the very heart of the Palatine, in front of the Temple of Apollo, and the altar upon it was named the *Roma Quadrata*. This name has been much discussed, and it has even been applied to the Palatine city itself, although it is an established fact that there is, strictly speaking, no connection between the two. The controversy has been resumed lately by Professor Luigi Pigorini in a paper still unpublished which was read at the sitting of the German Institute, December 17, 1890; and by Professor Otto Richter in his pamphlet *Die älteste Wohnstätte des römischen Volks*, Berlin, 1891.

In view of the ignorance of ancient writers on this subject, and the almost absurd definitions they give of the word, we had come to the conclusion that the altar had been removed or concealed by Augustus, when he built the Temple of Apollo and the Portico of the Danaids, in 28 B. C. A remarkable inscription discovered September 20, 1890 (to which I shall refer at length later), by mentioning the Roma Quadrata as existing A. D. 204, shows that our opinion was wrong, and that the old altar, the most venerable monument of Roman history, had survived the vicissitudes of time, and the transformation of the Palatine from the cradle of the city into the palace of the Cæsars.

In December, 1869, when the nuns of the Visitation were laying the foundations of a new wing of their convent on the area of the Temple of Apollo,[44] I saw a line of square pilasters at the depth of forty-one feet below the pavement of the Portico of the Danaids, and in the centre of the line a heap of stones, either of tufa or peperino, roughly squared. It is more than probable that, in 1869, I did not think of the Roma Quadrata, and of its connection with those remains, so deeply buried in the heart of the hill; but I am sure that a careful investigation of that sacred spot would lead to very important results.

THE ARA OF AIUS LOCUTIUS. In 1820, while excavations were proceeding near the western corner of the Palatine (at the spot marked No. 7, on the plan, page 106, of "Ancient Rome"), an altar was discovered, of archaic type, inscribed with the following dedication: "Sacred to a Divinity, whether male or female. Caius Sextius Calvinus, son of Caius, praetor, has restored this altar by decree of the Senate." Nibby and Mommsen believe Calvinus to be the magistrate mentioned twice by Cicero as a candidate against Glaucias in the contest for the praetorship of 125 B. C. They also identify the altar as (a restoration of) the one raised behind the Temple of Vesta, in the "lower New Street," in memory of the mysterious voice announcing the invasion of

Ara of Aius Locutius on the Palatine.

the Gauls, in the stillness of the night, and warning the citizens to strengthen the walls of their city. The voice was attributed to a local Genius, whom the people named Aius Loquens or Locutius. As a rule, the priests refrained from mentioning in public prayers the name and sex of new and slightly known divinities, especially of local Genii, to which they objected for two reasons: first, because there was danger of vitiating the ceremony by a false invocation; secondly, because it was prudent not to reveal the true name of these tutelary gods to the enemy of the commonwealth, lest in case of war or siege he could force them to abandon the defence of that special place, by mysterious and violent rites. The formula *si deus si dea,* "whether god or goddess," is a consequence of this superstition; its use is not uncommon on ancient altars; Servius describes a shield dedicated on the Capitol to the Genius of Rome, with the inscription: GENIO URBIS ROMÆ SIVE MAS SIVE FEMINA, "to the tutelary Genius of the city of Rome, whether masculine or feminine." The Palatine altar, of which I give an illustration, cannot fail to impress the student, on account of its connection with one of the leading events in history, the capture and burning of Rome by the Gauls, 390 B. C.

THE ARA DITIS ET PROSERPINÆ. On the 20th of September, 1890, the workmen employed in the construction of the main sewer on the left bank of the Tiber, between the Ponte S. Angelo and the church of S. Giovanni dei Fiorentini, found a mediæval wall, built of materials collected at random from the neighboring ruins. Among them were fragments of one or more inscriptions which described the celebrations of the *Ludi Sæculares* under the Empire. By the end of the day, seventeen pieces had been recovered, seven of which belonged to the records of the games celebrated under Augustus, in the year 17 B. C., the others to those celebrated under Septimius Severus and Caracalla, in the year 204 A. D. Later researches led to the discovery of ninety-six other fragments, making a total of one hundred and thirteen, of which eight are of the time of Augustus, two of the time of Domitian, and the rest date from Severus.

The fragments of the year 17 B. C., fitted together, make a block three metres high, containing one hundred and sixty-eight minutely inscribed lines. This monument, now exhibited in the Baths of Diocletian, was in the form of a square pillar enclosed by a projecting frame, with base and capital of the Tuscan order, and it measured, when entire, four metres in height. I believe that there is no inscription among the thirty thousand collected in volume vi. of the "Corpus" which makes a more profound impression on the mind, or appeals more to the imagination than this official report of a state

Pillar commemorating the *Ludi Sæculares.*

ceremony which took place over nineteen hundred years ago, and was attended by the most illustrious men of the age.

The origin of the sæcular games seems to be this: In the early days of Rome the northwest section of the Campus Martius, bordering on the Tiber, was conspicuous for traces of volcanic activity. There was a pool here called Tarentum or Terentum, fed by hot sulphur springs, the efficiency of which is attested by the cure of Volesus, the Sabine, and his family, described by Valerius Maximus. Heavy vapors hung over the springs, and tongues of flame were seen issuing from the cracks of the earth. The locality became known by the name of the fiery field (*campus ignifer*), and its relationship with the infernal realms was soon an established fact in folk-lore. An altar to the infernal gods was erected on the borders of the pool, and games were held periodically in honor of Dis and Proserpina, the victims being a black bull and a black cow. Tradition attributed this arrangement of time and ceremony to Volesus himself, who, grateful for the recovery of his three children, offered sacrifices to Dis and Proserpina, spread *lectisternia*, or reclining couches, for the gods, with tables and viands before them, and celebrated games for three nights, one for each child which had been restored to health. In the republican epoch they were called *Ludi Tarentini*, from the name of the pool, and were celebrated for the purpose of averting from the state the recurrence of some great calamity by which it had been afflicted. These calamities being contingencies which no man could foresee, it is evident that the celebration of the *Ludi Tarentini* was in no way connected with definite cycles of time, such as the *sæculum*.

Not long after Augustus had assumed the supreme power, the *Quindecemviri sacris faciundis* (a college of priests to whom the direction of these games had been intrusted from time immemorial) announced that it was the will of the gods that the *Ludi Sæculares* should be performed, and misrepresenting and distorting events and dates, tried to prove that the festival had been held regularly at intervals of 110 years, which was supposed to be the length of a *sæculum*. The games of which the Quindecemviri made this assertion were the Tarentini, instituted for quite a different purpose, but their suggestion was too pleasing to Augustus and the people to be despised. Setting aside all disputes about chronology and tradition, the celebration was appointed for the summer of the year 17 B. C.

Plan and section of the Altar of Dis and Proserpina.

What was the exact location of the sulphur springs, the Tarentum, and the altar of the infernal gods? I have reason to regard the discovery of the Altar of Dis and Proserpina as the most satisfactory I have made, especially because I made it, if I may so express myself, when away from Rome on a long leave of absence. It took place in the winter of 1886-87, during my visit to America. At that time the work of opening and draining the Corso Vittorio Emanuele had just reached a place which was considered *terra incognita* by the topographers, and indicated by a blank spot in the archæological maps of the city. I mean the district between the Vallicella (la Chiesa Nuova, the Palazzo Cesarini, etc.) and the banks of the Tiber near S. Giovanni dei Fiorentini. The reports spoke vaguely about the discovery of five or six parallel walls, built of blocks of peperino, of marble steps in the centre of this singular monument, of gates with marble posts and architraves, leading to the spaces between the six parallel walls, and finally, of a column with foliage carved upon its surface. On my return to Rome, in the spring of 1887, every trace of the monument had disappeared under the embankment of the Corso Vittorio Emanuele. I questioned foremen and workmen, I consulted the notebooks of the contractors, every day I visited the excavations which were still in progress, on each side of the Corso, for building the Cavalletti and Bassi palaces, and lastly, I examined the "column with foliage carved upon its surface," which in the mean time had been removed to the courtyard of the Palazzo dei Conservatori on the Capitol. This marble fragment, the only one saved from the excavations, gave me the clue to the mystery. It was not a column, it was a *pulvinus*, or volute, of a colossal marble altar, worthy of being compared, in size and perfection of work, with the Altar of Peace discovered under the Palazzo Fiano, with that of the Antonines discovered under the Monte Citorio, and with other such monumental structures. There was then no hesitation in determining the nature of the discoveries made in the Corso Vittorio Emanuele; an altar had been found there, and this altar must have been the one sacred to Dis and Proserpina, as no other is mentioned in history in the northwest section of the Campus Martius.

The drawings which illustrate my account of the discovery[45] prove that the altar rose from a platform twelve feet square, approached on all sides by three or four marble steps, that platform and altar were enclosed by three lines of wall at an interval of thirty-six feet from one another, and that on the east side of the square ran a *euripus*, or channel, eleven feet wide, and four feet deep, lined with stone blocks, the incline of which towards the Tiber is about 1:100. This last detail proves that when the rough altar of Volesus Sabinus was succeeded by the later noble structure, the pool was drained, and its feeding springs were led into the *euripus*, so that the patients seeking a cure for their ailments could bathe in or drink the miracle-working waters with greater ease. No attention whatever was paid to the discovery at the time it took place. Instead of reaching the ancient level, the excavation for the main sewer of the Corso Vittorio Emanuele was stopped at the wrong place, within three feet of the pavement; consequently whatever fragments of the altar, of inscriptions, or of works of art, were lying on the marble floor will lie there forever, as the building of the palaces on either side of the Corso, and the construction of the Corso itself, with its costly sewers, sidewalks, etc., have made further research impossible, at least with our present means.

Concerning the celebration which took place around this altar in the year 17 B. C., we already possessed ample information from such materials as the oracle of the Sibyl, referred to by Zosimus, the *Carmen Sæculare* of Horace, and the legends and designs on the medals struck for the occasion; but the official report, discovered September 20, 1890, produces an altogether different impression; it enables us actually to take part in the pageant, to follow with rapture Horace as he leads a chorus of fifty-four young men and girls of patrician birth, singing the hymn which he composed for the occasion.[46]

There is such a tone of simplicity and common-sense, such a display of method and mutual respect between Augustus, the Senate, and the Quindecemviri, in the official transactions which preceded, attended and followed the celebration, in the resolutions passed by the several bodies, in the proclamations addressed to the people, and in the arrangements for the festivities, which a mass of a million or more spectators was expected to attend, that a lesson in civic dignity could be learned from this report by modern governments and corporations.

The official report begins, or rather began (the first lines are missing), with the request presented by the Quindecemviri to the Senate to take their proposal into consideration, and grant the necessary funds, followed by a decree of the Senate accepting the proposal and inviting Augustus to take the direction of the festivities. The request was addressed to the Senate on February 17, by Marcus Agrippa, president of the Quindecemviri, standing before the seat of the consuls. What a scene to witness! We can picture to ourselves the two consuls, Gaius Furnius and Junius Silanus, clad in their official robes, listening to the speech of the great statesman, who is supported by twenty colleagues, all ex-consuls, and chosen among the noblest, richest, and most gallant patricians of the age. The Senate agrees that the preparations for the festival, the building of the temporary stages, hippodromes, tribunes, and scaffoldings shall be executed by the contractors (*redemptores*), and that the treasury officials shall provide the funds.

Lines 1-23 contain a letter from Augustus to the Quindecemviri detailing the programme of the ceremonies, the number and quality of persons who shall take part in it, the dates and hours, and the number and character of the victims. Two clauses of the imperial manifesto are especially noteworthy. First, that during the three days, June 1-3, the courthouses shall be closed, and justice shall not be administered. Second, that ladies who are wearing mourning shall lay aside that sign of grief for this occasion. The date of the manifesto is March 24.

Upon the receipt of this document the Quindecemviri meet and pass several resolutions: that the rules regarding the ceremonies shall be made known to the public by advertisement (*albo proposita*); that the mornings of May 26, 27, and 28, shall be set apart for the *distributio suffimentorum*, in which the Quindecemviri were wont to distribute among the citizens torches, sulphur and bitumen, for purification; and the mornings of May 29, 30, and 31, for the *frugum acceptio*, or distribution of wheat, barley, and beans. To avoid overcrowding, four centres of distribution are named, and each of them is placed under the supervision of four members of the college, making a total of sixteen delegates. The places indicated in the programme are the platform of the Capitolium, the area in front of the Temple of Jupiter Tonans, the Portico of the Danaids on the Palatine, and the Temple of Diana on the Aventine.

On May 23 the Senate meets in the Septa Julia—the ruins of which still exist, under the Palazzo Doria and the church of S. Maria in Via Lata—and passes two resolutions. Horace's hymn, vv. 17-20, alludes to the first: "O Goddess, whether you choose the title of Lucina or of Genitalis, multiply our offspring, and prosper the decree of the Senate in relation to the giving of women in wedlock, and the matrimonial laws." Among the penalties imposed on men and women who remained single between the ages of twenty and fifty years, was the prohibition against attending public festivities and ceremonies of state. The Senate, considering the extraordinary case of the *Ludi Sæculares*, which none among the living had seen or would ever see again, removes this prohibition. The second resolution provides for the erection of two commemorative pillars, one of bronze, the other of marble, upon which the official report of the celebration shall be engraved. The bronze pillar is probably lost forever, but the marble one is that recovered on the banks of the Tiber, September 20, 1890, the inscription on which I am endeavoring to explain.

The celebration in the strict sense of the word began at the second hour of the night of May 31. Sacrifices were offered to the Fates, on altars erected between the Tarentum and the banks of the Tiber, where S. Giovanni dei Fiorentini now stands; and the other ceremonies were performed on a wooden stage which was illuminated by lights and fires. This temporary theatre was not provided with seats, and the report calls it "a stage without a theatre." In the performances of the next day and in those of June 2 and 3, which took place on the Capitol and the Palatine, the following order was observed in the ceremonial pageant; first came Augustus as Emperor and Pontifex Maximus, next the Consuls, the Senate, the Quindecemviri and other colleges of priests, then followed the Vestal Virgins, and a group of one hundred and ten matrons (as many as there were years in the *sæculum*) selected from among the most exemplary *matres familiæ* above twenty-five years of age.

Twenty-seven boys and twenty-seven girls of patrician descent whose parents were both living (*patrimi et matrimi*) were enlisted on June 3, to sing the hymn composed expressly by Horace. "Carmen composuit Q. Horatius Flaccus," so the report says (line 149). The first stanzas of the beautiful canticle were sung when the procession was marching from the Temple of Apollo to that of Jupiter Capitolinus, the middle portion on the Capitol, and the last on the way back to the Palatine. The accompaniments were played by the orchestra and the trumpeters of the official choir (*tibicines et fidicines qui sacris publicis præsto sunt*). The wealth of magnificence and beauty which the Romans beheld on the morning of June 3, 17 B. c., we can see as in a dream, but it baffles description. Imagine the group of fifty-four young patricians clad in snow-white tunics, crowned with flowers, and waving branches of laurel, led by Horace down the Vicus Apollinis (the street which led from the Summa Sacra Via to the house of Augustus on the Palatine), and the Sacra Via, singing the praises of the immortal gods:— 82

"Quibus septem placuere colles!"

During those days and nights Augustus gave evidence of a truly remarkable strength of mind and body, never missing a ceremony, and himself performing the sacrifices. Agrippa showed less power of endurance than his friend and master. He appeared only in the daytime, helping the emperor in addressing supplications to the gods, and in immolating the victims.

ARA PACIS AUGUSTAE. Among the honors voted to Augustus by the Senate in the year 13 B. c., on the occasion of his triumphal return from the campaigns of Germany and Gaul, was the erection of a votive altar in the Curia itself. Augustus refused it, but consented that an altar should be raised in the Campus Martius and dedicated to Peace. Judging from the fragments which have come down to us, this *ara* was one of the most exquisite artistic productions of the golden age of Augustus. It stood in the centre of a triple square enclosure, on the west side of the Via Flaminia, the site of the present Palazzo Fiano. Twice its remains have been brought to light; once in 1554, when they were drawn by Giovanni Colonna,[47] and again in 1859, when the present duke of Fiano was rebuilding the southern wing of the palace on the Via in Lucina. Of the panels and basreliefs found in 1554, some were removed to the Villa 83

Medici and inserted in the front of the casino, on the garden side; others were transferred to Florence; those of 1859 have been placed in the vestibule of the Palazzo Fiano. They are well worth a visit.

The family of Augustus. Relief from the Ara Pacis, in the Gallery of the Uffizi, Florence.

ARA INCENDII NERONIANI. In the month of July, A. D. 65, half Rome was destroyed by the fire of Nero. The citizens, overwhelmed by the greatness of the calamity, and ignorant of its true cause, made a vow for the annual celebration of expiatory sacrifices, on altars expressly constructed for the purpose in each of the fourteen regions of the metropolis. The vow was, however, forgotten until Domitian claimed its fulfilment some twenty or twenty-five years later. One of these altars, which adjoined Domitian's paternal house on the Quirinal, has just been found near the church of S. Andrea del Noviziato, in the foundations of the new "Ministero della Casa Reale."

The altar, six metres long by three wide, built of travertine with a coating of marble, stands in the middle of a paved area of considerable size. The area is lined with stone cippi, placed at an interval of two and a half metres from one another. The following inscription has been found engraved on two of them: "This sacred area, marked with stone cippi, and enclosed with a hedge, as well as the altar which stands in the middle of it, was dedicated by the emperor Domitian in consequence of an unfulfilled vow made by the citizens at the time of the fire of Nero. The dedication is made subject to the following rules: that no one shall be allowed to loiter, trade, build, or plant trees or shrubs within the line of terminal stones; that on August 23 of each year, the day of the Volkanalia, the magistrate presiding over this sixth region shall sacrifice on this altar a red calf and a pig; that he shall address to the gods the following prayer (text missing)." The inscription has been read twice: once towards the end of the fifteenth century, when the cippus containing it was removed to S. Peter's and made use of in the new building, and again in 1644, when Pope Barberini was laying the foundations of S. Andrea al Quirinale, one of the most graceful and pleasing churches of modern Rome.

Let us now turn our attention to more imposing structures. The first temple in the excavation of which I took part was that of Jupiter Optimus Maximus on the Capitoline Hill.[48] Its discovery was due more to an intuition of the truth, than to actual recognition of existing remains. On November 7, 1875, while digging for the foundation of the new Rotunda in the garden which divides the Conservatori palace from that of the Caffarellis,—the residence of the German ambassador,—our workmen came upon a piece of a colossal fluted column of Pentelic marble, lying on a platform of squared stones, which were laid without mortar, in a decidedly archaic style. Were we in the presence of the remains of the famous Capitolium, or of one of the smaller temples within the Arx? To give this query a satisfactory answer, we must remember that the Capitoline Hill had two summits, one containing the citadel, or Arx, the other the Temple of Jupiter Optimus Maximus, the Capitolium. Ancient writers never use the two names promiscuously, or apply them indifferently to either summit or to the whole hill. The name of the hill is the *Capitoline*; not the *Capitol*, which means exclusively the portion occupied by the great temple. Suffice it to quote Livy's evidence (vi. 20), *ne quis in Arce aut Capitolio habitaret*, and also the passage of Aulus Gellius (v. 12) in which the shrine of Vedjovis is placed between the Arx and the Capitolium.

For many generations topographers tried to discover which summit was occupied by the citadel, and which by the temple. The Italian school, save a few exceptions, had always identified the site of the Aracœli with that of the temple, the Caffarelli palace with that of the citadel. The Germans upheld the opposite theory. In these circumstances it is not surprising that the discovery made November 7, 1875, should have excited us; because we saw at once our chance of settling the dispute, not theoretically, but with the evidence of facts.

The Temple of Jupiter Optimus Maximus, designed by Tarquinius Priscus, built by Tarquinius Superbus, and dedicated in 509 B. C. by the consul M. Horatius Pulvillus, stood on a high platform 207½ feet long, by 192½ feet broad. The front of the edifice, ornamented with three rows of columns, faced the south. The style of the architecture was purely Etruscan, and the intercolumniations were so wide as to require architraves of timber. The cella was divided into three sections, the middle one of which was sacred to Jupiter, that on the right to Minerva, that on the left to Juno Regina; the top of the pediment was ornamented with a terra-cotta quadriga. Of the same material was the statue of the god, with the face painted red, and the body dressed in a *tunica palmata* and a *toga picta*, the work of an Etruscan artist, Turianus of Fregenæ.

In 386 B. C. it was found necessary to enlarge the platform in the centre of which the temple stood; and as the hill was sloping, even precipitous, on three sides, it was necessary to raise huge foundation walls from the plain below to the level of the platform, a work described by Pliny (xxxvi. 15, 24) as prodigious, and by Livy (vi. 4) as one of the wonders of Rome.

THE WESTERN SUMMIT OF THE CAPITOLINE HILL (*R. Lanciani del.*)

On July 6, 83 B. C., four hundred and twenty-six years after its dedication by Horatius Pulvillus, an unknown malefactor, taking advantage of the abundance of timber used in the structure, set fire to it, and utterly destroyed the sanctuary which for four centuries had presided over the fates of the Roman Commonwealth. The incendiary, less fortunate than Erostratos, remained unknown, the suspicions cast at the time against Papirius Carbo, Scipio, Norbanus and Sulla having proved groundless. He probably belonged to the faction of Marius, because we know that Marius himself laid hands on the half-charred ruins of the temple, and pillaged several thousand pounds of gold.

Sulla the dictator undertook the reconstruction of the Capitolium, for which purpose he caused some columns of the temple of the Olympian Jupiter to be removed from Athens to Rome. Sulla's work was continued by Lutatius Catulus, and finished by Julius Cæsar in 46 B. C. A second restoration took place in the year 9 B. C. under Augustus, a third A. D. 74 under Vespasian, and the last in the year 82, under Domitian. It was therefore evident that, if the temple had not been literally obliterated since that time, its remains would show the characteristics of the age of Domitian, who is known to have made use of Pentelic marble in his reconstruction. We should also find these remains in the middle of a platform of the time of the kings, surrounded by foundation walls of the time of the republic. The accompanying plan shows how perfectly the remains discovered on the southwestern summit of the Capitoline Hill corresponded to this theory.

The platform, in the shape of a parallelogram, 183 feet broad and a few feet longer, is built of roughly squared blocks of *capellaccio*, exactly like certain portions of the Servian walls. Its area and height were reduced by one third, when the Caffarellis built their palace, in 1680. A sketch taken at that time by Fabretti and published in his volume "De Columna Trajana" shows that fourteen tiers of stone have disappeared. A portion of the same platform, discovered in 1865, by Herr Schloezer, Prussian minister to Pius IX., is represented on the next page.

The foundation walls, which Pliny and Livy enumerate among the wonders of Rome, have been, and are still being, discovered on the three sides of the hill which face the Piazza della Consolazione, the Piazza Montanara, and the Via di Torre de' Specchi. They are built of blocks of red tufa, with facing of travertine. The travertine facing is covered with inscriptions set up in honor of the great divinity of Rome by the kings and nations of the whole world. One cannot read these historical documents[49] without acquiring a new sense of the magnitude and power of the city.

These inscriptions are found mostly at the foot of the substructure, on the side towards the Piazza della Consolazione. The latest, found in the foundations of the Palazzo Moroni, contain messages of friendship and gratitude from kings Mithradates Philopator and Mithradates Philadelphos, of Pontus, from Ariobarzanes Philoromæus of Cappadocia and Athenais his queen, from the province of Lycia, from some townships of the province of Caria, etc.

As for the remains of the temple itself, the colossal column discovered November 7, 1875, in the Conservatori garden, is not the only one saved from the wreck. Flaminio Vacca, the sculptor and amateur-archæologist of the sixteenth century, says: "Upon the Tarpeian Rock, behind the Palazzo de' Conservatori, several pillars of Pentelic marble (*marmo statuale*) were lately found. Their capitals are so enormous that out of one of them I have carved the lion now in the Villa Medici. The others were used by Vincenzo de Rossi to carve the prophets and other statues which adorn the chapel of cardinal Cesi in the church of S. Maria della Pace. I believe the columns belonged to the Temple of Jupiter. No fragments of the entablature were found: but as the building was so close to the edge of the Tarpeian Rock, I suspect they must have fallen into the plain."

The correctness of this surmise is shown not only by the discovery of the dedicatory inscriptions, in the Piazza della Consolazione, just alluded to, but also from what took place in 1780, when the duca Lante della Rovere was excavating the foundations of a house, No. 13,

Via Montanera. The discoveries are described by Montagnani as "marble entablatures of enormous size and beautiful workmanship, with festoons and *bucranii* in the frieze. No one took the trouble to sketch them; they were destroyed on the spot. I have no doubt that they belonged to the temple seen by Vacca on the Monte Tarpeo, one hundred and eighty-six years ago."

All these indications, compared with the discovery of the platform, the substructure, and the column of Pentelic marble in the Conservatori garden, leave no doubt as to the real position of the Temple of Jupiter. To that piece of marble we owe the opportunity and the privilege of settling a dispute on Roman topography which had lasted at least three centuries.

The temple, rebuilt by Domitian, stood uninjured till the middle of the fifth century. In June, 455, the Vandals, under Genseric, plundered the sanctuary, its statues were carried off to adorn the African residence of the king, and half the roof was stripped of its gilt bronze tiles. From that time the place was used as a stone-quarry and lime-kiln to such an extent that only the solitary fragment of a column remains on the spot to tell the long tale of destruction. Another piece of Pentelic marble was found January 24, 1889, near the Tullianum (S. Pietro in Carcere). It belongs to the top of a column, and has the same number of flutings,—twenty-four. This fragment seems to have been sawn on the spot to the desired length, seven feet, and then dragged down the hill towards some stone-cutter's shop. Why it was thus abandoned, half way, in a hollow or pit dug expressly for it, there is nothing to show.

The Temple of Jupiter is represented in ancient monuments of the class called pictorial reliefs. I have selected for my illustration one of the panels from the triumphal arch of Marcus Aurelius, near S. Martina, because it contains a good sketch of the reliefs of the pediment, with Jupiter seated between Juno and Minerva. The temple itself is most carelessly drawn, the number of columns being reduced by one half, that is, from eight to four.[50]

There is one interesting feature of the Capitolium, which is not well known among those who do not make a profession of archæology. It was used as a place for advertising State acts, deeds, and documents, in order that the public might take notice of them and be informed of what was going on in the administrative, military, and political departments. This fact is known from a clause appended to imperial letters-patent by which veterans were honorably discharged from the army or navy, and privileges bestowed on them in recognition of their services. These deeds, known as *diplomata honestæ missionis*, were engraved on bronze tablets shaped like the cover of a book, the original of which was hung somewhere in the Capitolium, and a copy taken by the veteran to his home. The originals are all gone, having fallen the prey of the plunderers of bronze in Rome, but copies are found in great numbers in every province of the Roman empire from which men were drafted.[51] These copies end with the clause:—

"Transcribed (and compared or verified) from the original bronze tablet which is hung in Rome, in the Capitolium"—and here follows the designation of a special place of the Capitolium, such as,—

"On the right side of the shrine of the *Fides populi romani*" (December 11, a. d. 52).

"On the left side of the *ædes Thensarum*" (July 2, a. d. 60).

"On the pedestal of the statue of Quintus Marcius Rex, behind the temple of Jupiter" (June 15, 64).

"On the pedestal of the *ara gentis Iuliæ*, on the right side, the statue of Bacchus" (March 7, 71).

"On the vestibule, on the left wall, between the two archways" (May 21, 74).

"On the pedestal of the statue of Jupiter Africus" (December 2, 76).

"On the base of the column, on the inner side, near the statue of Jupiter Africus" (September 5, 85).

"On the tribunal by the trophies of Germanicus, which are near the shrine of the *Fides*" (May 15, 86).

Comparing these indications of localities with the dates of the diplomas,—there are sixty-three in all,—it appears that they were not hung at random, but in regular order from monument to monument, until every available space was covered. In the year 93 there was not an inch left, and the Capitol is mentioned no more as a place for exhibiting or advertising the acts of Government. From that year they were hung *"in muro post templum divi ad Minervam,"* that is, behind the modern church of S. Maria Liberatrice.

THE TEMPLE OF ISIS AND SERAPIS. In the spring of 1883, in surveying the tract of ground between the Collegio Romano and the Baths of Agrippa, formerly occupied by the Temple of Isis and Serapis, and in collecting archæological information concerning it, I was struck by the fact that, every time excavations were made on either side of the Via di S. Ignazio for building or restoring the houses which line it, remarkable specimens of Egyptian art had been brought to light. The annals of discoveries begin with 1374, when the obelisk now in the Piazza della Rotonda was found, under the apse of the church of S. Maria sopra Minerva, together with the one now in the Villa Mattei von Hoffman. In 1435, Eugenius IV. discovered the two lions of Nektaneb I. which are now in the Vatican, and the two of black basalt now in the Capitoline Museum. In 1440 the reclining figure of a river-god was found and buried again. The Tiber of the Louvre and the Nile of the Braccio Nuovo seem to have come to light during the pontificate of Leo X.; at all events it was he who caused them to be removed to the Vatican. In 1556 Giovanni Battista de Fabi found, and sold to cardinal Farnese, the reclining statue of Oceanus now in Naples. In 1719 the Isiac altar now in the Capitol was found under the Biblioteca Casanatense. In 1858 Pietro Tranquilli, in restoring his house,—the nearest to the apse of la Minerva,—came across the following-named objects: a sphinx of green granite,

92

93

the head of which is a portrait of Queen Haths'epu, the oldest sister of Thothmes III., who was famous for her expedition to the Red Sea, recently described by Dümmichen;[52] a sphinx of red granite, believed to be a Roman replica; a group of the cow Hathor, the living symbol of Isis, nursing the young Pharaoh Horemheb; the portrait statue of the grand dignitary Uahábra, a good specimen of Saïtic art; a column of the temple, covered with high reliefs, which represented a procession of bald-headed priests holding canopi in their hands; a capital, carved with papyrus leaves and lotus flowers; and a fragment of an Egyptian basrelief in red granite, with traces of polychromy.

In 1859 Augusto Silvestrelli, the owner of the next house, on the same side of the Via di S. Ignazio, found five capitals of the same style and size, which, I believe, are now in the Museo Etrusco Gregoriano. Inasmuch as no excavation had ever been made under the pavement of the street itself, which is public property, and as there was no reason why that strip of public property should not contain as many works of art as the houses about it, I asked the municipal authorities to try the experiment, and my proposal was accepted at once.

The work began on Monday, June 11, 1883. It was difficult, because we had to dig to a depth of twenty feet between houses of very doubtful solidity. First to appear, at the end of the third day, was a magnificent sphinx of black basalt, the portrait of King Amasis. It is a masterpiece of the Saïtic school, perfected even in the smallest details, and still more impressive for its historical connection with the conquest of Egypt by Cambyses.

The cartouches bearing the king's name appear to have been purposely erased, though not so completely as to render the name illegible. The nose, likewise, and the *urœus*, the symbol of royalty, were hammered away at the same time. The explanation of these facts is given by Herodotos. When Cambyses conquered Saïs, Amasis had just been buried. The conqueror caused the body to be dragged out of the royal tomb, then flogged and otherwise insulted, and finally burnt, the maximum of profanation, from an Egyptian point of view. His name was erased from the monuments which bore it, as a natural consequence of the *memoriæ damnatio*. This sphinx is the surviving testimonial of the eventful catastrophe.

The Sphinx of Amasis.

When, six or seven centuries later, a Roman governor of Egypt, or a Roman merchant from the same province, singled out this work of art, to be shipped to Rome as a votive offering for the Temple of Isis, ignorant of the historical value of its mutilations, he had the nose and the *urœus* carefully restored. Now both are gone again, and there is no danger of a second restoration. I may remark, as a curious coincidence, that, as the name of Amasis is erased from the sphinx, so that of Hophries, his predecessor, is erased from the obelisk discovered in the same temple, and now in the Piazza della Minerva. In these two monuments of the Roman Iseum we possess a synopsis of Egyptian history between 595 and 526 B. C.

The second work, discovered June 17, was an obelisk which was wonderfully well preserved to the very top of the pinnacle, and covered with hieroglyphics. It was quarried at Assuan, from a richly colored vein of red granite, and was brought to Rome, probably under Domitian, together with the obelisk now in the Piazza del Pantheon. The two monoliths are almost identical in size and workmanship, and are inscribed with the same cartouches of Rameses the Great. The one which I discovered was set up, in 1887, to the memory of our brave soldiers who fell at the battle of Dogali. The site selected for the monument, the square between the railway station and the Baths of Diocletian, is too large for such a comparatively small shaft.

Two days later, on the 19th, we discovered two *kynokephaloi* or *kerkopithekoi*, five feet high, carved in black porphyry. The monsters are sitting on their hind legs, with the paws of the forearms resting on the knees. Their bases contain finely-cut hieroglyphics, with the cartouche of King Necthor-heb, of the thirtieth Sebennitic dynasty. One of these *kynokephaloi*, and also the obelisk, were certainly seen in 1719 by the masons who built the foundations of the Biblioteca Casanatense. For some reason unknown to us, they kept their discovery a secret. Many other works of art were discovered before the close of the excavations, in the last days of June. Among them were a crocodile in red granite, the pedestal of a candelabrum, triangular in shape, with sphinxes at the corners; a column of the temple, with reliefs representing an Isiac procession; and a portion of a capital. From an architectural point of view, the most curious discovery was that the temple itself, with its colonnades and double cella, had been brought over, piece by piece, from the banks of the Nile to those of the Tiber. It is not an imitation; it is a purely original Egyptian structure, shaded first by the palm-trees of Saïs, and later by the pines of the Campus Martius.

The earliest trustworthy account we have of its existence is given by Flavius Josephus. He relates how Tiberius, after the assault of Mundus against Paulina,[53] condemned the priests to crucifixion, burned the shrine, and threw the statue of the goddess into the Tiber. Nero restored the sanctuary; it was, however, destroyed again in the great conflagration, A. D. 80. Domitian was the second restorer; Hadrian, Commodus, Caracalla, and Alexander Severus improved and beautified the group, from time to time. At the beginning of the fourth century of our era it contained the *propylaia*, or pyramidal towers with a gateway, at each end of the *dromos*; one near the present church of S. Stefano del Cacco, one near the church of S. Macuto. They were flanked by one or more pairs of obelisks, of which six have been recovered up to the present

Obelisk of Rameses the Great.

time, namely, one now in the Piazza della Rotonda, a second in the Piazza della Minerva, a third in the Villa Mattei, a fourth in the Piazza della Stazione, a fifth in the Sphæristerion at Urbino, and fragments of a sixth in the Albani collection.

From the propylaia, a *dromos*, or sacred avenue, led to the double temple. To the dromos belong the two lions in the Museo Etrusco Gregoriano, the two lions in the Capitoline Museum, the sphinx of Queen Hathsèpu in the Barracco collection, the sphinx of Amasis and the Tranquilli sphinx in the Capitol, the cow Hathor and the statue of Uahábra in the Museo Archeologico in Florence, the *kynokephaloi* of Necthor-heb, the *kynokephalos* which gave the popular name of *Cacco* (ape) to the church of S. Stefano, the statue formerly in the Ludovisi Gallery, the Nile of the Braccio Nuovo, the Tiber of the Louvre, the Oceanus at Naples, the River-God buried in 1440, the Isiac altars of the Capitol and of the Louvre, the tripod, the crocodile and sundry other fragments which were found in 1883. Of the temple itself we possess two columns covered with mystic bas-reliefs, seven capitals,—one in the Capitol, the others in the Vatican,—and two blocks of granite from the walls of the cella, one in the Barberini gardens, one in the Palazzo Galitzin.

The last historical mention we possess of this admirable Egyptian museum of ancient Rome was found by Delille in the "Cod. Parisin." 8064, in which the attempt by Nicomachus Flavianus to revive the pagan religion in 394 A. D. is minutely described.[54] The reaction caused by this final outburst of fanaticism must have been fatal to the temple. The masterpieces of the dromos were upset, and otherwise damaged, the faces of the *kynokephaloi* and the noses and paws of the sphinxes were knocked off, and statues of Pharaohs, gods, priests, dignitaries, and Pastophoroi were hurled from their pedestals, and broken to pieces. When this wholesale destruction took place, the pavement of the temple was still clear of the rubbish and loose soil. The sphinx of Amasis, found June 14, was lying on its left side on the bare pavement; the two apes had fallen on their backs. No attempt, however, was made to overthrow the obelisks, at least the one which I discovered. When the monolith fell, in the eighth or ninth century, the floor of the Iseum was already covered with a bed of rubbish five feet thick. To this fact we owe the wonderful preservation of the obelisk, the soft, muddy condition of the soil having eased the weight of the fall.

Students have wondered at the existence, in our time, of such a mine of antiquities in this quarter of the Campus Martius, where it appears as if, in spite of the feverish search for ancient marbles, this spot had escaped the attention of the excavators of the past four or five centuries. It did not escape their attention. The whole area of the Iseum, save a few recesses, has been explored since the Middle Ages, but the search was made to secure marble, which could be burnt into lime, or turned into new shapes. Of what use would porphyry, or granite, or basalt be for such purposes? These materials are useless for the lime-kiln, and too hard to be worked anew, and accordingly they were left alone. In the excavations of 1883 I found the best evidence that such was the case. The obelisk is of granite; its pedestal of white marble. The obelisk escaped destruction, but the pedestal was split, and made ready for the lime-kiln.

THE TEMPLE OF NEPTUNE. The discoveries made in 1878 in the Piazza di Pietra, on the site of the Temple of Neptune, rank next in importance to those just described. In repairing a drain which runs through the Via de' Bergamaschi to the Piazza di Pietra, the foundations of an early mediæval church, dedicated to S. Stephen (Santo Stefano del Trullo) were unearthed, together with historical inscriptions, pieces of columns of *giallo antico*, and other architectural fragments. On a closer examination of the discoveries, I was able to ascertain that the whole church had been built with spoils from the triumphal arch of Claudius in the Piazza di Sciarra, and from the Temple of Neptune in the Piazza di Pietra. To enable the reader to appreciate the value of the discovery, I must begin with a short description of the temple itself.

Dio Cassius (liii. 27) states that, in 26 B. C., Marcus Agrippa built the Portico of the Argonauts, with a temple in the middle of it, called the Poseidonion (ΠΟΣΕΙΔΩΝΙΟΝ), in token of his gratitude to the god of the seas for the naval victories he had gained over the foes of the commonwealth; but the beautiful ruins still existing in the Piazza di Pietra do not belong to Agrippa's work, nor to the golden age of Roman art. They belong to the restoration of the temple which was made by Hadrian after the great fire of A. D. 80, by which the Neptunium, or Poseidonion, was nearly destroyed. The characteristic feature of

One of the Provinces from the Temple of Neptune.

the temple was a set of thirty-six bas-reliefs representing the thirty-six provinces of the Roman Empire at the beginning of the Christian era. These reliefs were set into the basement of the temple, so as to form the pedestals of the thirty-six columns of the peristyle, while the intercolumniations, or spaces between the pedestals, were occupied by another set of bas-reliefs representing the military uniforms, flags and weapons which were peculiar to each of the provinces. The fifteen provinces and fourteen trophies belonging to the colonnade of the Piazza di Pietra, that is, to the north side of the temple, have all been accounted for. Four provinces were found during the pontificate of Paul III. (1534-50), two during that of Innocent X. (1644-55), two during that of Alexander VII. (1655-1667), three in our excavations of 1878, and four either are still in the ground or have perished in a lime-kiln. Here again we have an instance of the shameful dispersion of the spoils of ancient Rome. We have this wing of the temple still standing in all its glory, in the Piazza di Pietra; we have eleven pedestals out of fifteen, and as many panels for the intercolumniations; the others are *probably* within our reach, and we have beautiful pieces of the entablature with its rich carvings. The temple, entablature, and nearly all the trophies and provinces are public property; nothing would be easier than to restore each piece to its proper place, and make this wing of the Neptunium one of the most perfect relics of ancient Rome. Alas! three provinces and two trophies have emigrated to Naples with the rest of the Farnese marbles, one has been left behind in the portico of the Farnese palace in Rome, five provinces and four trophies are in the Palazzo dei Conservatori, two are in the Palazzo Odescalchi, one is in the Palazzo Altieri, two pieces of the entablature are used as a rustic seat in the Giardino delle Tre Pile on the Capitol, and another has been used in the restoration of the Arch of Constantine.

101

THE TEMPLE OF AUGUSTUS. It is a remarkable fact that, at the beginning of archæological research in the Renaissance, there was great enthusiasm over a few strange monuments of little or no interest, the existence of which would have been altogether unknown but for an occasional mention in classical texts. As a rule, the cinquecento topographers give a prominent place in their books to the *columna Mænia*, the *columna Lactaria*, the *senaculum mulierum*, the *pila Tiburtina*, the *pila Horatia* and other equally unimportant works which, for reasons unknown to us, had forcibly struck their fancy. The fashion died out in course of time, but never entirely. Some of these more or less fanciful structures still live in our books, and in the imagination of the people. The place of honor, in this line, belongs to Caligula's bridge, which is supposed to have crossed the valley of the Forum at a prodigious height, so as to enable the young monarch to walk on a level from his Palatine house to the Temple of Jupiter on the Capitol. This bridge is not only mentioned in guide-books, and pointed out to strangers on their first visit to the Forum, but is also drawn and described in works of a higher standard,[55] in which the bridge is represented from "remains concealed under a house, which have been carefully examined and measured, as well as drawn by architectural draughtsmen of much experience."

The bridge never existed. Caligula made use of the roofs of edifices which were already there, spanning only the gaps of the streets with temporary wooden passages. This is clearly stated by Suetonius in chapters xxii. and xxxvii. and by Flavius Josephus, "Antiq. Jud." xix. 1, 11. From the palace at the northeast corner of the Palatine, he crossed the roof of the *templum divi Augusti*, then the *fastigium basilicæ Juliæ*, and lastly the Temple of Saturn close to the Capitolium. The Street of Victory which divided the emperor's palace from the Temple of Augustus, the Street of the Tuscans which divided the temple from the basilica, and the Vicus Iugarius between the basilica and the Temple of Saturn, were but a few feet wide and could easily be crossed by means of a *passerelle*. We are told by Suetonius and Josephus how Caligula used sometimes to interrupt his aerial promenade midway, and throw handfuls of gold from the roof of the basilica to the crowd assembled below. I have mentioned this bridge because the words of Suetonius, *supra templum divi Augusti ponte transmisso*, gave me the first clew towards the identification of the splendid ruins which tower just behind the church of S. Maria Liberatrice, between it and the rotunda of S. Teodoro.

102

The position of Caligula's palace at the northeast corner of the Palatine being well known, as also the site of the Basilica Julia, it is evident that the building which stands between the two must be the Temple of Augustus. This conclusion is so simple that I wonder that no one had mentioned it before my first announcement in 1881. The last nameless remains adjoining the Forum have thus regained their place and their identity in the topography of this classic quarter.

The construction of a temple in honor of the deified founder of the empire was begun by his widow Livia, and Tiberius, his adopted son, and completed by Caligula. An inscription discovered in 1726, in the

103

Plan of the Temple of Augustus.

Columbaria of Livia on the Appian Way, mentions a C. Julius Bathyllus, sacristan or keeper of the temple. Pliny (xii. 19, 42) describes, among the curiosities of the place, a root of a cinnamon-tree, of extraordinary size, placed by Livia on a golden tray. The relic was destroyed by fire in the reign of Titus. Domitian must have restored the building, because the rear wall of the temple, the *murus post templum divi Augusti ad Minervam*, is mentioned in contemporary documents as the place on which state notices were posted. It has been excavated but once, in June, 1549, when the Forum, the Sacra Via and the Street of the Tuscans were ransacked to

Remains of the Temple of Augustus, from a sketch by Ligorio.

supply marbles and lime for the building of S. Peter's. Two documents show the wonderful state of preservation in which the temple was found. One is a sketch, taken in 1549, by Pirro Ligorio, which, through the kindness of Professor T. H. Middleton,[56] I reproduce from the original, in the Bodleian Library; the other is a description of the discovery by Panvinius.[57] The place was in such good condition that even the statue and altar of Vortumnus, described by Livy, Asconius, Varro and others, were found lying at the foot of the steps of the temple.

104

THE SACELLUM SANCI, or Shrine of Sancus on the Quirinal.[58] The worship of *Semo Sancus Sanctus Dius Fidius* was imported into Rome at a very early period, by the Sabines who first colonized the Quirinal Hill. He was considered the Genius of heavenly light, the son of Jupiter *Diespiter* or *Lucetius*, the avenger of dishonesty, the upholder of truth and good faith, whose mission upon earth was to secure the sanctity of agreements, of matrimony, and hospitality. Hence his various names and his identification with the Roman Hercules, who was likewise invoked as a guardian of the sanctity of oaths (*me-Hercle, me-Dius Fidius*). There were two shrines of Semo Sancus in ancient Rome, one built by the Sabines on the Quirinal, near the modern church of S. Silvestro, from which the *Porta Sanqualis* of the Servian walls was named, the other built by the Romans on the Island of the Tiber (S. Bartolomeo) near the Temple of Jupiter Jurarius. Justin, the apologist and martyr, laboring under the delusion that Semo Sancus and Simon the Magician were the same, describes the altar on the island of S. Bartolomeo as sacred to the latter.[59] He must have glanced hurriedly at the first three names of the Sabine god,—SEMONI SANCO DEO,—and translated them ΣΙΜΩΝΙ ΔΕΩ ΣΑΓΚΤΩ. The altar on which these names were written, the very one seen and described by S. Justin, was discovered on the same island, in July, 1574, during the pontificate of Gregory XIII. The altar is preserved in the Galleria Lapidaria of the Vatican Museum, in the first compartment (*Dii*).

105

The shrine on the Quirinal is minutely described by classical writers. It was hypæthral, that is, without a roof, so that the sky could be seen by the worshippers of the "Genius of heavenly light." The oath *me-Dius Fidius* could not be taken except in the open air. The chapel contained relics of the kingly period, the wool, distaff, spindle, and slippers of Tanaquil, and brass *clypea* or medallions, made of money confiscated from Vitruvius Vaccus.

Its foundations were discovered in March, 1881, under what was formerly the convent of S. Silvestro al Quirinale, now the headquarters of the Royal Engineers. The monument is a parallelogram in shape, thirty-five feet long by nineteen feet wide, with walls of travertine, and decorations of white marble; and it is surrounded by votive altars and pedestals of statues. I am not sure whether the remarkable work of art which I shall describe presently was found in this very place, but it is a strange coincidence that, during the progress of the excavations at S. Silvestro, a statue of Semo Sancus and a pedestal inscribed with his name should have appeared in the antiquarian market of the city.

The statue, reproduced here from a heliogravure, is life-sized, and represents a nude youth, of archaic type. His attitude may be compared to that of some early representations of Apollo, but the expression of the face and the modelling of some parts of the body are realistic rather than conventional. Both hands are missing, so that it is impossible to state what were the attributes of the god. Visconti thinks they may have been the *avis Sanqualis* or *ossifraga*, and the club of Hercules. The inscription on the

106

Statue of Semo Sancus.

pedestal is very much like that seen by S. Justin:—

SEMONI . SANCO . DEO . FIDIO . SACRUM . DECURIA . SACER-
DOT[UM] BIDENTALIUM.

According to Festus, *bidentalia* were small shrines of second-rate divinities, to whom *bidentes*, lambs two years old, were sacrificed. For this reason the priests of Semo were called *sacerdotes bidentales*. They were organized, like a lay corporation, in a *decuria* under the presidency of a *magister quinquennalis*. Their residence, adjoining the chapel, was ample and commodious, with an abundant supply of water. The lead pipe by which this was distributed through the establishment was discovered at the same time and in the same place with the bronze statues of athletes described in chapter xi. of my "Ancient Rome."

The pipe has been removed to the Capitoline Museum, the statue and its pedestal have been purchased by Pope Leo XIII. and placed in the Galleria dei Candelabri, and the foundations of the shrine have been destroyed.

CHAPTER III.

CHRISTIAN CHURCHES.

The large number of churches in Rome.—The six classes of the earliest of these.—I. Private oratories.—The houses of Pudens and Prisca.—The evolution of the church from the private house.—II. Scholæ.—The memorial services and banquets of the pagans.—Two extant specimens of early Christian scholæ.—That in the Cemetery of Callixtus.—III. Oratories and churches built over the tombs of martyrs and confessors.—How they came to be built.— These the originals of the greatest sanctuaries of modern Rome.—S. Peter's.— The origin of the church.—The question of S. Peter's residence and execution in Rome.—The place of his execution and burial.—The remarkable discovery of graves under the *baldacchino* of Urban VIII.—The basilica erected by Constantine.—Some of its monuments.—The chair and statue of S. Peter.— The destruction of the old basilica and the building of the new.—The vast dimensions of the latter.—Is S. Peter's body really still under the church?—The basilica of S. Paul's outside the walls.—The obstacles to its construction.—The fortified settlement of Johannipolis which grew up around it.—The grave of S. Paul.—IV. Houses of confessors and martyrs.—The discoveries of padre Germano on the Cælian.—The house of the martyrs John and Paul.—V. Pagan monuments converted into churches.—Every pagan building capable of holding a congregation was thus transformed at one time or another.—Examples of these in and near the Coliseum.—VI. Memorials of historical events.—The chapel erected to commemorate the victory of Constantine over Maxentius.—That of Santa Croce a Monte Mario.

Rome, according to an old saying, contains as many churches as there are days in the year. This statement is too modest; the "great catalogue" published by cardinal Mai[60] mentions over a thousand places of worship, while nine hundred and eighteen are registered in Professor Armellini's "Chiese di Roma." A great many have disappeared since the first institution, and are known only from ruins, or inscriptions and chronicles. Others have been disfigured by "restorations." Without denying the fact that our sacred buildings excel in quantity rather than quality, there is no doubt that as a whole they form the best artistic and historic collection in the world. Every age, from the apostolic to the present, every school, every style has its representatives in the churches of Rome.

The assertion that the works of mediæval architects have been destroyed or modernized to such an extent as to leave a wide gap between the classic and Renaissance periods, must have been made by persons unacquainted with Rome; the churches and the cloisters of S. Saba on the Aventine, of SS. Quattro Coronati on the Cælian, of S. Giovanni a Porta Latina, of SS. Vincenzo e Anastasio alle Tre Fontane, of S. Lorenzo fuori le Mura, are excellent specimens of mediæval architecture. Let students, archæologists, and architects provide themselves with a chronological table of our sacred buildings, and select the best specimens for every quarter of a century, beginning with the oratory of Aquila and Prisca, mentioned in the Epistles, and ending with the latest contemporary creations; they cannot find a better subject for their education in art and history.

From the point of view of their origin and structure, the churches of Rome of the first six centuries may be divided into six classes:—

I. Rooms of private houses where the first prayer-meetings were held.

II. Scholæ (memorial or banqueting halls in public cemeteries), transformed into places of worship.

III. Oratories and churches built over the tombs of martyrs and confessors.

IV. Houses of confessors and martyrs.

V. Pagan monuments, especially temples, converted into churches.

VI. Memorials of historical events.

In treating this subject we must bear in mind that early Christian edifices in Rome were never named from a titular saint, but from their founder, or from the owner of the property on which they were established. The same rule applies to the suburban cemeteries, which were always named from the owner of the ground above them, not from the martyrs buried within. The statement is simple; but we are so accustomed to calling the Lateran basilica "S. Giovanni," or the oratory of Pudens "S. Pudentiana," that their original names (Basilica Salvatoris, and Ecclesia Pudentiana) have almost fallen into oblivion.

I shall select from each of the six classes such specimens as I believe will convey an impression of its type to the mind of the reader.

I. Private Oratories. "In the familiar record of the first days of the Christian church we read how the men of Galilee, who returned to Jerusalem after the ascension, 'went up into the upper chamber,' which was at once their dwelling-place and their house of prayer and of assembly. There, at the first common meal, the bread was broken and the cup passed around in remembrance of the last occasion on which they had sat at table with Christ. There too they assembled for their first act of church government, the election of a successor to the apostate Judas. All is simple and domestic, yet we have here the beginnings of what became in time the most wide-reaching and highly organized of human systems. An elaborate hierarchy, a complicated theology were to arise out of the informal conclave, the memorial meal; and in like manner, out of the homely meeting-place of the disciples would be developed the costly and beautiful forms of the Christian temple."[61]

110

Rome possesses authentic remains of the "houses of prayer" in which the gospel was first announced in apostolic times. Five names are mentioned in connection with the visit of Peter and Paul to the capital of the empire, and two houses are mentioned as those in which they found hospitality, and were able to preach the new doctrine. One of these, belonging to Pudens and his daughters Pudentiana and Praxedes, stands halfway up the Vicus Patricius (Via del Bambin Gesù) on the southern slope of the Viminal; the other, belonging to Aquila and Prisca (or Priscilla), on the spur of the Aventine which overlooks the Circus Maximus. Both have been represented through the course of centuries, and are represented now, by a church, named from the owner the *Titulus Pudentis*, and the *Titulus Priscæ*. Archæologists have tried to trace the genealogy of Pudens, the friend of the apostles; but, although it seems probable that he belonged to the noble race of the Cornelii Æmilii, the fact has not yet been clearly proved. Equally doubtful are the origin and social condition of Aquila and his wife Prisca, whose names appear both in the Acts and in the Epistles. We know from these documents that, in consequence of the decree of banishment which was issued against the Jews by the emperor Claudius, Aquila and Prisca were compelled to leave Rome for a while, and that on their return they were able to open a small oratory—*ecclesiam domesticam*—in their house. This oratory, one of the first opened to divine worship in Rome, these walls which, in all probability, have echoed with the sound of S. Peter's voice, were discovered in 1776 close to the modern church of S. Prisca; but no attention was paid to the discovery, in spite of its unrivalled importance. The only memorandum of it is a scrap of paper in Codex 9697 of the Bibliothèque Nationale in Paris, in which a man named Carrara speaks of having found a subterranean chapel near S. Prisca, decorated with paintings of the fourth century, representing the apostles. A copy of the frescoes seems to have been made at the time, but no trace of it has been found. I cannot understand how, in an age like ours, so enthusiastically

111

devoted to archæological, historical, and religious research, no attempt has since been made to bring this venerable oratory to light.

In the same excavations of 1776 was found a bronze tablet, which had been offered to Gaius Marius Pudens Cornelianus, by the people of Clunia (near Palencia, Spain) as a token of gratitude for the services which he had rendered them during his governorship of the province of Tarragona. The tablet, dated April 9, A. D. 222, proves that the house owned by Aquila and Prisca in apostolic times had subsequently passed into the hands of a Cornelius Pudens; in other words, that the relations formed between the two families during the sojourn of the apostles in Rome had been faithfully maintained by their descendants. Their intimate connection is also proved by the fact that Pudens, Pudentiana, Praxedes, and Prisca were all buried in the Cemetery of Priscilla on the Via Salaria.[62]

A very old tradition, confirmed by the "Liber Pontificalis," describes the modern church of S. 112 Pudentiana as having been once the private house of the same Pudens who was baptized by the apostles, and who is mentioned in the epistles of S. Paul.[63] Here the first converts met for prayers; here Pudentiana, Praxedes and Timotheus, daughters and son of Pudens, obtained from Pius I. the institution of a regular parish-assembly (*titulus*), provided with a baptismal font; and here, for a long time, were preserved some pieces of household furniture which had been used by S. Peter. The tradition deserves attention because it was openly accepted at the beginning of the fourth century. The name of the church at that time was simply Ecclesia Pudentiana, which means "the church of Pudens," its owner and founder. An inscription discovered by Lelio Pasqualini speaks of a Leopardus, *lector de Pudentiana*, in the year 384; and in the mosaic of the apse the Redeemer holds a book, on the open page of which is written: "The Lord, defender of the church of Pudens." In course of time the ignorant people changed the word Pudentiana, a possessive adjective, into the name of a saint; and the name Sancta Pudentiana usurped the place of the genuine one. It appears for the first time in a document of the year 745.

The connection of the house with the apostolate of SS. Peter and Paul made it very popular from the beginning. Laymen and clergymen alike contributed to transform it into a handsome church. Pope Siricius (384-397), his acolytes Leopardus, Maximus and Ilicius, and Valerius Messalla, prefect of the city (396-403), ornamented it with mosaics, colonnades, and marble screens, and built on the west side of the Vicus Patricius a portico more than a thousand feet 113 long, which led from the Subura to the vestibule of the church.

In 1588 Cardinal Enrico Caetani disfigured the building with unfortunate restorations. He laid his hands even on the mosaics of the apse, considered by Poussin the best in Rome, as they are the oldest (A. D. 398), and mutilated the figures of two apostles, a portion of the foreground and the historical inscription. His architect, Francesco Ricciarelli da Volterra, while excavating the foundations for one of the pilasters of the new dome, made a discovery, which is described by Gaspare Celio[64] in the following words:—

"While Francesco Volterra was restoring the church of S. Pudentiana, and building the foundations of the dome, the masons discovered a marble group of the Laocoön, broken into many pieces. Whether from ill will or from laziness, they left the beautiful work of art at the bottom of the trench, and brought to the surface only a leg, without the foot, and a wrist. It was given to me, and I used to show it with pride to my artist friends, until some one stole it. It was a replica of the Belvedere group, considerably larger, and so beautiful that many believe it to be the original described by Pliny (xxvi. 5). The ancients, like the moderns, were fond of reproducing masterpieces. If the replica of the Pietà of Michelangelo, which we admire in the church of S. Maria dell' Anima, had been found under the ground, would we not consider it a better work than the original in S. Peter's? Francesco Volterra complained to me many times about the slovenliness of the masons; he says that, working by contract (*a cottimo*), they were afraid they should get no reward for the trouble of bringing the group to the surface."

Remains of the House of Pudens,
discovered in 1870.

Remains of the house of Pudens were found in 1870. They occupy a considerable area under the neighboring houses.[65]

The theory accepted by some modern writers as regards the transformation of these halls of prayer into regular churches is this. The prayer-meetings were held in the *tablinum* (A) or reception room of the house, which, as shown in the accompanying plan, opened on the *atrium* or court (B), and this was surrounded by a portico or peristyle (C). In the early days of the gospel the *tablinum* could easily accommodate the small congregation of converts; but, as this increased in numbers and the space became inadequate, the faithful were compelled to occupy that section of the portico which was in front of the meeting hall. When the congregation became still larger, there was no other way of accommodating it, and sheltering it from rain or sun, than by covering the court either with an awning or a roof. There is very little difference between this arrangement and the plan of a Christian basilica. The *tablinum* becomes an apse; the court, roofed over, becomes the nave; the side wings of the peristyle become the aisles.

Among the Roman churches whose origin can be traced to the hall of meeting, besides those of Pudens and Prisca already mentioned, the best preserved seems to be that built by Demetrias at the third milestone of the Via Latina, near the "painted tombs." Demetrias, daughter of Anicius Hermogenianus, prefect of the city, 368-370, and of Tyrrania Juliana, a friend of Augustine and Jerome, enlarged the oratory already existing in the *tablinum* of the Anician villa, and transformed it into a beautiful church, afterwards dedicated to S. Lorenzo. Church and villa were discovered in 1857,

Plan of Pompeian House.

and, together with the painted tombs of the Via Latina, are now the property of the nation. The stranger could not find a pleasanter afternoon drive. The church is well preserved, and still contains the metric inscription in praise of Demetrias which was composed by Leo III. (795-816).[66]

II. SCHOLÆ. The laws of Rome were very strict in regard to associations, which, formed on
the pretence of amusement, charity, or athletic sports, were apt to degenerate into political
sects. Exception was made in favor of the *collegia funeraticia*, which were societies formed
to provide a decent funeral and place of burial for their members. An inscription discovered at
Civita Lavinia quotes the very words of a decree of the Senate on this subject: "It is permitted
to those who desire to make a monthly contribution for funeral expenses to form an
association." These clubs or colleges collected their subscriptions in a treasure-chest, and out
of it provided for the obsequies of deceased members. Funeral ceremonies did not cease
when the body or the ashes was laid in the sepulchre. It was the custom to celebrate on the
occasion a feast, and to repeat that feast year by year on the birthday of the dead, and on
other stated days. For the holding of these feasts, as well as for other meetings, special
buildings were erected, named *scholæ*; and when the societies received gifts from rich
members or patrons, the benefaction frequently took the shape of a new lodge-room, or of a

117

ground for a new cemetery, with a building for meetings."[67] The Christians took advantage of the freedom accorded to funeral colleges, and associated themselves for the same purpose, following as closely as possible their rules concerning contributions, the erection of lodges, the meetings, and the αγαπαι or love feasts; and it was largely through the adoption of these well-understood and respected customs that they were enabled to hold their meetings and keep together as a corporate body through the stormy times of the second and third centuries.

Two excellent specimens of *scholæ* connected with Christian cemeteries and with meetings of the faithful have come down to us, one above the Catacombs of Callixtus, the other above those of Soter.

The first edifice has the shape of a square hall with three apses,—*cella trichora*. It is built over the part of the catacombs which was excavated at the time of Pope Fabianus (A. D. 236-250), who is known to have raised *multas fabricas per cœmeteria*; it is probably his work, as the style of masonry is exactly that of the first half of the third century. The original *schola* was covered by a wooden roof, and had no façade or door. In the year 258, while Sixtus II., attended by his deacons Felicissimus and Agapetus, was presiding over a meeting at this place in spite of the prohibition of Valerian, a body of men invaded the *schola*, murdered the bishop and his acolytes, and razed the building nearly to the level of the ground. Half a century later, in the time of Constantine, it was restored to its original shape, with the addition of a vaulted roof and a façade. The line which separates the old foundations of Fabianus from the restorations of the age of peace is clearly visible. Later the *schola* was changed into a church and dedicated to the memory of Syxtus, who had lost his wife there, and of Cæcilia, who was buried in the crypt below. It became a great place of pilgrimage, and the itineraries mention it as one of the leading stations on the Appian Way.

When de Rossi first visited the place, fifty years ago, this famous *schola* or church of Syxtus and Cæcilia was used as a wine-cellar, while the crypts of Cæcilia and Cornelius were used as vaults. Thanks to his initiative the monument has again become the property of the Church of Rome; and after a lapse of ten or twelve centuries divine service was resumed in it on the twentieth day of April of the present year. Its walls have been covered with inscriptions found in the adjoining cemetery.

The theory suggested by modern writers with regard to the *scholæ* is very much the same as that concerning the *tablinum* of private houses. At first the small building was sufficient to meet the wants of a small congregation; with the increase of the members it became a *presbiterium*, or place reserved for the bishop or the clergy, while the audience stood outside, under the shelter of a tent, or a roof supported by upright beams. Here also we have all the architectural elements of the Christian basilica.

The name *schola*, in its original meaning, has never died out in Rome; and as in the Middle Ages we had the *scholæ* of the Saxons, the Greeks, the Frisians, and the Lombards, so we have in the present day those of the Jews (*gli scoli degli ebrei*).

III. ORATORIES AND CHURCHES BUILT OVER THE TOMBS OF MARTYRS AND CONFESSORS. The sacred buildings of this class are, or were formerly, outside the walls, as burial was not allowed within city limits. To explain their origin and to understand their significance we must bear in mind the following rules. The action of the Roman law towards the Christians, that is, towards persons accused of atheism and rebellion against the Empire, resulted in the execution of those who were convicted. Except in extraordinary cases, the body of the victim could be claimed by relatives and friends and buried with due honors. In chapters vi. and vii. instances will be quoted of the erection of imposing tombs to the memory of Roman patricians, generals and magistrates, who were put to death under the imperial régime. The same privileges of burial were granted to the Christians, who preferred, however, the modesty and safety of a grave in the heart of the catacombs to the pompous luxury of a mausoleum above ground. The grave of a martyr was an object of consideration, and was often visited by pilgrims, who adorned it with wreaths and lights on the anniversary of his execution. After the end of the persecutions the first thought of the victorious church was to honor the memory of those who had fought so gallantly for the common cause, and who at the sacrifice of their lives had hastened the advent of the days of freedom and peace. No better altar than those graves could be chosen for the celebration of divine service; but they were sunk deep in the ground, and the cubicula of the catacombs were hardly capable of containing the officiating clergy, much less the multitudes of the faithful. Touching the graves, removing them to a more suitable place, was out of the question; in the eyes of the early 120 Christians no more impious sacrilege could be perpetrated. There was but one way left to deal with the difficulty; that of cutting away the rock over and around the grave, and thereby gaining such space as was deemed sufficient for the erection of a basilica. The excavation was done in conformity with two rules,—that the tomb of the martyr should occupy the place of honor in the middle of the apse, and that the body of the church should be to the *east* of the tomb, except in cases of "force majeure," as when a river, a public road, or some other such obstacle made it necessary to vary this principle.

Such is the origin of the greatest sanctuaries of Christian Rome. The churches of S. Peter on the Via Cornelia, S. Paul on the Via Ostiensis, S. Sebastian on the Via Appia, S. Petronilla on the Via Ardeatina, S. Valentine on the Via Flaminia, S. Hermes on the Via Salaria, S. Agnes on the Via Nomentana, S. Lorenzo on the Via Tiburtina, and fifty other historical structures, owe their existence to the humble grave which no human hand was allowed to transfer to a more suitable and healthy place.

When these graves were not very deep, the floor of the basilica was almost level with the ground, as in the case of S. Peter's, S. Paul's, and S. Valentine's; in other cases it was sunk so deep in the heart of the hill that only the roof and the upper tier of windows were seen above the ground, as in the basilicas of S. Lorenzo, S. Petronilla, etc. There are two or three basilicas built, or rather excavated, entirely under ground. The best specimen is that of S. Hermes on the old Via Salaria.

It soon became evident that edifices sunk in such awkward places could hardly answer their purpose, on account of dampness and the want of air and light. Several steps were taken to 121 remedy the evil. Large portions of the hills were cut away so as to make the edifice free on one or two sides at least, and outlets for rain or spring water provided. We have a description of the system of drainage of S. Peter's, written by its originator, Pope Damasus, in a poem the original of which, discovered by Pope Paul V., in 1607, is preserved in the Grotte Vaticane:

—

"The hill was abundant in springs; and the water found its way to the very graves of the saints. Pope Damasus determined to check the evil. He caused a large portion of the Vatican Hill to be cut away; and by excavating channels and boring *cuniculi* he drained the springs so as to make the basilica dry and also to provide it with a steady fountain of excellent water."[68]

The Acqua Damasiana is still in use, and has the honor of supplying the apartments of the Pope. Its feeding-springs are located at S. Antonino, twelve hundred yards west of S. Peter's. The aqueduct of Damasus, restored in 1649 by Innocent X., is neatly built in the old Roman style; the channel is four feet nine inches high, three feet three inches wide, and runs through the clay of the hill at a depth of ninety-eight feet. The principal fountain, in the Cortile di S. Damaso, was designed by Algardi in 1649.

Apparently the works accomplished for the same purpose at S. Lorenzo fuori le Mura, by Pope Pelagius II. (579-590), were no less important. They are described in another poem, a modern copy of which (1860) is to be seen on the side of the mosaic in the apsidal arch. The poem relates how the hill of Cyriaca was cut away, and how, in consequence of the excavation, the church became light, accessible, and free from the danger of landslips and inundations. The importance of the work of Pelagius is rather exaggerated by the composer of the poem. The church was never free from dampness and want of air and light until the pontificate of Pius IX., who cut away another section of the hill.

The damage done to the catacombs by the builders of these sunken basilicas is incalculable. Thousands of graves must have been sacrificed for the embellishment of one.

The reader cannot expect to find in these pages a description of this class of basilicas; that of S. Peter's alone would require several volumes. I have in my modest library not less than twenty-two volumes on the subject, an insignificant fraction of the Petrine literature. And what do we know about S. Peter's? Very little in comparison with the amount of knowledge that lies yet unpublished in the volumes of Grimaldi,[69] in the archives of the Vatican, in epigraphic, historical and diplomatic documents scattered among various European libraries.

The history of the building has yet to be written. Duchesne's "Liber Pontificalis" and de Rossi's second volume of the "Inscriptiones Christianae" provide the necessary foundations for such a work. Let us hope that the Vatican will soon find its own Rohault de Fleury.[70]

The following sketch of the origin of the two leading sacred edifices of Rome may answer the scope of the present chapter. But let me repeat once again the declaration that I write about the monuments of ancient Rome from a strictly archæological point of view, avoiding questions which pertain, or are supposed to pertain, to religious controversy. For the archæologist the presence and execution of SS. Peter and Paul in Rome are facts established beyond a shadow of doubt by purely monumental evidence. There was a time when persons belonging to different creeds made it almost a case of conscience to affirm or deny *a priori* those facts, according to their acceptance or rejection of the tradition of any particular church. This state of feeling is a matter of the past, at least for those who have followed the progress of recent discoveries and of critical literature. However, if my readers think that I am assuming as proved what they still consider subject for discussion, I beg to refer them to

122

123

some of the standard works published on this subject by writers who are above the suspicion of partiality. Such are Döllinger's "First Age of Christianity" (translated by Henry Nutcombe Oxenham, second edition, London, Allen, 1867); Bishop Lightfoot's "Apostolic Fathers," part ii., London, Macmillan, 1885, one of the most beautiful and conclusive works on early Christian history and literature; and de Rossi's "Bullettino di archeologia cristiana," for 1877. Bishop Lightfoot justly remarks that when Ignatius—the second apostolic father, a contemporary of Trajan—writes to the Romans "I do not command you, like Peter and Paul," the words are full of meaning, if we suppose him to be alluding to the personal relations of the two apostles with the Roman Church. In fact, the reason for his use of this language is the recognition of the visit to Rome of S. Peter as well as S. Paul, which is persistently maintained in early tradition; and thus it is a parallel to the joint mention of the two apostles in "Clement of Rome" (p. 357). Döllinger adds: "That S. Peter worked in Rome is a fact so abundantly proved and so deeply imbedded in the earliest Christian history, that whoever treats it as a legend ought in consistency to treat the whole of the earliest church history as legendary, or at least, quite uncertain. His presence in Corinth is obviously connected with his journey to Rome, and no one will accept the one and deny the other (see Cor. i. 12; iii. 22; xi. 22, 23; Clement's Ep. 47, etc.) Clement again reminds the Corinthians of the 'martyrdom of Peter and Paul ... among us,' meaning Rome. The very mention implies that S. Peter's martyrdom was a well-known fact, and it is inconceivable that his execution should have been known and not the place where it occurred, or that the place could have been forgotten, and a wrong one substituted some years later. And when Ignatius writes to the Romans—'I do not command you like Peter and Paul; they were apostles'—it is clear, without any explanation, that he desires to remind them of the two men who, as founders and teachers, had been the glory of the Church."

The Ebionite document, called "The Preaching of Peter," produced about the time of Ignatius, or very soon after, and used by Heracleon in Hadrian's time, is manifestly founded on the undisputed fact of S. Peter having labored at Rome. It is inconceivable that the author of the Ebionite document should have put forward a groundless fable, about the theatre of S. Peter's operations, at a time when many who had seen him must have been still alive. Eusebius, who had the writings of Papias (and Hegesippos) before him, maintains with Clement, that S. Peter wrote his Epistle at Rome (Euseb. ii. 15). Papias, a disciple of S. John, speaking of this epistle declares that "Babylon" means expressly the capital of the empire. Hegesippos, a Christian Jew of Palestine, who came to Rome in the first half of the second century, makes Linus the first bishop after the apostles, in accordance with Irenæus, who says: "After Peter and Paul had founded the Roman church and set it in order, they gave over the episcopate to Linus." If we consider that Hegesippos came to Rome to investigate, among other things, the succession of local bishops for the short period of eighty-three years, that he certainly spoke with persons whose fathers could remember the presence of the apostles, we cannot help accepting his evidence as conclusive.

The main objection brought forward by the opponents is that, after the incident at Antioch, we have no positive knowledge of the actions and travels of S. Peter. Still, there is nothing to contradict the assumption of his journey to Rome, and his confession and execution there. The fact was so generally known that nobody took the trouble to write a precise statement of it, because nobody dreamed that it could be denied. How is it possible to imagine that the primitive Church did not know the place of the death of its two leading apostles? In default of written testimony let us consult monumental evidence.

There is no event of the imperial age and of imperial Rome which is attested by so many noble structures, all of which point to the same conclusion,—the presence and execution of the apostles in the capital of the empire. When Constantine raised the monumental basilicas over their tombs on the Via Cornelia and the Via Ostiensis; when Eudoxia built the church ad Vincula; when Damasus put a memorial tablet in the Platonia ad Catacumbas; when the houses of Pudens and Aquila and Prisca were turned into oratories; when the name of Nymphæ Sancti Petri was given to the springs in the catacombs of the Via Nomentana; when the twenty-ninth day of June was accepted as the anniversary of S. Peter's execution; when Christians and pagans alike named their children Peter and Paul; when sculptors, painters, medallists, goldsmiths, workers in glass and enamel, and engravers of precious stones, all began to reproduce in Rome the likenesses of the apostles, at the beginning of the second century, and continued to do so till the fall of the empire; must we consider them all as laboring under a delusion, or as conspiring in the commission of a gigantic fraud? Why were such proceedings accepted without protest from whatever city, from whatever community, if there were any other which claimed to own the genuine tombs of SS. Peter and Paul? These arguments gain more value from the fact that the evidence on the opposite side is purely negative. It is one thing to write of these controversies at a distance from the scene of the events, in the seclusion of one's own library; but quite another to study them on the spot, and to follow the events where they took place. If my readers had the opportunity of witnessing the discoveries made lately in the Cemeterium Ostrianum, and the Platonia ad Catacumbas; or of examining Grimaldi's manuscripts and drawings relating to the old basilica of Constantine; or Carrara's account of the discoveries made in 1776 in the house of Aquila and Prisca, they would surely banish from their minds the last shade of doubt.

Besides the works of Döllinger, Lightfoot, and de Rossi referred to above, there are thirty or forty which deal with the same question, as to whether S. Peter was ever at Rome. The list of them is given in volume xviii. of the "Encyclopædia Britannica," p. 696, no. 1.

Two roads issued from the bridge called *Vaticanus*, *Neronianus*, or *Triumphalis*, the remains of which are still seen at low water between S. Giovanni dei Fiorentini and the hospital of S. Spirito,—the Via Triumphalis, described in chapter vi., which corresponds to the modern Strada di Monte Mario, and joins the Clodia at la Giustiniana; and the Via Cornelia, which led to the woodlands west of the city, between the Via Aurelia Nova and the Triumphalis. When the apostles came to Rome, in the reign of Nero, the topography of the Vatican district, which was crossed by the Via Cornelia, was as follows:—

On the left of the road was a circus begun by Caligula, and finished by Nero; on the right a line of tombs built against the clay cliffs of the Vatican. The circus was the scene of the first sufferings of the Christians, described by Tacitus in the well-known passage of the "Annals," xv. 45. Some of the Christians were covered with the skins of wild beasts so that savage dogs might tear them to pieces; others were besmeared with tar and tallow, and burnt at the stake; others were crucified (*crucibus adfixi*), while Nero in the attire of a vulgar *auriga* ran his races around the goals. This took place A. D. 65. Two years later the leader of the Christians shared the same fate in the same place. He was affixed to a cross like the others, and we know exactly where. A tradition current in Rome from time immemorial says that S. Peter was executed *inter duas metas* (between the two metæ), that is, in the *spina* or middle line of Nero's circus, at an equal distance from the two end goals; in other words, he was executed at the foot of the obelisk which now towers in front of his great church. For many centuries after the peace of Constantine, the exact spot of S. Peter's execution was marked by a chapel called the chapel of the "Crucifixion." The meaning of the name, and its origin, as well as the topographical details connected with the event, were lost in the darkness of the Middle Ages. The memorial chapel lost its identity and was believed to belong to "Him who was crucified," that is, to Christ himself. It disappeared seven or eight centuries ago. At the same time the words *inter duas metas*, by which the spot was so exactly located, were deprived of their genuine significance. The name *meta* was generally applied to tombs of pyramidal shape; of which two were still conspicuous among the ruins of Rome: the pyramid of Caius Cestius near the Porta S. Paolo, which was called *Meta Remi*, and that by the church of S. Maria Traspontina, in the quarter of the Vatican which was called *Meta Romuli*. The consequences of this mistake were remarkable; to it we owe the erection of two noble monuments, the church of S. Pietro in Montorio, and the "Tempietto del Bramante," in the court of the adjoining convent. It seems that in the thirteenth century, when some one[71] determined to raise a memorial of S. Peter's execution *inter duas metas*, he chose this spot on the spur of the Janiculum, because it was located at an equal distance from the meta of Romulus at la Traspontina, and that of Remus at the Porta S. Paolo!

The line of the Via Cornelia, which ran parallel with the north side of the circus, can be traced with precision by the help of the classical, or pagan, tombs discovered at various times along its borders. Let us start from the site of the modern Piazza di S. Pietro. Sante Bartoli, *mem.* 56-57, says that while Pope Alexander VII. was building the left wing of Bernini's portico, and the fountain of the southern semicircle, a tomb was discovered with a bas-relief above the door representing a marriage-scene ("vi era un bellissimo bassorilievo di un matrimonio antico"). On July 19, 1614, three others were found in the *atrium*, in one of which was the sarcophagus of Claudia Hermione, the renowned pantomimist. The best discovery, that of pagan tombs exactly on the line with that of S. Peter's, was made in the presence of Grimaldi, November 9, 1616. "On that day," he says, "I entered a square sepulchral room (10 ft. × 11 ft.), the ceiling of which was ornamented with designs in painted stucco. There was a

129

medallion in the centre, with a figure in high relief. The door opened on the Via Cornelia, which was on the same level. This tomb is located under the seventh step in front of the middle door of the church. I am told that the sarcophagus now used as a fountain, in the court of the Swiss Guards, was discovered at the time of Gregory XIII. in the same place, and that it contained the body of a pagan."

We come now to the decisive point, the discoveries made in the time of Urban VIII., when the foundations of his bronze baldacchino were sunk to a great depth, in close proximity to the tomb of S. Peter. The genuineness of the account is proved by the fact that in spite of its great bearing on the question, so little importance was attached to it that, had not Professor Palmieri and Cavaliere Armellini unearthed it from the sacred dust of the Vatican archives, in which it had been buried for three and a half centuries, we should still have been wholly ignorant of its existence.

The account published by Armellini[72] proves that S. Peter must have been buried in a small plot surrounded by other tombs, and probably protected by an enclosing wall. There were graves which in later ages had been dug in confusion, one above the other, by persons wishing to lie as near as possible to the remains of the apostle; but those of the time of the persecution were arranged in parallel lines,[73] and consisted of plain marble coffins bearing no name, and containing one or two bodies, which were dressed like mummies, with bands of darkish linen wound about the body and head. This statement is corroborated by other evidence. In 1615, when Paul V. built the stairs leading to the Confession and the crypts, "several bodies were found lying in coffins, tied with linen bands, as we read of Lazarus in the Gospel: *ligatus pedibus et manibus institis*. One body only was attired in a sort of pontifical robe. Notwithstanding the absence of written indications we thought they were the graves of the ten bishops of Rome buried *in Vaticano*." So speaks Giovanni Severano on page 20 of his book "Memorie sacre delle sette chiese di Roma," which was printed in 1629. Francesco Maria Torrigio, who witnessed the exhumations with cardinal Evangelista Pallotta, adds that the linen bands were from two to three inches wide, and that they must have been soaked in aromatics. One of the coffins bore, however, the name LINVS.[74] Let us now refer to the "Liber Pontificalis," the authority of which as an historical text-book cannot be doubted, since the critical publication of Louis Duchesne.[75] After describing the "deposition of S. Peter in the Vatican, near the circus of Nero, between the Via Aurelia and the Via Triumphalis, *iuxta locum ubi crucifixus est* (near the place of his crucifixion)," it proceeds to say that Linus "was buried side by side with the remains of the blessed Peter, in the Vatican, October 24." Even if we were disposed to doubt Torrigio's correctness in copying the name of the second bishop of Rome,[76] the fact of his burial in this place seems to be certain, because Hrabanus Maurus, a poet of the ninth century, speaks of Linus's tomb as visible and accessible, in the year 822. Another man was present at the discoveries enumerated by Torrigio and Severano; the master-mason Benedetto Drei, whose drawing, printed in 1635, has become very rare.

The reader will remark how perfectly Drei's sketch fits the written accounts of the other eye-witnesses, even in the detail of the child's grave—"*sepoltura di un bambino*,"—which is distinctly mentioned by them.

The privileges which the Roman law allowed to sepulchres, even of criminals, made it possible for the Christians to keep these graves in good order, with impunity. However, they ran a great risk under Elagabalus. Among the many extravagances in which this youth indulged in connection with the circus, such as driving a chariot drawn by four camels, or letting loose thousands of poisonous snakes among the spectators, Lampridius mentions a race of four quadrigæ drawn by elephants, which was to be run in the Vatican; and as the track inside the circus was obviously too narrow for such an attempt, another was prepared outside by removing or destroying those tombs of the Via Cornelia which stood in the way.[77] It is more than probable that the body of S. Peter was at that time transferred to a temporary place of shelter at the third milestone of the Via Appia, which I shall have opportunity to describe in the seventh chapter.[78]

After the defeat of Maxentius in the plains of Torre di Quinto, Constantine "raised a basilica over the tomb of the blessed Peter, which he enclosed in a bronze case. The altar above was decorated with spiral columns carved with vines which he had brought over from Greece."[79]

The basilica was erected hurriedly at the expense of the adjoining circus. Constantine took advantage of its three northern walls, which supported the seats of the spectators on the side of the Via Cornelia, to rest upon them the left wing of the church, and built new foundations for the right wing only. His architect seems to have been rather negligent in his measurements, because the tomb of S. Peter did not correspond exactly with the axis of the nave, and was not in the centre of the apse, being some inches to the left.

The columns were collected from everywhere. I have discovered in one of the note-books of Antonio da Sangallo the younger a memorandum of the quality, quantity, size, color, etc., of one hundred and thirty-six shafts. Nearly all the ancient quarries are represented in the collection, not to speak of styles and ages. An exception must be made in favor of the twelve columns of the Confession, mentioned above, which, according to the "Liber Pontificalis," were brought over from Greece (*columnæ vitineæ quas de Græcia perduxit*: i. 176). I doubt the correctness of the statement; they appear to me a fantastic Roman work of the third century.

PLAN OF THE GRAVES SURROUNDING THAT OF S. PETER
DISCOVERED AT THE TIME OF PAUL V.
(From a rare engraving by Benedetto Drei, head master mason to
the Pope. The site of the tomb of S. Peter and the Fenestella are
indicated by the author)

At all events the surmise of the "Liber Pontificalis" shows how little credit is to be attached to the tradition that they once belonged to the Temple of Solomon at Jerusalem.[80] There are eleven left: of which eight ornament the balconies under the dome; two, the altar of S. Mauritius, and one (reproduced in our illustration) the Cappella della Pietà, the first on the right. It is called the *colonna santa* (the holy column), because it was formerly used for the exorcism of evil spirits. It was enclosed in a marble *pluteus* by Cardinal Orsini, in 1438.

The walls of the church were patched with fragments of tiles (*tegolozza*) and stone, except the apse and the arches, which were built of good bricks bearing the name of the emperor:—

Dominus Noster CONSTANTINVS AV*Gustus.*

Grimaldi says that he could not find two capitals or two bases alike. He says also that the architraves and friezes differed from one intercolumniation to another, and that some of them were inscribed with the names and praises of Titus, Trajan, Gallienus, and others. On each side of the first gateway, at the foot of the steps, were two granite columns, with composite capitals, representing the bust of the emperor Hadrian framed in acanthus leaves.

The accompanying illustration, which was copied from an engraving of Ciampini, shows the aspect of the interior in the year 1588.

It gives a fairly good idea of the decorations of the nave, in their general outline; but fails to show the details of Constantine's patchwork. His system of structure may be better understood by referring to another of his creations, the basilica of S. Lorenzo fuori le Mura, of which a section of the interior is illustrated on p. 135.

The atrium or quadri-portico was entered by three gateways, the middle one of which had doors of bronze inlaid with silver. The *nielli* represented castles, cities, and territories which were subject to the apostolic see. The doors were stolen in 1167, and carried to Viterbo as trophies of war.

The Colonna Santa.

View of a section of the Nave of old S. Peter's (South Side).

The fountain in the centre of the atrium was a masterpiece of the time of Symmachus (498-514), who had a great predilection for buildings connected with hygiene and cleanliness, such as baths, fountains, and *necessaria*.[81] The fountain is described in my "Ancient Rome," p. 286; let me add here the particulars concerning its destruction.

The structure was composed of a square tabernacle supported by eight columns of red porphyry, with a dome of gilt bronze. Peacocks, dolphins, and flowers, also of gilt bronze, were placed on the four architraves, from which jets of water flowed into the basin below. The border of the basin was made of ancient marble bas-reliefs, representing panoplies, griffins, etc. On the top of the structure were semicircular bronze ornaments worked "à jour," that is, in open relief, without background, and crowned by the monogram of Christ. This gem of the art of the sixth century was ruthlessly destroyed by Paul V. The eight columns of porphyry, one of which was ornamented with an imperial bust in high relief, have disappeared, and so have the bas-reliefs of the border of the fountain, although Grimaldi claims to have saved one. The bronzes were removed to the garden of the Vatican, but, with the exception of the pine-cone and two peacocks, they were doomed to share the fate of the marbles. In 1613 the semicircular pediments, the four dolphins, two of the peacocks, and the dome were melted to provide the ten thousand pounds of metal required for the casting of the statue of the Madonna which was placed by Paul V. on the column of S. Maria Maggiore.

The most important monument of the atrium, after the fountain, was the tomb of the emperor Otho II. († 983), or what was believed to be his tomb, as some contemporary writers attribute it to Cencio, prefect of Rome, who died 1077. The body lay in a marble

136

sarcophagus, which was screened by slabs of serpentine, the whole being surmounted by a porphyry cover supposed to have come from Hadrian's mausoleum. The mosaic picture above represented the Saviour between SS. Peter and Paul. This historical monument was demolished by Carlo Maderno in the night of October 20, 1610. The coffin was removed to the Quirinal and turned into a water-trough. Grimaldi saw it last, near the entrance gate from the side of the Via dei Maroniti. The panels of serpentine were used in the new building, the picture of the Saviour was removed to the Grotte; the cover of porphyry was turned upside down, and made into a baptismal font.

The Fountain of Symmachus.

The church was entered by five doors, named respectively (from left to right) the Porta *ludicii*, *Ravenniana*, *argentea* or *regia maior*, *Romana*, and *Guidonea*. The first was called the "Judgment Door," because funerals entered or passed out through it. The name "Ravenniana" seems to have originated in the barracks of marine infantry of the fleet of Ravenna, detailed for duty in Rome, or else from the name "Civitas Ravenniana" given to the Trastevere in the epoch of the decadence. It was reserved for the use of men, as the fourth or Romana was for women, and the fifth, Guidonea, for tourists and pilgrims. The main entrance, called the "Royal," or "Silver Door," was opened only on grand occasions. Its name was derived from the silver ornaments affixed to the bronze by Honorius I. (A. D. 626-636) in commemoration of the reunion of the church of Histria with the See of Rome. According to the "Liber Pontificalis" nine hundred and seventy-five pounds of silver were used in the work. There were the figures of S. Peter on the left and S. Paul on the right, surrounded by halos of precious stones. They were the prey of the Saracens in 845. Leo IV. restored them to a certain extent, changing the subject of the silver *nielli*. In the year 1437, Antonio di Michele da Viterbo, a Dominican lay brother, was commissioned by Pope Eugenius IV. to carve new side doors in wood, while Antonio Filarete and Simone Bardi were asked to model and cast, in bronze, those of the middle entrance.

On entering the nave the visitor was struck by the simplicity of Constantine's design, and by the multitude and variety of later additions, by which the number of altars alone had been increased from one to sixty-eight. Ninety-two columns supported an open roof, the trusses of which were of the kingpost pattern. In spite of frequent repairs, resulting from fires, decay, and age, some of these trusses still bore the mark of Constantine's name. They were splendid specimens of timber. Filippo Bonanni, whose description of S. Peter's deserves more credit than all the rest together, except Grimaldi's manuscripts,[82] says that on February 21, 1606, he examined and measured the horizontal beam of the first truss from the façade, which Carlo Maderno had just lowered to the floor; it was seventy-seven feet long and three feet thick. The same writer copies from a manuscript diary of Rutilio Alberini, dated 1339, the following story relating to the same roof: "Pope Benedict XII. (1334-1342) has spent eighty thousand gold florins in repairing the roof of S. Peter's, his head carpenter being maestro Ballo da Colonna. A brave man he was, capable of lowering and lifting those tremendous beams as if they were motes, and standing on them while in motion. I have seen one marked with the name of the builder of the church (CON*stantine*); it was so huge that all kinds of animals had bored their holes and nests in it. The holes looked like small caverns, many yards long, and gave shelter to thousands of rats." Grimaldi climbed the roof at the beginning of 1606, and describes it as made of three kinds of tiles,—bronze, brick, and lead. The tiles of gilt bronze were cast in the time of the emperor Hadrian for the roof of the Temple of Venus and Rome. Pope Honorius I. (625-640) was allowed by Heraclius to make use of them for S. Peter's. The brick tiles were all stamped with the seal of King Theodoric, or with the motto BONO ROMÆ (for the good of Rome). The lead sheets bore the names of various Popes, from Innocent III. (1130-1138) to Benedict XII. All these precious materials for the chronology and history of the basilica have disappeared, save a few planks from the roof, with which the doors of the modern church were made.

139

Another sight must have struck the pilgrim as he first crossed the threshold, that of the "triumphal arch" between the nave and the transept, glistening with golden mosaics. We owe to Prof. A. L. Frothingham, Jr., of Baltimore, the knowledge of this work of art, he having found the description of it by cardinal Jacobacci in his book "De Concilio" (1538). The mosaics represented the emperor Constantine being presented by S. Peter to the Saviour, to whom he was offering a model of the basilica. It was destroyed, with the dedicatory inscription, in 1525.[83]

The baptistery erected by Pope Damasus after the discovery of the springs of the Aqua Damasiana, and restored by Leo III. (795-816), stood at the end of the north transept.[84] One of its inscriptions contained the verse—

"Una Petri sedes unum verumque lavacrum,"—

an allusion both to the baptismal font and to the "chair of S. Peter's," upon which the Popes sat after baptizing the neophytes. The cathedra is mentioned by Optatus Milevitanus, Ennodius of Pavia, and by more recent authors, as having changed place many times, until Alexander VII., with the help of Bernini and Paul Schor, placed it in a case of gilt bronze at the end of the apse. It has been minutely examined and described several times by Torrigio, Febeo, and de Rossi. I saw it in 1867. The framework and a few panels of the relic may possibly date from apostolic times; but it was evidently largely restored after the peace of the Church. The upright supports at the four corners were whittled away by early pilgrims.

140

141

The Chair of S. Peter; after photograph from original. — *A* Oak wood, much decayed, and whittled by pilgrims. *B* Acacia wood, inlaid with ivory carvings.

Another work of art deserves attention, because its origin, age, and style are still matters of controversy. I mean the bronze statue of S. Peter (see p. 142) placed against the right wall of the nave, near the S. Andrew of Francis de Quesnoy. Without attempting a discussion which would be inconsistent with the spirit of this book, I can safely state that the theories suggested by modern Petrographists, from Torrigio to Bartolini, deserve no credit. The statue is not the Capitoline Jupiter transformed into an apostle; nor was it cast with the bronze of that figure; it never held the thunderbolt in the place of the keys of heaven. The statue was cast as a portrait of S. Peter; the head belongs to the body; the keys and the uplifted fingers of the right hand are essential and genuine details of the original composition. The difficulty, and it is a great one, consists in stating its age. There is no doubt that Christian sculptors modelled excellent portrait-statues in the second and third centuries: as is proved by that of Hippolytus (see p. 143), discovered in 1551 in the Via Tiburtina, and now in the Lateran Museum, a work of the time of Alexander Severus.

There is no doubt also that there is a great similarity between the two, in the attitude and inclination of the body, the position of the feet, the style of dress, and even the lines of the folds. But portrait-statues of bronze may belong to any age; because, while the sculptor in marble is obliged to produce a work of his own hands and conception, and the date of a marble statue can therefore be determined by comparison with other well-known works, the caster in bronze can easily reproduce specimens of earlier and better times by taking a mould from a good original, altering the features slightly, and then casting it in excellent bronze. This seems to be the case with this celebrated image. I know that the current opinion makes it contemporary with the erection of Constantine's basilica; but to this I cannot subscribe on account of the comparatively modern shape of the keys. One of two things must be true,— either that these keys are a comparatively recent addition, in which case the statue may be a work of the fourth century, or they were cast together with the figure. If the latter be the fact the statue is of a comparatively recent age. Doubts on the subject might be dispelled by a careful examination of these crucial details, which I have not been able to undertake to my satisfaction.

Bronze Statue of S. Peter.

The destruction of old S. Peter's is one of the saddest events in the history of the ruin of Rome. It was done at two periods and in two sections, a cross wall being raised in the mean time in the middle of the church to allow divine service to proceed without interruption, while the destruction and the rebuilding of each half was accomplished in successive stages.

Statue of S. Hippolytus.

The work began April 18, 1506, under Julius II. It took exactly one century to finish the western section, from the partition wall to the apse. The demolition of the eastern section began February 21, 1606. Nine years later, on Palm Sunday, April 12, 1615, the jubilant multitudes witnessed the disappearance of the partition wall, and beheld for the first time the new temple in all its glory.

It seems that Paul V., Borghese, to whom the completion of the great work is due, could not help feeling a pang of remorse in wiping out forever the remains of the Constantinian basilica. He wanted the sacred college to share the responsibility for the deed, and summoned a consistory for September 26, 1605, to lay the case before the cardinals. The report revealed a remarkable state of things. It seems that while the foundations of the right side of the church built by Constantine had firmly withstood the weight and strain imposed upon them, the foundation of the left side, that is, the three walls of the circus of Caligula, which had been

144

built for a different purpose, had yielded to the pressure so that the whole church, with its four rows of columns, was bending sideways from right to left, to the extent of three feet seven inches. The report stated that this inclination could be noticed from the fact that the frescoes of the left wall were covered with a thick layer of dust; it also stated that the ends of the great beams supporting the roof were all rotten and no longer capable of bearing their burden. Then cardinal Cosentino, the dean of the chapter, rose to say that, only a few days before, while mass was being said at the altar of S. Maria della Colonna, a heavy stone had fallen from the window above, and scattered the congregation. The vote of the sacred college was a foregone conclusion. The sentence of death was passed upon the last remains of old S. Peter's; a committee of eight cardinals was appointed to preside over the new building, and nine architects were invited to compete for the design. These were Giovanni and Domenico Fontana, Flaminio Ponzio, Carlo Maderno, Geronimo Rainaldi, Nicola Braconi da Como, Ottavio Turiano, Giovanni Antonio Dosio, and Ludovico Cigoli. The competition was won by Carlo Maderno, much to the regret of the Pope, who was manifestly in favor of his own architect, Flaminio Ponzio. The execution of the work was marked by an extraordinary accident. On Friday, August 27, 1610, a cloud-burst swept the city with such violence that the volume of water which accumulated on the terrace above the basilica, finding no outlet but the winding staircases which pierced the thickness of the walls, rushed down into the nave in roaring torrents and inundated it to a depth of several inches. The Confession and tomb of the apostle were saved only by the strength of the bronze door.

It is very interesting to follow the progress of the work in Grimaldi's diary, to witness with him the opening and destruction of every tomb worthy of note, and to make the inventory of its contents. The monuments were mostly pagan sarcophagi, or bath basins, cut in precious marbles; the bodies of Popes were wrapped in rich robes, and wore the "ring of the fisherman" on the forefinger. Innocent VIII., Giovanni Battista Cibo (1484-1492), was folded in an embroidered Persian cloth; Marcellus II., Cervini (1555), wore a golden mitre; Hadrian IV., Breakspeare (1154-1159), is described as an undersized man, wearing slippers of Turkish make, and a ring with a large emerald. Callixtus III. and Alexander VI., both of the Borgia family, have been twice disturbed in their common grave: the first time by Sixtus V., when he removed the obelisk from the spina of the circus to the piazza; the second by Paul V. on Saturday, January 30, 1610, when their bodies were removed to the Spanish church of Montserrat, with the help of the marquis of Billena, ambassador of Philip III., and of cardinal Çapata.

Grimaldi asserts that Michelangelo's plan of a Greek cross had not only been designed on paper, but actually begun. When Pope Borghese and Carlo Maderno determined upon the Latin cross, not only the foundations of the front had been finished according to Michelangelo's design, but the front itself, with its coating of travertine, had been built to the height of several feet. The construction of the dome was begun on Friday, July 15, 1588, at 4 P. M. The first block of travertine was placed *in situ* at 8 P. M. of the thirtieth. The cylindrical portion or drum (*tamburo*) which supports the dome proper was finished at midnight of December 17, of the same year, a marvellous feat to have accomplished. The dome itself was begun five days later, and finished in seventeen months. If we remember that the experts of the age had estimated ten years as the time required to accomplish the work, and one million gold scudi as the cost, we wonder at the power of will of Sixtus V., who did it in two years and spent only one fifth of the stated sum.[85] He foresaw that the political persecution from the crown of Spain and the daily assaults, almost brutal in their nature, which he had to endure from count d'Olivare, the Spanish ambassador, would shorten his days, and consequently manifested but one desire: that the dome and the other great works undertaken for the embellishment and sanitation of the city should be finished before his death. Six hundred skilled craftsmen were enlisted to push the work of the dome night and day; they were excused from attending divine service on feast days, Sundays excepted. We may form an idea of the haste felt by all concerned in the enterprise, and of their determination to sacrifice all other interests to speed, by the following anecdote. The masons, being once in need of another receptacle for water, laid their hands on the tomb of Pope Urban VI., dragged the marble sarcophagus under the dome on the edge of a lime-pit, and emptied it of its contents. The golden ring was given to Giacomo della Porta, the architect, the bones were put aside in a corner of the building, and the coffin was used as a tank from 1588 to 1615.

S. PETER'S IN 1588. (From an engraving by Ciampini)

When we consider that the building-materials—stones, bricks, timber, cement, and water— had to be lifted to a height of four hundred feet, it is no wonder that five hundred thousand pounds of rope should have been consumed, and fifteen tons of iron. The dome was built on a framework of most ingenious design, resting on the cornice of the drum so lightly that it seemed suspended in mid air. One thousand two hundred large beams were employed in it.

Fea and Winckelmann assert that the lead sheets which cover the dome must be renewed eight or ten times in a century. Winckelmann attributes their rapid decay to the corrosive action of the sirocco wind; Fea to the variations in temperature, which cause the lead to melt in summer, and crack in winter.

The size and height, the number of columns, altars, statues, and pictures,—in short, the *mirabilia* of S. Peter's,—have been greatly exaggerated. There is no necessity of exaggeration when the truth is in itself so astonishing. Readers fond of statistics may consult the works of Briccolani and Visconti.[86] The basilica is approached by a square 1256 feet in diameter. The nave is six hundred and thirteen feet long, eighty-eight wide, one hundred and thirty-three high; the transept is four hundred and forty-nine feet long. The cornice and the mosaic inscription of the frieze are 1943 feet long. The dome towers to the height of four hundred and forty-eight feet above the pavement, with a diameter on the interior of 139.9 feet, a trifle less than that of the Pantheon. The letters on the frieze are four feet eight inches high. The old church contained sixty-eight altars and two hundred and sixty-eight columns; while the modern one contains forty-six altars,—before which one hundred and twenty-one lamps are burning day and night,—and seven hundred and forty-eight columns, of marble, stone and bronze. The statues number three hundred and eighty-six, the windows two hundred and ninety.

It is easy to imagine to what surprising effects of light and shade such vastness of proportion lends itself on the occasion of illuminations. These were made both inside (Holy Thursday and Good Friday) and outside (Easter, and June 29). The outside illumination required the use of forty-four hundred lanterns, and of seven hundred and ninety-one torches, and the help of three hundred and sixty-five men. It has not been seen since 1870. I have heard from old friends who remember the illumination of the interior, which was given up more than half a century ago, that no sight could be more impressive. In the darkness of the night, a cross studded with thirteen hundred and eighty lights shone like a meteor at a prodigious height, while the multitude crowding the church knelt and prayed in silent rapture.

Before leaving the Vatican let me answer a doubt which may naturally have occurred to the mind of the reader, as it has long perplexed the author. After the many vicissitudes to which the place has been subject, from the time of Elagabalus to the pillage of the constable de Bourbon, can we be sure that the body of the founder of the Roman Church is still lying in its grave under the great dome of Michelangelo, under the canopy of Urban VIII., under the high altar of Clement VIII.? After considering the case from its various aspects, and weighing all the circumstances which have attended each of the barbaric invasions, I cannot see any reason why we should disbelieve the popular opinion. The tombs of S. Peter and S. Paul have been exposed but once to imminent danger, and that happened in 846, when the Saracens took possession of their respective churches and plundered them at leisure. Suppose the crusaders had taken possession of Mecca: their first impulse would have been to wipe the tomb of the Prophet from the face of the earth, unless the keepers of the Kaabah, warned of their approach, had time to conceal or protect the grave by one means or another. Unfortunately, we know very little about the Saracenic invasion of 846; still it seems certain that Pope Sergius II. and the Romans were warned days or weeks beforehand of the landing of the infidels, by a despatch from the island of Corsica. Inasmuch as the churches of S. Peter and S. Paul were absolutely defenceless, in their outlying positions, I am sure that steps were taken to conceal or wall in the entrance to the crypts and the crypts themselves, unless the tombs were removed bodily to shelter within the city walls. An argument, very little known but of great value, seems to prove that the relics were saved.

The "Liber Pontificalis" describes, among the gifts of Constantine, a cross of pure gold, weighing one hundred and fifty pounds, which he placed over the gold lid of the coffin. The golden cross bore the following inscription in *niello* work, "Constantine the emperor and Helena the empress have richly decorated this royal crypt, and the basilica which shelters it." If this precious object is there, the remains must *a fortiori* be there also. Here comes the decisive test. In the spring of 1594, while Giacomo della Porta was levelling the floor of the church above the Confession, removing at the same time the foundations of the Ciborium of Julius II., the ground gave way, and he saw through the opening what nobody had beheld since the time of Sergius II.,—the grave of S. Peter,—and upon it the golden cross of Constantine. On hearing of the discovery, Pope Clement VIII., accompanied by cardinals Bellarmino, Antoniano, and Sfrondato, descended to the Confession, and with the help of a torch, which Giacomo della Porta had lowered into the hollow space below, could see with his own eyes and could show to his followers the cross, inscribed with the names of Constantine and Helena. The impression produced upon the Pope by this wonderful sight was so great that he caused the opening to be closed at once. The event is attested not only by a manuscript deposition of Torrigio, but also by the present aspect of the place. The materials with which Clement VIII. sealed the opening, and rendered the tomb once more invisible and inaccessible, can still be seen through the "cataract" below the altar.

Wonder has been manifested at the behavior of Constantine towards S. Paul, whose basilica at the second milestone of the Via Ostiensis appears like a pigmy structure in comparison to that of S. Peter. Constantine had no intention of placing S. Paul in an inferior rank, or of showing less honor to his memory. He was compelled by local circumstances to raise a much smaller building to this apostle. As before stated, there were three rules which builders of sacred memorial edifices had to observe: first, that the tomb-altar of the saint in whose honor the building was to be erected should not be molested or moved from its original place either vertically or horizontally; second, that the edifice should be adapted to the tomb so as to give it a place of honor in the centre of the apse; third, that the apse and the front of the edifice should look towards the east. The position of S. Peter's tomb in relation to the circus of Nero and the cliffs of the Vatican was such as to give the builders of the basilica perfect freedom to extend it in all directions, especially lengthwise. This was not the case with that of S. Paul,

151

which was only a hundred feet distant from an obstacle which could not be overcome,—the high-road to Ostia, the channel by which the city of Rome was fed. The road to Ostia ran *east* of the grave; hence the necessity of limiting the size of the church within these two points. Discoveries made in 1834, when the foundations of the present apse were strengthened, and again in 1850, when the foundations of the baldacchino of Pius IX. were laid,[87] have enabled Signor Paolo Belloni, the architect, to reconstruct the plan of the original building of Constantine. His memoir[88] is full of useful information well illustrated. One of his illustrations, representing the comparative plans of the original and modern churches, is here reproduced.

The plan needs no comment, but one particular cannot be omitted. In the course of the excavations for the baldacchino, the remains of classical columbaria were found a few feet from the grave of the apostle, with their inscriptions still in place. He must, therefore, have been buried, like S. Peter, in a private area, surrounded by pagan tombs.

In 386 Valentinian, Theodosius, and Arcadius asked Flavius Sallustius, prefect of the city, to submit to the Senate and the people a scheme for the reconstruction *a fundamentis* of the basilica, so as to make it equal in size and beauty to that of the Vatican. To fulfil this project, without disturbing either the grave of the apostle or the road to Ostia, there was but one thing to do; this was to change the orientation of the church from east to west, and extend it at pleasure towards the bank of the Tiber. The consent of the S. P. Q. R. was easily obtained, and the magnificent temple, which lasted until the fire of July 15, 1823, was thus raised so as to face in a direction opposite to the usual one.

152

The Burning of S. Paul's, July 15, 1823. (From an old print.)

The name of Pope Siricius, who was then governing the church, can still be seen engraved on one of the columns, formerly in the left aisle, now in the north vestibule:—

SIRICIVS EPISCOPVS A   Ω TOTA MENTE DEVOTVS.

Another rare monument of historical value, in spite of its humble origin, came to light at the 153 beginning of the last century, and was published by Bianchini and Muratori, who failed, however, to explain its meaning. It is a brass label once tied to a dog's collar, with the inscription "[I belong] to the basilica of Paul the apostle, rebuilt by our three sovereigns [Valentinianus, Theodosius, and Arcadius]. I am in charge of Felicissimus the shepherd." Such inscriptions were engraved on the collars of dogs, and slaves, so that in case they ran away from their masters, their legal ownership would be known at once by the police, or whoever chanced to catch them.

In course of time the basilica became the centre of a considerable group of buildings, especially of monasteries and convents. There were also chapels, baths, fountains, hostelries, porticoes, cemeteries, orchards, farmhouses, stables, and mills. This small suburban city was exposed to a constant danger of pillage, on account of its location on the high-road from the coast. In 846 it was ransacked by the Saracens, before the Romans could come to the rescue. For these considerations, Pope John VIII. (872-882) determined to put the church of S. Paul and its surroundings under shelter, and to raise a fort that could also command the approach to Rome from this most dangerous side.

The construction of Johannipolis, by which the history of the classical and early mediæval fortifications of Rome is brought to a close, is described by one document only: an inscription above the gate of the castle, which was copied first by Cola di Rienzo, and later by Pietro Sabino, professor of rhetoric in the Roman archigymnasium (Sapienza), towards the end of the fifteenth century. A few fragments of this remarkable document are still preserved in the cloister of the monastery. It states that Pope John VIII. raised a wall for the defence of the 154 basilica of S. Paul's and the surrounding churches, convents, and hospices, in imitation of that built by Leo IV. for the protection of the Vatican suburb. The determination to fortify the sacred buildings at the second milestone of the Via Ostiensis was taken, as I have just said, in consequence of the inroads of the Saracens, which, under the pontificate of John, had become so frequent. The atrocities which marked their second landing on the Roman coast were so appalling that the whole of Europe was shaken with terror. Having failed in his attempt to secure help from Charles the Bald, John placed himself at the head of such scanty forces as he could gather from land and sea, under the pressure of events. Ships from several harbors in the Mediterranean met in the roads of Ostia; and on hearing that the hostile fleet had sailed from the bay of Naples, the Pope set sail at once. The gallant little squadron confronted the infidels under the cliffs of Cape Circeo, and inflicted upon them such a bloody defeat that the danger was averted, at least for a time. The church galleys came back to the mouth of the Tiber, laden with a considerable booty.

It seems that the advance fort of Johannipolis was finished and consecrated by Pope John soon after the naval battle of Cape Circeo (A. D. 877), because the inscription above referred to speaks of him as a *triumphant* leader,—SEDIS APOSTOLICÆ PAPA JOHANNES OVANS.

The location of this fortified outpost could not have been more judiciously selected. It commanded the roads from Ostia, Laurentum, and Ardea, those, namely, from which the pirates could most easily approach the city. It commanded also the water-way by the Tiber, and the towpaths on each of its banks. It is a great pity that no stone of this historical wall should be left standing. It saved the city from further invasions of the African pirates, as the *agger* of Servius Tullius had saved it, centuries before, from the attacks of the Carthaginians. I have examined the ground between S. Paul's, the Fosso di Grotta Perfetta, the Vigna de Merode, at the back of the apse, and the banks of the river, without finding a trace of the fortification. I believe, however, that the wall which encloses the garden of the monastery on the south side runs on the same line with John's defences, and rests on their foundations. We must not wonder at the disappearance of Johannipolis, when we have proofs that even the quadri-portico, by which the basilica was entered from the riverside, has been allowed to disappear through the negligence and slovenliness of the monks. Pope Leo I. erected in the centre of the quadri-portico a fountain crowned by a Bacchic Kantharos, and wrote on its epistyle a brilliant epigram, inviting the faithful to purify themselves bodily and spiritually, before presenting themselves to the apostle within. When Cola di Rienzo visited the spot, towards the middle of the fourteenth century, the monument was still in good condition. He calls it "the vase of waters (*cantharus aquarum*), before the main entrance (of the church) of the blessed Paul." One century later the whole structure had become a heap of ruins. Fra Giocondo da Verona looked in vain for the inscription of Leo I.; he could only find a fragment "lying among the nettles and thorns" (*inter orticas et spineta*). The same indifference was shown towards the edifices by which the basilica was surrounded. They fell, or were overthrown, one by one.

In 1633, when Giovanni Severano wrote his book on the Seven Churches, only one bit of ruins could be identified, the door and apse of the church of S. Stephen, to which a powerful convent had once been attached. Stranger still is the total destruction of the portico, two thousand yards long, which connected the city gate—the Porta Ostiensis—with the basilica. This portico was supported by marble columns, one thousand at least, and its roof was covered with sheets of lead. Halfway between the gate and S. Paul's, it was intersected by a church, dedicated to an Egyptian martyr, S. Menna. The church of S. Menna, the portico, its thousand columns, even its foundation walls, have been totally destroyed. A document discovered by Armellini in the archives of the Vatican says that some faint traces of the building (*vestigia et parietes*) could be still recognized in the time of Urban VI. This is the last mention made by an eye-witness.

Here, also, we find the evidence of the gigantic work of destruction pursued for centuries by the Romans themselves, which we have been in the habit of attributing to the barbarians alone. The barbarians have their share of responsibility in causing the abandonment and the desolation of the Campagna; they may have looted and damaged some edifices, from which there was hope of a booty; they may have profaned churches and oratories erected over the tombs of martyrs; but the wholesale destruction, the obliteration of classical and mediæval monuments, is the work of the Romans and of their successive rulers. To them, more than to the barbarians, we owe the present condition of the Campagna, in the midst of which Rome remains like an oasis in a barren solitude.

S. Paul was executed on the Via Laurentina, near some springs called *Aquæ Salviæ*, where a memorial chapel was raised in the fifth century. Its foundations were discovered in 1867, under the present church of S. Paolo alle Tre Fontane (erected in the seventeenth century by Cardinal Aldobrandini) together with historical inscriptions written in Latin and Armenian. I have also to mention another curious discovery. The apocryphal Greek Acts of S. Paul, edited by Tischendorff,[89] assert that the apostle was beheaded near these springs under a stone pine. In 1875, while the Trappists, who are now intrusted with the care of the Abbey of the Tre Fontane, were excavating for the foundations of a water-tank behind the chapel, they found a mass of coins of Nero, together with several pine-cones fossilized by age, and by the pressure of the earth.

Tombstone of S. Paul.

The "Liber Pontificalis," i. 178, asserts that Constantine placed the body of S. Paul in a coffin of solid bronze; but no visible trace of it is left. I had the privilege of examining the actual grave December 1, 1891, lowering myself from the *fenestella* under the altar. I found myself on a flat surface, paved with slabs of marble, on one of which (placed negligently in a slanting direction) are engraved the words: PAVLO APOSTOLO MART · · ·

The inscription belongs to the fourth century. It has been illustrated since by my kind and learned friend, Prof. H. Grisar, to whom I am indebted for much valuable information on subjects which do not come exactly within my line of studies.[90]

IV. Houses of Confessors and Martyrs. This class of sacred buildings has been splendidly illustrated by the discoveries made by Padre Germano dei Passionisti under the church of SS. Giovanni e Paolo on the Cælian. The good work of Padre Germano is not unknown in America, thanks to Prof. A. L. Frothingham, who has described it in the "American Journal of Archæology." The discoverer himself will shortly publish a voluminous account with the title: *La casa dei SS. Giovanni e Paolo sul monte celio.*

The church has the place of honor in early itineraries of pilgrims, because of its peculiarity in containing a martyr's tomb *within* the walls of the city. William of Malmesbury says: "Inside the city, on the Cælian hill, John and Paul, martyrs, lay in their own house, which was made into a church after their death." The Salzburg Itinerary describes the church as "very large and beautiful." The account of the lives of the two brothers, and of their execution under Julian the apostate, is apocryphal; but no one who has seen Padre Germano's excavations will deny the essential fact, that in this noble Roman house of the Cælian some one was put to death for his faith, and that over the room in which the event took place a church was built at a later age.

Tradition attributes its construction to Pammachius, son of Bizantes, the charitable senator, and friend of S. Jerome, who built an hospice at Porto for the use of pilgrims landing from countries beyond the sea. The church, according to the rule, was not named from the martyrs to whose memory it was sacred, but from the founders; and it became known first as the *Titulus Bizantis,* later as the *Titulus Pammachii.*

159

Strictly speaking, there was no transformation, but a mere superstructure. The Roman house was left intact, with its spacious halls, and classical decorations, to be used as a crypt, while the basilica was raised to a much higher level. The murder of the saints seems to have taken place in a narrow passage (*fauces*) not far from the *tablinum* or reception room. Here we see the *fenestella confessionis*, by means of which pilgrims were allowed to behold and touch the venerable grave. Two things strike the modern visitor: the variety of the fresco decorations of the house, which begin with pagan genii holding festoons, a tolerably good work of the third century, and end with stiff, uncanny representations of the Passion, of the ninth and tenth centuries; second, the fact that such an important monument should have been buried and forgotten, so that its discovery by Padre Germano took us by surprise. The upper church, the "beautiful and great" Titulus Pammachii, was treated with almost equal contempt by Cardinal Camillo Paolucci and his architect, Antonio Canevari, who "modernized" it at the end of the seventeenth century. The "spirit of the age" which lured these *seicento* men into committing such archæological and artistic blunders, placed no boundary upon its evil work. It attacked equally the great mediæval structures and their contents. To quote one instance: in the vestibule of this church was the tomb of Luke, cardinal of SS. Giovanni e Paolo, the friend of S. Bernard, the legate at the council of Clermont. It was composed of an ancient sarcophagus, resting on two marble lions. During the "modernization" of the seventeenth century, the coffin was turned into a water-trough, and cut half-way across so as to make it fit the place for which it was intended. Had it not happened that the inscription was copied by Bruzio before the mutilation of the coffin, we should have remained entirely ignorant of its connection with the illustrious friend of S. Bernard. But let us forget these sad experiences,

160

and step into the beautiful garden of the convent, which, large as it is, with its dreamy avenues of ilexes, its groves of cypress and laurel, and its luxuriant vineyards, is all included within the limits of one ancient temple, that of the Emperor Claudius (*Claudium*).

The view from the edge of the lofty platform over the Coliseum, the Temple of Venus and Rome, and the slopes of the Palatine, is fascinating beyond conception, and as beautiful as a dream. No better place could be chosen for the study of the next class of Roman places of worship, which comprises:—

V. PAGAN MONUMENTS CONVERTED INTO CHURCHES. The experience gained in twenty-five years of active exploration in ancient Rome, both above and below ground, enables me to state that every pagan building which was capable of giving shelter to a congregation was transformed, at one time or another, into a church or a chapel. Smaller edifices, like temples and mausoleums, were adapted bodily to their new office, while the larger ones, such as thermæ, theatres, circuses, and barracks were occupied in parts only. Let not the student be deceived by the appearance of ruins which seem to escape this rule; if he submits them to a patient investigation, he will always discover traces of the work of the Christians. How many times have I studied the so-called Temple of the Sibyl at Tivoli without detecting the faint traces of the figures of the Saviour and the four saints, which now appear to me distinctly visible in the niche of the cella. And again, how many times have I looked at the Temple of Neptune in the Piazza di Pietra,[91] without noticing a tiny figure of Christ on the cross in one of the flutings of the fourth column on the left. It seems to me that, at one period, there must have been more churches than habitations in Rome.

I shall ask the reader to walk over the Sacra Via from the foot of the Temple of Claudius, on the ruins of which we are still sitting, to the summit of the Capitol, and see what changes time has wrought on the surroundings of this pathway of the gods.

The Coliseum, which we meet first, on our right, was bristling with churches. There was one at the foot of the Colossus of the Sun, where the bodies of the two Persian martyrs, Abdon and Sennen, were exposed at the time of the persecution of Decius. There were four dedicated to the Saviour (*S. Salvator in Tellure, de Trasi, de Insula, de rota Colisei*), a sixth to S. James, a seventh to S. Agatha (*ad caput Africæ*), besides other chapels and oratories within the amphitheatre itself.

Proceeding towards the Summa Sacra Via and the Arch of Titus we find a church of S. Peter nestled in the ruins of the vestibule of the Temple of Venus (the S. Maria Nova of later times).

Popular tradition connected this church with the alleged fall of Simon the magician,—so vividly represented in Francesco Vanni's picture, in the Vatican,—and two cavities were pointed out in one of the paving-stones of the road, which were said to have been made by the knees of the apostle when he was imploring God to chastise the impostor. The paving-stone is now kept in the church of S. Maria Nova. Before its removal from the original place it gave rise to a curious custom. People believed that rainwater collected in the two holes was a miracle-working remedy; and crowds of ailing wretches gathered around the place at the approach of a shower.

On the opposite side of the road, remains of a large church can still be seen at the foot of the Palatine, among the ruins of the baths attributed to Elagabalus. Higher up, on the platform once occupied by the "Gardens of Adonis" and now by the Vigna Barberini, we can visit the church of S. Sebastiano, formerly called that of S. Maria in Palatio or in Palladio.

I am unable to locate exactly another famous church, that of S. Cesareus de Palatio, the private chapel which Christian emperors substituted for the classic Lararium (described in "Ancient Rome," p. 127). Here were placed the images of the Byzantine princes, sent from Constantinople to Rome, to represent in a certain way their rights. The custody of these was intrusted to a body of Greek monks. Their monastery became at one time very important, and was chosen by ambassadors and envoys from the east and from southern Italy as their residence during their stay in Rome.

The basilica of Constantine is another example of this transformation. Nibby, who conducted the excavations of 1828, saw traces of religious paintings in the apse of the eastern aisle. They are scarcely discernible now.

The temple of the Sacra Urbs, and the heroön of Romulus, son of Maxentius, became a joint church of SS. Cosma and Damiano, during the pontificate of Felix IV. (526-530); the Temple of Antoninus and Faustina was dedicated to S. Lorenzo; the Janus Quadrifrons to S. Dionysius, the hall of the Senate to S. Adriano, the offices of the Senate to S. Martino, the Mamertine prison to S. Peter, the Temple of Concord to SS. Sergio e Bacco.

The same practice was followed with regard to the edifices on the opposite side of the road. The Virgin Mary was worshipped in the Templum divi Augusti, in the place of the deified founder of the empire; and also in the Basilica Julia, the northern vestibule of which was transformed into the church of S. Maria de Foro. Finally, the Ærarium Saturni transmitted its classic denomination to the church of S. Salvatore in Ærario.

In drawing sheet no. xxix. of my archæological map of Rome, which represents the region of the Sacra Via, I have had as much to do with Christian edifices as with pagan ruins.[92]

VI. Memorials of Historical Events. The first commemorative chapel erected in Rome is perhaps contemporary with the Arch of Constantine, and refers to the same event, the victory gained by the first Christian emperor over Maxentius in the plain of the Tiber, near Torre di Quinto.

The existence of this chapel, called the *Oratorium Sanctæ Crucis* ("the oratory of the holy cross"), is frequently alluded to in early church documents. The name must have originated from a monumental cross erected on the battlefield, in memory of Constantine's vision of the "sign of Christ" (the monogram   ). In the procession which took place on S. Mark's day, from the church of S. Lorenzo in Lucina to S. Peter's, through the Via Flaminia and across the Ponte Milvio, the first halt was made at S. Valentine's,[93] the second at the chapel of the Holy Cross. The "Liber Pontificalis," in the Life of Leo III. (795-816), speaks of this strange ceremony. It was called the "great litany," and occurred on the twenty-third of April, the day on which the Romans used to celebrate the Robigalia. The Christian litany and the pagan ceremony had the same purpose, that of securing the blessing of Heaven upon the fields, and averting from them the pernicious effects of late spring frosts. The rites were nearly the same, the principal one being a procession which left Rome by the Porta Flaminia, and passed across the Ponte Milvio to a suburban sanctuary. The end of the pagan pilgrimage was a temple of the god Robigus or the goddess Robigo, situated at the fifth milestone of the Via

Claudia; that of the Christian the monumental cross near the same road, and ultimately the basilica of S. Peter's. In course of time the oratory and cross lost their genuine meaning; they were thought to mark the spot on which the miraculous vision had appeared to Constantine on the eve of battle. This was not the case, however, because Eusebius, to whom the emperor himself described the event, says that the luminous sign appeared to him before the commencement of military operations, which means before he crossed the Alps and took possession of Susa, Turin, and Vercelli. But, if the heavenly apparition of the "sign of Christ" on Monte Mario is historically without foundation, the existence of the oratory is not. Towards the end of the twelfth century it was in a ruinous state, and converted probably into a stable or a hay-loft. The last archæologist who mentions it is Seroux d'Agincourt. He describes the ruins "on the slopes of the hill of the Villa Madama," and gives a sketch of the paintings which appeared here and there on the broken walls. Armellini and myself have explored the beautiful woods of the Villa Madama in all directions without finding a trace of the building. It was probably destroyed in the disturbances of 1849.

The noble house of the Millini, to whom the Mons Vaticanus owes its present name of Monte Mario (from Mario Millini, son of Pietro and grandson of Saba), while building their villa on the highest ridge, in 1470, raised a chapel in place of the one which had been profaned, and called it Santa Croce a Monte Mario. It was held in great veneration by the Romans, who made pilgrimages to it in times of public calamities, such as the famous plague (*contagio-moria*) of Alexander VII. I well remember this interesting little church, before its disappearance in 1880. Its pavement, according to the practice of the time, was inlaid with inscriptions from the catacombs, whole or in fragments, twenty-four of which are now preserved in the Lipsanotheca (Palazzo del Vicario, Piazza di S. Agostino). They contain a curious list of names, like *Putiolanus* (so called from his birth-place, Pozzuoli) or *Stercoria*, a name which seems to have been taken up by devout people, as a sign of humility. Another inscription over the door of the sacristy spoke of a restoration of the building in 1696; a third, composed by Pietro and Mario Mellini in 1470, sang the praises of the cross. The most important record, however, was engraved on a slab of marble at the left of the entrance:—

"This oratory was first built in the year of the jubilee, MCCCL, by Pontius, bishop of Orvieto and vicar of the city of Rome."

The inscription, besides proving that the removal of the oratory from its original site to the summit of the mountain had been accomplished before the age of the Millini, is the only historical record of the jubilee of 1350, which attracted to Rome enormous multitudes, so that pilgrims' camps had to be provided both inside and outside the walls. Petrarca and king Louis of Hungary (then on his way back from Apulia) were among the visitors. Bishop Pontius of Orvieto, Ponzio Perotti, is also an historical man. He was intrusted with the government of the city in consequence of the attempted assassination of his predecessor, cardinal Annibaldo, by a partisan of Cola di Rienzo.

This chapel, to which so many interesting souvenirs were attached, which owed its origin to one of the greatest battles in history, which commanded one of the finest panoramas in the world, is no more. It was sacrificed in 1880 to the necessity of raising a fortress on the hill. No sign is left to mark its place.

CHAPTER IV.

IMPERIAL TOMBS.[94]

The death and burial of Augustus.—His will.—The Monumentum Ancyranum.—Description and history of his mausoleum.—Its connection with the Colonnas and Cola di Rienzo.—Other members of the imperial family who were buried in it.—The story of the flight and death of Nero.—His place of burial.—Ecloge, his nurse.—The tomb of the Flavian emperors, Templum Flaviæ Gentis.—Its situation and surroundings.—The death of Domitian.—The mausolea of the Christian emperors.—The tomb and sarcophagus of Helena, mother of Constantine.—Those of Constantia.—The two rotundas built near St. Peter's as imperial tombs.—Discoveries made in them in the fifteenth and sixteenth centuries.—The priceless relics of Maria, wife of Honorius.—Similar instances of treasure-trove in ancient and modern times.

The Mausoleum of Augustus. Ancient writers have left detailed accounts of the last hours of the founder of the Roman Empire. On the morning of the nineteenth of August, anno Domini 14, feeling the approach of death, Augustus inquired of the attendants whether the outside world was concerned at his precarious condition; then he asked for a mirror, and composed his body for the supreme event, as he had long before prepared his mind and soul. Of his friends and the officers of the household he took leave in a cheerful spirit; and as soon as he was left alone with Livia he passed away in her arms, saying, "Livia, may you live happily, as we have lived together from the day of our marriage." His death was of the kind he had desired, peaceful and painless. Ευθανασιαν (an easy end) was the word he used longingly, whenever he heard of any one dying without agony. Once only in the course of the malady he seemed to lose consciousness, when he complained of forty young men crowding around the bed to steal away his body. More than a wandering mind, Suetonius thinks this was a vision or premonition of an approaching event, because forty prætorian soldiers were really to carry the bier in the funeral march. The great man died at Nola, in the same villa and room in which his father, Octavius, had passed away years before. His body was transported from village to village, from city to city, along the Appian Way, by the members of each municipal council in turn; and, to avoid the intense heat of the Campanian and Pontine lowlands, the procession marched only at night, the bier being kept in the local sanctuaries or town halls during the day. Thus Bovillae (le Frattocchie, at the foot of the Alban hills) was reached. The whole Roman knighthood was here in attendance; the body was carried in triumph, as it were, over the last ten miles of the road, and deposited in the vestibule of the palace on the Palatine Hill.

Military funeral evolutions; from the base of the Column of Antoninus.

Meanwhile proposals were made and resolutions passed in the Senate, which went far beyond anything that had ever been suggested in such contingencies of state. One of the members recommended that the statue of Victory which stood in the Curia should be carried before the hearse, that lamentations should be sung by the sons and daughters of the senators, and that the pageant, on its way to the Campus Martius, should march through the Porta Triumphalis, which was never opened except to victorious generals. Another member suggested that all classes of citizens should put aside their golden ornaments and all articles of jewelry, and wear only iron finger-rings; a third, that the name of "August" should be transferred to the month of September, because the lamented hero was born in the latter and had died in the former. These exaggerated expressions of grief were suppressed, however, and the funeral was organized with the grandest simplicity. The body was placed in the Forum, in front of the Temple of Julius Cæsar, from the *rostra* of which Tiberius read a panegyric. Another oration was delivered at the opposite end of the Forum by Drusus, the adopted son of Tiberius. Then the senators themselves placed the bier on their shoulders, leaving the city by the Porta Triumphalis. The procession formed by the Senate, the high priesthood, the knights, the army, and the whole population skirted the Circus Flaminius and the Septa Julia, and by the Via Flaminia reached the *ustrinum*, or sacred enclosure for cremation. As soon as the body had been placed on the pyre the "march past" began in the same order, the officers and men of the various army corps making their evolutions or *decursiones*. This word, taken in a general sense, means a long march by soldiers made in a given time and without quitting the ranks; when referring to a funeral ceremony it signifies special evolutions performed three times, in honor of distinguished generals. A *decursio* is represented on the base of the column of Antoninus Pius, now in the Giardino della Pigna. In that which I am describing, officers and men threw on the pyre the decorations which Augustus had awarded them for their bravery in battle. The privilege of setting fire to the *rogus* was granted to the captains of the legions whom he had led so often to victory. They approached with averted faces, and, uttering a last farewell, performed their act of duty and respect. The cremation accomplished, and while the glowing embers were being extinguished with wine and perfumed waters, an eagle rose from the ashes as if carrying the soul of the hero to Heaven. Livia and a few officers watched the place for five days and nights, and finally collected the ashes in a precious urn, which they placed in the innermost crypt of the mausoleum which Augustus had built in the Campus Martius forty-two years before.

The Apotheosis of an Emperor; from the base of the Column of Antoninus.

Of this monument we have a description by Strabo, and ruins which substantiate the description in its main lines. It was composed of a circular basement of white marble, two hundred and twenty-five feet in diameter, which supported a cone of earth, planted with cypresses and evergreens. On the top of the mound the bronze statue of the emperor towered above the trees.

This type of sepulchral structure dates almost from prehistoric times, and was in great favor with the Etruscans. The territories of Vulci, near the Ponte dell' Abbadia, and of Veii, near the Vaccareccia, are dotted with these mounds, which the peasantry call *cocumelle*. Augustus made the type popular among the Romans, as is proved by the large number of tumuli which date from his age, on the Via Salaria, the Via Labicana, and the Via Appia.

His tomb was entered from the south, the entrance being flanked by monuments of great interest, such as the obelisks now in the Piazza del Quirinale and the Piazza di S. Maria Maggiore; the copies of the decrees of the Senate in honor of the personages buried within; and, above all, the *Res gestæ divi Augusti*, a sort of political will, autobiography, and apology, the importance of which surpasses that of any other document relating to the history of the Roman Empire.

This was written by Augustus towards the end of his life. He ordered his executors to have it engraved on bronze pillars on each side of the entrance to his mausoleum. That his will was duly executed by Livia, Tiberius, Drusus, and Germanicus, his heirs and trustees, is proved by the frequent allusions to the document made by Suetonius and Velleius, and also by the copies which have come down to us, not from Rome or Italy, but from the remote provinces of Galatia and Pisidia.

173

It was customary in ancient times to raise temples in honor of the rulers of the empire, and to ornament them with their images and eulogies. These were called *Augustea* or *ædes Augusti et Romæ* in the western provinces, σεβαστεια in eastern or Greek-speaking countries,[95] Ancyra (Angora), the capital of Galatia, and Apollonia, the capital of Pisidia, were the foremost among the Asiatic cities to pay this honor to the founder of the empire.

The Ancyran temple owes its preservation to the Christians, who made use of it as a church from the fourth to the fifteenth centuries, and also to the Turks, who have turned it into a mosque associated with the Hadji Beiram. The temple and its invaluable epigraphic treasures became known towards the middle of the sixteenth century. In 1555 an embassy was sent by the emperor Ferdinand II. to Suleiman, the khalif, who was then residing at Amasia.[96] It so happened that the head of the mission, Ogier Ghislain Busbecq, and his assistant, Antony Wrantz, bishop of Agram, were fond of archæological investigation. They were struck by the importance of the Augusteum at Ancyra; and with the help of their secretaries, they made a tolerably good copy of its inscriptions. Since 1555 the place has been visited many times, notably by Edmond Guillaume, in 1861, and by Humann, in 1882.[97] There are two copies of the will of Augustus engraved on the marble wall of the temple: one in Latin, which is in the pronaos, on either side of the door; the other in Greek, on the outer wall of the cella. Both were transcribed (or translated) "from the original, engraved on the bronze pillars at the mausoleum in Rome." The document is divided into three parts, and thirty-five paragraphs. The first part describes the honors conferred on Augustus,—military, civil, and sacerdotal; the

174

second gives the details of the expenses which he sustained for the benefit and welfare of the public; the third relates his achievements in peace and war; and some of the facts narrated are truly remarkable. He says, for instance, that the Roman citizens who fought under his orders and swore allegiance to him numbered five hundred thousand, and that more than three hundred thousand completed the term of their engagement, and were honorably dismissed from the army. To each of these he gave either a piece of land, which he bought with his own money, or the means of purchasing it in other lands than those assigned to military colonies. Since, at the time of his death, one hundred and sixty thousand Roman citizens were still serving under the flag, the number of those killed in battle, disabled by disease, or dismissed for misconduct, in the course of fifty-five years[98] is reduced to forty thousand. The percentage is surprisingly low, considering the defective organization of the military medical staff, and the length and hardships of the campaigns which were conducted in Italy (Mutina), Macedonia (Philippi), Acarnania (Actium), Sicily, Egypt, Spain, Germany, Armenia and other countries. The number of men-of-war of large tonnage, which were captured, burnt, or sunk in battle, is stated at six hundred. In the naval engagement against Sextus Pompeius, off Naulochos, he sank twenty-eight vessels, and captured or burnt two hundred and fifty-five; so that only seventeen out of a powerful fleet of three hundred could make their escape.

Thrice he took the census of the citizens of Rome; the first time in the year 29-28 B. C., when 4,063,000 souls were counted; the second in the year 8 B. C., showing 4,233,000; the third in 14 A. D., with 4,937,000. Under his peaceful rule, therefore, there was an increase of 874,000 in the number of Roman citizens. He remarks with pride that, while from the beginning of the history of Rome to his own age the gate of the Temple of Janus had been shut but twice, as a sign that peace was prevailing over land and sea, he had been able to close it three times in the course of fifty years. His liberalities are equally surprising. Sometimes they took the form of free distributions of corn, oil, or wine; sometimes of an allowance of money. He asserts that he spent in gifts the sum of six hundred and twenty millions of sestertii, nearly twenty-six millions of dollars. Adding to this sum the cost of purchasing lands for his veterans in Italy (six hundred millions) and in the provinces (two hundred and sixty millions), of giving pecuniary rewards to his veterans (four hundred millions), of helping the public treasury (one hundred and fifty millions), and the army funds (one hundred and seventy millions), besides other grants and bounties, the amount of which is not known, we reach a total expenditure for the benefit of his people of ninety-one million dollars.

I need not speak of the material renovation of the city, which he found of brick and left of marble. Roads, streets, aqueducts, bridges, quays, places of amusement, places of worship, parks, gardens, public offices, were built, opened, repaired, and decorated with incredible profusion. Suetonius says that, on one occasion alone, he offered to Jupiter Capitolinus sixteen thousand pounds of gold and fifty millions' worth of jewels. In the year 28 B. C. not less than eighty-two temples were rebuilt in Rome itself.

Were we not in the presence of official statistics and of state documents, we should hardly feel inclined to believe these enormous statements. We must remember, too, that the work of

175

176

Augustus was seconded and imitated with equal magnitude by his wealthy friends and advisers, Marcius Philippus, Lucius Cornificius, Asinius Pollio, Munatius Plaucus, Cornelius Balbus, Statilius Taurus, and above all by Marcus Agrippa, to whom we owe the aqueducts of the Virgo and Julia, the Pantheon, the Thermæ, the artificial lake (*stagnum*), the Portico of the Argonauts, the Temple of Neptune, the Portico of Vipsania Palta, the Diribitorium, the Septa, the Campus Agrippæ, a bridge on the Tiber, and hundreds of other costly structures. During the twelve months of his ædileship, in 19 B. C., he rebuilt the network of the city sewers, adding many miles of new channels, erected eight hundred and five fountains, and one hundred and thirty water reservoirs. These edifices were ornamented with three hundred bronze and marble statues, and four hundred columns.

We have seen works of perhaps greater importance accomplished in our age; but, as Baron de Hübner remarks, in speaking of another great man, Sixtus V., they are the joint product of government, national credit, speculation, and public and private capital; and they are facilitated by wonderful mechanical contrivances. The transformation of Rome at the time of Augustus was the work of a few wealthy citizens, whose names will forever be connected with their splendid creations.

The gates of the Mausoleum of Augustus were opened for the last time in A. D. 98, for the reception of the ashes of Nerva. We hear no more of it until the year 410, when the Goths ransacked the imperial vaults. No harm, however, seems to have been done to the building itself at that time. Like the mausolea of Metella, on the Appian Way, and Hadrian, on the right bank of the Tiber, it was subsequently converted into a stronghold, and occupied by the Colonnas. Its ultimate destruction, in 1167, marks one of the great occurences in the history of mediæval Rome.

Between the counts of Tusculum, partisans of the German Empire, and the Romans, devoted to their independent municipal government, there was a feud of long standing, which had resulted occasionally in open violence. In 1167, Alexander III. being Pope, the Romans decided to strike the decisive blow on the Tusculans, as well as on their allies, the Albans. The cardinal of Aragona, the biographer of Alexander III., states that towards the end of May, when the cornfields begin to ripen, the Romans sallied forth on their expedition against Count Raynone, much against the Pope's will; and having crossed the frontier of his estate, set fire to the crops, uprooted trees and vineyards, ruined farmhouses, killed cattle, and laid siege to the city itself. Raynone, knowing how precarious his position was, implored the help of the emperor Frederic, who was at that time encamped near Ancona. The request was granted, and a body of German warriors returned with the ambassadors to the rescue of Tusculum. They soon perceived that, although the Romans had the advantage of numbers, they were so imperfectly drilled and so insubordinate that the chances were equal for both sides. The battle was opened at nine o'clock on the morning of Whit-Monday, May 30, 1167. The twelve hundred Germans, led by Christian, archbishop of Mayence, and three hundred Tusculans, led by Raynone, gallantly attacked the advance guard of the Roman army, which numbered thirty thousand men. Overcome by panic, the Romans fled and disbanded at the first encounter. They were closely followed from valley to valley, and slain in such numbers that scarcely one third of them reached the walls of Aurelian in safety. The local memories of the battle still survive, after a lapse of eight centuries; the valley which leads from the villa of Q. Voconius Pollio (Sassone) to Marino being still called by the peasantry "la valle dei morti."

On the following day an embassy was sent to Archbishop Christian and Count Raynone begging leave to bury the dead. The permission was granted, with the humiliating clause that the number of dead and missing should be reported at Tusculum. The legend says that the number ascertained was fifteen thousand, which is an exaggeration. Contemporary historians speak of only two thousand dead and three thousand prisoners, who were sent to Viterbo. The chronicle of Sikkardt adds that the Romans were encamped near Monte Porzio; that the battle lasted only two hours, and that the dead were buried in the church of S. Stefano, at the second milestone of the Via Latina, with the following inscription:—

MILLE DECEM DECIES ET SEX DECIES QVOQVE SENI,—

which, if genuine, proves that the number of killed in battle was only eleven hundred and sixty-six, that is, 1,000+100+60+6.

179

The connection of the Mausoleum of Augustus with this mediæval battle of Cannæ is easily explained. The mausoleum had been selected by the Colonnas for their stronghold in the Campus Martius, and it was for their interest to keep it in good repair. As happens in cases of crushing defeats, when the succumbing party must find an excuse and an opportunity for revenge, the powerful Colonnas were accused of high treason, namely, of having led the advance-guard of the Romans into an ambush. Consequently they were banished from the city, and their castle on the Campus Martius was destroyed. Thus perished the Mausoleum of Augustus.

The history of its ruins, however, does not end with the events just described. Most important of all, they are associated with the fate of Cola di Rienzo. His biographer, in Book III. ch. xxiv., says that the body of the Tribune was allowed to remain unburied, for two days and one night, on some steps near S. Marcello. Giugurta and Sciarretta Colonna, leaders of the aristocratic faction, ordered the body to be dragged along the Via Flaminia, from S. Marcello to the mausoleum which had been occupied and fortified by that powerful family once more in 1241. In the mean time, the Jews had gathered in great numbers around the "Campo dell' Augusta," as the ruins were then called. Thistles and dry brushwood were collected and set afire, and the body thrown into the flames; this extemporized pyre being fed with fresh fuel until every particle of the corpse was consumed. A strange coincidence, that the same monument which the founder of the empire, the oppressor of Roman liberty, had chosen for his own burial-place, should serve, thirteen centuries later, for the cremation of him who tried to restore popular freedom! Here is the description of the event by a contemporary: "Along this street (the Corso of modern days) the corpse was dragged as far as the church of S. Marcello. There it was hung by the feet to a balcony, because the head had been crushed and lost, piece by piece, along the road; so many wounds had been inflicted on the body that it might be compared to a sieve (crivello); the entrails were protruding like a bull's in the butchery; he was horribly fat, and his skin white, like milk tinted with blood. Enormous was

180

his fatness,—so great as to give him the appearance of an ox (*bufalo*). The body hung from the balcony at S. Marcello for two days and one night, while boys pelted it with stones. On the third day it was removed to the Campo dell' Augusta, where the Jewish colony, to a man, had congregated; and although the pyre had been made only with thistles, in which those ruins abounded, the fat from the corpse kept the flames alive until their work was accomplished. Not an atom of the great champion of the Romans was left."

I need not remind the reader that the house near the Ponte Rotto, and opposite the Temple of Fortuna Virilis, which guides attribute to Cola di Rienzo, has no connection with him.[99] He was born and lived many years near the church of S. Tommaso in Capite Molarum, between the Palazzo Cenci and the synagogue of the Jews, on the left bank of the Tiber. The church is still in existence, although it has changed its mediæval name into that of S. Tommaso a' Cenci.

The house by the Ponte Rotto, just referred to, has still another name in folk-lore; it is called the *House of Pilate*. The denomination is not so absurd as it at first seems; it brings us back to bygone times, when passion-plays were performed in Rome in a more effective way than they are now exhibited at Oberammergau. They took place, not on a wooden stage, so suggestive of conventionality, but in a quarter of the city most wonderfully adapted to represent the Via Dolorosa of Jerusalem, from the houses of Pilate and Caiaphas to the summit of Calvary.

The passion-play began at a house, Via della Bocca della Verità, No. 37, which is still called the "Locanda della Gaiffa," a corruption of *Gaifa*, or *Caiaphas*. From this place the procession moved across the street to the "Casa di Pilato," as the house of Crescenzio was called, where the scenes of the Ecce Homo, the flagellation, and the crowning with thorns, were probably enacted. The Via Dolorosa corresponds to our streets of the Bocca della Verità, Salara, Marmorata, and Porta S. Paolo; there must have been stations at intervals for the representation of the various episodes, such as the meeting with the Virgin Mary, the fainting under the cross, the meeting with Veronica and with the man from Cyrene. The performance culminated on the summit of the Monte Testaccio, where three crosses were erected. One is still there.

Readers who have had an opportunity of studying the Via Dolorosa at Jerusalem will be struck by the resemblance between the original and its Roman imitation. The latter must have been planned by crusaders and pilgrims on their return from the Holy Land towards the end of the thirteenth century. Every particular, even those which rest on doubtful tradition, was repeated here, such as that referring to the house of the rich man, and to the stone in front of it on which Lazarus sat. A ruin half-way between the house of Pilate, by the Ponte Rotto, and the Monte Testaccio, or Calvary, is still called the Arco di S. Lazaro.

The Mausoleum of Augustus was explored archæologically for the first time in 1527, when the obelisk now in the Piazza di S. Maria Maggiore was found on the south side, near the church of S. Rocco. On July 14, 1519, Baldassarre Peruzzi discovered and copied some fragments of the original inscriptions *in situ*; but the discovery made in 1777 casts all that preceded it into the shade. In the spring of that year, while the corner house between the

Corso and the Via degli Otto Cantoni (opposite the Via della Croce) was being built, the *ustrinum*, or sacred enclosure for the cremation of the members of the imperial family, came to light, lined with a profusion of historical monuments. Strabo describes the place as paved with marble, enclosed with brass railings, and shaded by poplars. The marble pavement was found at a depth of nineteen feet below the sidewalk of the Corso. The first object to appear was the beautiful vase of *alabastro cotognino*, now in the Vatican Museum (Galleria delle Statue), three feet in height, one and one half in diameter, with a cover ending in a lotus flower, the thickness of the marble being only one inch. The vase had once contained the ashes of one of the imperial personages in the mausoleum; either Alaric's barbarians or Roman plunderers must have left it in the *ustrinum*, after looting its contents.

The marble pedestals lining the borders of the square were of two kinds: some were intended to indicate the spot on which each prince had been cremated, others the place where the ashes had been deposited. The former end with the formula HIC CREMATVS (or CREMATA) EST, the latter with the words HIC SITVS (or SITA) EST.

Augustus was not the first member of the family to occupy the mausoleum. He was preceded by Marcellus (28 B. C.) whose premature fate is so admirably described by Virgil (Æneid, vi. 872); by Marcus Agrippa, in 14 B. C.; by Octavia, the sister of Augustus, in the year 13; by Drusus the elder, in the year 9; and by Caius and Lucius, nephews of Augustus. After Augustus, the interments of Livia, Germanicus, Drusus, son of Tiberius, Agrippina the elder, Tiberius, Antonia wife of Drusus, Claudius, Brittannicus, and Nerva are registered in succession. Of these great and, in many cases, admirable men and women, ten funeral cippi have been found in the *ustrinum*, some by the Colonnas before they were superseded by the Orsinis in the possession of the place, some in the excavations of 1777.

The fate of two of them cannot fail to impress the student of the history of the ruins of Rome. The pedestal of Agrippina the elder, daughter of Agrippa, wife of Germanicus, and mother of Caligula, and that of her eldest son Nero, were hollowed out during the Middle Ages, turned into standard measures for solids, and as such placed at the disposal of the public in the portico of the city hall. The pedestal of Nero perished during the renovation of the Conservatori Palace at the time of Michelangelo; that of Agrippina is still there.

The fate of this noble woman is described by Tacitus in the sixth book of the Annals; she was banished by Tiberius to the island of Pandataria, now called Ventotiene, where she spent the last three years of her life in solitude and grief. In 33 A. D.—the most memorable date in Christian chronology—she either starved herself to death voluntarily, or was starved by order of her persecutor. On hearing of her death the emperor eulogized his own clemency, because, instead of strangling the princess and exposing her body on the Gemonian steps, he had allowed her to die a peaceful death in that island. No honors were paid to her memory, but as soon as Caligula succeeded Tiberius in the government of the empire, he sailed to Pandataria, collected the ashes of his mother and relatives, and ultimately placed them in the mausoleum. The cippus represented in the illustration below is manifestly the work of Caligula, because mention is made on it of his accession to the throne. The hole excavated in it in the Middle

Ages is capable of holding three *hundred* pounds of grain, as shown by the legend RVGIATELLA DE GRANO, engraved in Gothic letters above the municipal coat of arms. The three armorial shields below belong to the three syndics, or conservatori, by whose authority the standard measure was made. Another inscription, engraved in 1635 on the opposite side, says: "The S.P.Q.R. pay honor to the memory of the noble and courageous woman who voluntarily put an end to her life" (and here follows a witticism of doubtful taste on the *bread* which she denied herself, and on the *breadstuffs*, for the measurement of which her tomb had been used).

The other cippi found in the *ustrinum* mention four other children of Germanicus, among them Caius Cæsar, the lovely child who was so much beloved by Augustus, and so deeply

The Cippus of Agrippina the Elder, made into a measure for grain.

regretted by him. A statue representing the youth with the attributes of a Cupid was dedicated by Livia in the temple of the Capitoline Venus, and another one was placed by Augustus in his own bedroom, on entering and leaving which he never missed kissing the cherished image.

The Mausoleum of Augustus and its precious contents have not escaped the spoliation and desecration which seem to be the rule both in past and modern times. The building is used now as a circus. Its basement is concealed by ignoble houses; the urn of Agrippina is kept in the courtyard of the Palazzo dei Conservatori; three others have been destroyed, and six belong to the Vatican Museum.

THE TOMB OF NERO. The defection of the last Roman legion was announced to Nero while at dinner in the Golden House. On hearing the news, he tore up the letters, upset the table, dashed upon the floor two marvellous cups, called *Homeric*, because their chiselling represented scenes from the Iliad; and having borrowed from Locusta a phial of poison, went out to the Servilian gardens. He then despatched a few faithful servants to Ostia with orders to keep a squadron of swift vessels in readiness for his escape. After this he inquired of the officers of the prætorian guards if they were willing to accompany him in his flight; some found an excuse, others openly refused; one had the courage to ask him: "Is death so hard?" Then various projects began to agitate his mind; now he was ready to beg for mercy from Galba, his successful opponent; now to ask help from the Parthian refugees, and again to dress himself in mourning, and appear barefooted and unshaven before the public by the rostra, and implore pardon for his crimes; in case that should be refused, to ask permission to exchange the imperial power for the governorship of Egypt. He was ready to carry this project into execution, but his courage failed at the last moment, as he knew that the exasperated people would tear him to pieces before he could reach the Forum. Towards evening he calmed his mind in the hope that there would be time enough to make a decision if he waited until the next day. As midnight approached he awoke, to find that the Prætorians detailed at the gates of the Servilian gardens had retired to their barracks. Servants were sent to rouse the friends sleeping in the villa, but none of them returned. He went around the apartments, finding them closed and deserted. On re-entering his own room he saw that his private attendants had run away, carrying the bed-covers, and the phial of poison. Then he seemed determined to put an end to his life by throwing himself from one of the bridges; but again his courage failed, and he begged to be shown a hiding-place. It was at this supreme moment that Phaon the freedman offered him his suburban villa, situated between the Via Salaria and the Via Nomentana, four miles outside the Porta Collina. The proposal was accepted at once; and barefooted, and dressed in a tunic, with a mantle of the commonest material about his shoulders, he jumped on a horse and started for the gate, accompanied by only four men,— Phaon, Epaphroditus, Sporus, and another whose name is not given.

Head of Nero, in the Capitoline Museum.

The incidents of the flight were terrible enough to deprive the imperial fugitive of the last spark of hope. The sky was overcast, and heavy black clouds hung close to the earth, the stillness of nature being occasionally broken by claps of thunder. The earth shook just as he was riding past the prætorian camp. He could hear the shouts of the mutinous soldiers cursing his name, while Galba was proclaimed his successor. Farther on, the fugitives met several men hurrying towards the town in search of news. Nero heard some of them telling one another to be sure to run in search of him. Another passer inquired the news from the palace. Before reaching the Ponte Nomentano, Nero's horse, frightened by a corpse which was lying on the roadside, gave a start. The slouched hat and handkerchief, with which the emperor was trying to conceal his face, slipped aside, and just at that moment a messenger from the prætorian camp recognized him, and by force of habit gave the military salute.

Beyond the bridge the Via Nomentana divides: the main road, on the right, leads to Nomentum (Mentana); the left to the territory of Ficulea (la Cesarina). It is now called the Strada delle Vigne Nuove. Nero and his followers took this country road. The particulars given by Suetonius suit the present aspect and the nature of the district so exactly that we can follow the four men step by step to the walls of Phaon's villa. The slopes of the hills were then, as they are now, uncultivated, and covered with bushes. There is still a path on the banks of the Fosso della Cecchina, leading to the rear wall of the villa, *aversum villæ parietem*; and the hillsides are still honeycombed with pozzolana quarries, the *angustiæ cavernarum* of Suetonius. The villa extends on the tableland, or ridge, between the valleys of la Cecchina and Melaina. Its main gate corresponds exactly with the gate of the Vigna Chiari, the first of the "vigne nuove" on the right as one goes from Rome, at a distance of six kilometres from the threshold of the Porta Collina. For a radius of a thousand feet around the gate, we meet with the typical remains of a Roman villa of the first century,—porticoes, water tanks, and substructions, from the platform of which there is a lovely view over the wooded plains of the Tiber and the Anio, the city, and the hills of the Vatican, and of the Janiculum, which frame the panorama. The site is pleasant, secluded, and quiet, so that it well fulfilled the wish for a *secretior latetra* expressed by Nero in his hopeless condition. The fugitives dismounted at the turn of the Strada delle Vigne Nuove, and let the horses loose among the brambles. Not wishing to be seen in the open road, they followed the lower path on the banks of the Cecchina, which was concealed by a thick growth of canes. It was necessary to bore a hole in the rear wall of the villa, and while this was being done, Nero quenched his thirst from a pond of stagnant water, near the opening of the pozzolana quarries. Once inside the villa, he was asked to lie down on a couch covered with a peasant's mantle, and was offered a piece of stale bread, and a glass of tepid water. Food he refused, but touched the rim of the cup with his parched lips. It is curious to read in Suetonius of the many grimaces the

189

wretch made before he could determine to kill himself; he made up his mind to do so only when he heard the tramping of the horsemen whom the Senate had sent to arrest him. He then put the dagger into his throat, aided in giving the last thrust by his freedman Epaphroditus. The centurion sent to take him alive arrived before he expired. To him Nero addressed these last words: "Too late! Is this your fidelity?" He gradually sank, his countenance assuming such a frightful expression that all who were present fled in horror. Icelus, freedman of Galba, the newly elected emperor, gave his consent to a decent funeral. Ecloge and Alexandra, his nurses, Acte his mistress, and the three faithful men who had accompanied him in his flight, provided the necessary funds, about five thousand dollars. The body was cremated, wrapped in a sheet of white woven with gold, the same that he had used on his bed New Year's night. The three women collected the ashes and placed them in the tomb of the Domitian family, which stood on the spur of the Pincian Hill which is behind the present church of S. Maria del Popolo. The urn was of porphyry, the altar upon which it stood of Carrara marble, and the tomb itself of Thesian marble. A pathetic discovery has just been made in the Vigna Chiari, on the exact spot of Nero's suicide, by my friend, Cav. Rodolfo Buti, that of the tomb of Claudia Ecloge, the old woman who was so devoted to her nursling. The epitaph is a plain marble slab containing only a name. But this simple inscription, read amid the ruins of Phaon's villa, with every detail of the scene of the suicide before one's eyes, makes more impression on the feelings than would a great monument to her memory. As she could not be buried within or near the family vault of the Domitii on the Pincian, she selected the spot where Nero's remains had been cremated.

190

> "When Nero perished by the justest doom
>   Which ever the destroyer yet destroy'd,
> Amidst the roar of liberated Rome,
>   Of nations freed, and the world overjoy'd,
> Some hands unseen strew'd flowers upon his tomb,—
>   Perhaps the weakness of a heart not void
> Of feeling for some kindness done, when power
> Had left the wretch an uncorrupted hour.'[100]

The original epitaph of Claudia Ecloge has been removed to the Capitoline Museum, where it seems lost among so many other objects of interest; but the student who will select the Vigne Nuove for an afternoon excursion will find there a facsimile, placed by our archæological commission on the front wall of the Casino di Vigna Chiari.

THE TOMB OF THE FLAVIAN EMPERORS. The Via del Quirinale-Venti Settembre, which leads from the Quirinal Palace to the Porta Pia, corresponds exactly to the old Alta Semita, which was a street of such importance, on account of its length, straightness, and surroundings, that the whole region (the sixth) was named from it. For our present purpose we shall take into consideration only the first part, between the Quirinal Palace and the Quattro Fontane. It was bordered on the north side by the Temple of Quirinus, discovered and demolished in 1626, and by the Capitolium Vetus, the old Capitol, also destroyed in 1625, by Pope Barberini.

191

The opposite side of the street was lined with private mansions of families who were eminent in the history of the republic and the empire. The first belonged to Pomponius Atticus, the friend of Cicero, and to his descendants the Pomponii Bassi. Cicero locates it between the Temple of Quirinus and the Temple of Health, that is, near the present church of S. Andrea al Quirinale; and precisely here, in November, 1558, the house was discovered by Messer Uberto Ubaldini, in such perfect condition that the family documents and deeds, inscribed on bronze, were still hanging on the walls of the *tablinum*,—a fact that is recorded only twice in the annals of Roman excavations.[101] The house, seen and described by Manuzio and Ligorio, stood at the corner of the Alta Semita and a side street called "The Pomegranate" (*ad malum punicum*), and was profusely adorned with statues, colonnades, spacious halls, etc. One of the bronze tablets, which was saved from the ruins, and is now exhibited in the Gallery of the Uffizi, at Florence, states that the municipal council of Ferentinum, assembled in the Temple of Mercury, had placed the city under the guardianship of Pomponius Bassus, A. D. 101. The patronage was accepted by the gallant patrician, and *tabulæ hospitales* were exchanged between the parties.

192

When his majesty king Humbert laid out a new garden, in 1887, on the site of this house, I hoped to come across some of the ruins described by Manuzio and Ligorio. But nothing was found, except a marble statue, of no especial value, which is now preserved in the royal palace.

Plan of the Alta Semita.

Another illustrious man lived near the Temple of Health,—Valerius Martial the epigrammatist. He distinctly says so in his "Epigrams" (x. 58; xi. 1). Was the house his own, or did he dwell in it as a tenant or guest? I believe he was the guest of his wealthy relative and countryman G. Valerius Vegetus, consul A.D. 91, whose city residence occupied half the site of the present building of the Ministry of War, on the Via Venti Settembre.

The residence has been explored three times, at least; the first in 1641, the second in 1776, the last in the autumn of 1884. Judging from this last exploration, which was conducted in my presence, and described by my late friend Capannari in the "Bullettino Comunale" of 1885, the palace of Valerius Vegetus must have been built and decorated on a grand scale. Martial, like all poets, if not actually in financial difficulties, was never a rich man, much less the owner of a private residence in a street and quarter in which the land alone represented a fortune.

193

Between the two palaces just described, the Pomponian and the Valerian, in the space now occupied by the Palazzo Albani and the church and convent of S. Carlino alle Quattro Fontane, there was an humbler house, which belonged to Flavius Sabinus, brother of Vespasian. Here the emperor Domitian was born, October 24, A. D. 50. The house which stood at the corner of the Alta Semita and the "Pomegranate" street was converted by him into a family memorial, or mausoleum, after the death of his father and brother. Here were buried, besides Vespasian and Titus, Flavius Sabinus, Julia, daughter of Titus, and ultimately Domitian himself.

The story of his death is as follows: After murdering his cousin Flavius Clemens, the Christian prince whose fate I have described in chapter i., his life became an intolerable burden to him. The fear that some one would suddenly rise to revenge the innocent blood into which he had dipped his hands made him tremble every moment for his life; so much so that he caused the porticos of the imperial palace to be encrusted with Phengite marble, in the brilliant surface of which he could see the reflection of his followers and attendants, and could watch their proceedings even if they were at quite a distance behind him. For several weeks he was frightened by thunderbolts. Once the Capitol was struck, next the family tomb on the Quirinal, which he had officially styled Templum Flaviæ Gentis; and another time the imperial palace and even his own bedroom. He was heard to mutter to himself in despair, "Let them strike: who cares?" On another occasion a furious cyclone wrenched the dedicatory tablet from the pedestal of his equestrian statue in the Forum. He also dreamed that Minerva, the protecting divinity of his happier days, had suddenly disappeared from his private chapel. What frightened him most, however, was the fate of Askletarion the fortune-teller. Having asked what sort of death Askletarion expected, the answer was: "I shall very soon be torn to pieces by dogs." To persuade himself and his friends that these predictions deserved no credit, Domitian, who had just received a very sad warning from the oracle of the Fortuna Prænestina, caused the necromancer to be killed at once, and his remains to be enclosed in a well-guarded tomb. But while the cremation was in progress, a hurricane swept the *ustrinum*, and frightened away the attendants, so that the half-charred remains did fall a prey to the dogs. The story was related to the emperor that very evening while he was at supper.

The details of the assassination, which took place a few days later, on September 18, A. D. 96, in the forty-fifth year of his age, and the fifteenth of his reign, are not well known, because, with the exception of the four murderers, the deed was witnessed only by a little boy, to whom Domitian had given the care of the images of the gods in the bedroom. The names of the conspirators are Saturius, the head valet de chambre, Maximus, a freedman of a lower class, Clodianus, an orderly, and Stephanus, who was the head of the party. He was led to commit the crime in the hope that the embezzlements of which he was guilty in his management of the property of Flavia Domitilla, niece of the emperor, would never be discovered, or punished. To avoid suspicion, he appeared for several days before the attempt with his arm bandaged, and in a sling, so that he could carry a concealed weapon with impunity even in the presence of his intended victim. The boy stated at the inquest that Domitian died like a brave man, fighting unarmed against his assailants. The moment he saw Stephanus drawing his dagger he told the boy to hand him quickly the poniard under the pillow of his bed, and to run for help; but he found only the empty scabbard, and all the doors were locked. The emperor fell at the seventh stroke.

The corpse was removed to a garden which his nurse Phyllis owned, on the borders of the Via Latina; and the ashes were secretly mingled with those of his niece Julia, another nursling of Phyllis, and deposited in the family mausoleum on the Quirinal. The mausoleum, which rose in the middle of the atrium of the old Flavian house, was discovered and destroyed towards the middle of the sixteenth century. Ligorio describes the structure as a round temple, with a pronaos of six columns of the composite order. The excavations were made at the expense of cardinal Sadoleto. He found among other things a beautiful marble statue of Minerva, with a shield in the left hand and a lance in the right. The villa of cardinal Sadoleto was afterwards bought by messer Uberto Ubaldini, who levelled everything to the ground, and uprooted the very foundations of the building. In so doing he discovered several headless marble statues. Flaminio Vacca adds, that the columns were of *bigio africano*, fourteen feet high.

The reader will easily understand, that were I to pass in review the tombs of all the rulers of the Roman Empire, from Trajan to Constantine, the present chapter would exceed the allotted length of the entire book. The Mausoleum of Hadrian, on which the history of the city is written century by century, down to our days; the Column of Trajan, in the foundations of which the ashes of the best of Roman princes are buried; the tomb of Geta, built in the shape of a septizonium, on the Appian Way; the artificial hill of the Monte del Grano, believed to be the tomb of Alexander Severus, and his wife and mother, in the very depths of which the Capitoline sarcophagus and the Portland vase were found: all these monuments would furnish abundant material for archæological, artistic, and historical discussion. My purpose is, however, to mention only subjects illustrated by recent and little-known discoveries, or else to select such representative specimens as may help the reader to compare pagan with Christian art and civilization. For this reason, and to save unavoidable repetitions, I pass over the fate of the emperors of the second and third centuries, and resume my description with those who came to power after the peace of the church.

Remains of Geta's Mausoleum.

MAUSOLEA OF CHRISTIAN EMPERORS. The first Christian members of the imperial family, Helena, mother of Constantine, and Constantia, his daughter, were buried in separate tombs, one on the Via Labicana, at the place formerly called *ad duas Lauros* and now Torre Pignattara, the other near the church of S. Agnese, on the Via Nomentana.

Helena's mausoleum at Torre Pignattara (so called from the *pignatte*, or earthen vases built into the vault to lighten its weight) is round in shape, and contains seven niches or recesses for sarcophagi. One of these sarcophagi, famous in the history of art, was removed from its position as early as the middle of the twelfth century by Pope Anastasius IV., who selected it for his own resting-place. It was taken to the Lateran basilica, where it appears to have been much injured by the hands of indiscreet pilgrims. In 1600 it was carried from the vestibule to the tribune, and thence to the cloister-court. When Pius VI. added it to the wonders of the Vatican Museum, it was subjected to a thorough process of restoration which employed twenty-five stone-cutters for a period of nine years.

198

The reliefs upon it are tolerably well executed, but lack invention and novelty. They are partly borrowed from an older work, partly combined from various sources in an extraordinary manner; horsemen hovering in the air, and below them, prisoners and corpses scattered around. They are intended to represent a triumphal procession, or possibly a military *decursio*, to which allusion has been made above.

It may appear indiscreet and even insulting on the part of Anastasius IV. to have removed the remains of a canonized empress from this noble sarcophagus in order to have his own placed in it; but we must bear in mind that although the Torre Pignattara has all the appearance of a royal mausoleum, and although the ground on which it stands is known to have belonged to the crown, Eusebius and Socrates deny that Helena was buried in Rome. Their assertion is contradicted by the "Liber Pontificalis" and by Bede, and above all by the similarity between this porphyry coffin and the one discovered in the second mausoleum of which I have spoken, —that of S. Constantia, on the Via Nomentana.

SARCOPHAGUS OF HELENA, MOTHER OF CONSTANTINE

When the love of splendor which was characteristic of the Romans of the decadence induced them to take possession of the enormous block of primeval stone of which this second sarcophagus was made, the art of sculpture had already degenerated; all that it could accomplish was to impart to this mass of rock more of an architectural than a plastic shape. The representations with which the sarcophagus is adorned or disfigured, as the case may be, if met with elsewhere would scarcely attract our attention. On the sides are festoons enclosing groups of winged boys gathering grapes; on the ends are similar figures treading out the

199

grapes. This sarcophagus was removed to the Hall of the Greek Cross by the same enlightened Pope Pius VI.

The Mausoleum of S. Constantia.

The same vintage scenes are represented in the beautiful mosaics with which the vault of the mausoleum is encrusted, and from this circumstance the monument received the erroneous name of the Temple of Bacchus, at the time of the Renaissance. There is no doubt that this is the tomb of the princess whose name it bears. Amianus Marcellinus, Book XXI., chapter i., says that the three daughters of Constantine—Helena, wife of Julian, Constantina, wife of Gallus Cæsar, and Constantia, who had vowed herself to chastity, and to the management of a congregation of virgins which she had established at S. Agnese—were all buried in the same place.

200

The study of these two structures may help us greatly to explain the origin and purpose of the two rotundas which are known to have existed on the south side of S. Peter's, in the arena of Nero's circus. One of them, dedicated to S. Petronilla, was destroyed in the sixteenth century; the other, called the Church of S. Maria della Febbre, met with the same fate during the pontificate of Pius VI. Their exact situation in relation to the modern basilica is shown by the accompanying diagram.

Mention of the structure, with its classical denomination of "Mausileos," appears in the life of Stephen II. (A. D. 752). To fulfil a promise which he had made to Pepin, king of France, that the remains of Petronilla, who was believed to be the daughter of Peter, should be no longer 201 exposed to barbaric profanations in their original resting-place on the Via Ardeatina, but put under the shelter of the Leonine walls near the remains of her supposed father, he selected one of these two rotundas, which became known as the "chapel of the kings of France." The early topographers of the Renaissance, ignorant of its history, gave a wrong name to the building, calling it the Temple of Apollo. That it was, however, of Christian origin, is proved not only by the fact that a temple could never have been built across the *spina* of the circus, and by the technical details of its construction, which show it to be a work of the end of the fourth or the beginning of the fifth century, but also by historical evidence. In 423 Honorius was buried in the mausoleum close by S. Peter's (*juxta beati Petri apostoli atrium in mausoleo*). In 451 the remains of the Emperor Theodosius II. were removed from

Constantinople to the *mausoleum ad apostolum Petrum*. In 483 Basilius, prefect of the Prætorium, summoned the leaders of the clergy and of the laity to the mausoleum *quod est apud beatissimum Petrum*. A precious engraving by Bonanni, No. lxxiv. of his volume on the Vatican, represents the outside of one of the rotundas, the nearest to the obelisk of the circus. The architecture of the building, so similar to the tomb of S. Helena at Torre Pignattara, gives some conception of the enormous downfall of Roman art and civilization, when we compare it with the tombs of Augustus and Hadrian.

The discovery of the imperial graves which filled the two rotundas did not take place at one and the same time. Their profanation and robbery was accomplished in various stages, by various persons; and so little has been said or written about them, that only in these last years has de Rossi been able to reconstruct in its entirety this chapter in the history of the destruction of Rome.

ROTUNDA AND OBELISK SOUTH OF OLD S. PETER'S. (After Bonanni)

In the chronicle of Nicolò della Tuccia of Viterbo is the following entry, dated 1458: "On the 27th day of June, news was circulated in Viterbo that two days before a great discovery had been made in S. Peter's of Rome. A priest of that church, having manifested the wish to be buried in the chapel of S. Petronilla, in the tribune on the right, where the story of the emperor Constantine was painted in ancient times, they found, while digging there, a tomb of exquisite marble, containing a sarcophagus, and inside of it, a smaller coffin of cypress wood overlaid with silver. This silver, of eleven carats standard, weighed eight hundred and thirty-two pounds. The bodies were wrapped in a golden cloth which yielded sixteen pounds of that precious metal. It was said that the bodies were those of Constantine and his little son. No written record or sign was found except a cross made in this shape: The Pope, Callixtus III., took possession of everything and sent the gold and silver to the mint." We hear no more of the imperial mausoleum during the sixty following years. In the diary of Marcantonio Michiel, of Venice, the next discovery is registered under the date of December 4, 1519: "A few days ago, while excavations were going on in the chapel of the kings of France, for the rebuilding of one of the altars, several antique coffins were found, and in one of them the bones of an old Christian prince, wrapped in a pall of gold cloth and surrounded with articles of jewelry. There was a necklace with a cross-shaped pendant, believed to be worth three thousand ducats. I know that a certain jeweller offered that amount of money for the dress alone to Giuliano Lena, who was in charge of the excavations. The Pope attached great importance to the jewels, although it was found out afterwards that they were not worth two thousand ducats, on account of some flaws in the stones, and of injury wrought by time on their mounting. The prospect of finding more made them overturn the whole pavement of the chapel." Another entry of the same diary, under the date of December 23, says: "The treasure-trove in the chapel of the kings of France consists of eight pounds of gold from the melting of dresses, of a cross of gold, dotted with emeralds, and of a second plain one, the value of all being a little over one thousand ducats. The Pope made a present of some to the chapter of S. Peter's that they might make a new reliquary for the skull of S. Petronilla."

The search was doubtless irregular, imperfect and careless, as is proved by other and far richer discoveries which were made in 1544. Unfortunately, if the accounts we have of these are complete, no drawings were made before the dispersion of the objects. The only sketches which have reached us represent a few perfume bottles found inside the grave. Of these *flacons* there are two sets of drawings, one in a codex of marchese Raffaelli di Cingoli, f. 43, with the legend, "Five goblets of agate discovered in the foundations of S. Peter's during the pontificate of Paul III. in the tomb of Maria, daughter of Stilicho and wife of Honorius;" the other in the codex of Fulvio Orsino, No. 3439 of the Vatican Library.

The discovery took place in 1544. A greater treasure of gems, gold, and precious objects has never been found in a single tomb. The beautiful empress was lying in a coffin of red granite, clothed in a state robe woven of gold. Of the same material were the veil, and the shroud which covered the head and breast. The melting of these materials produced a considerable amount of pure gold, its weight being variously stated at thirty-five or forty pounds. Bullinger puts it at eighty, with manifest exaggeration. At the right of the body was placed a casket of solid silver, full of goblets and smelling-bottles, cut in rock crystal, agate, and other precious stones. There were thirty in all, among which were two cups, one round, one oval, decorated with figures in high relief, of exquisite taste, and a lamp, made of gold and crystal, in the shape of a corrugated sea-shell, the hole for the oil being protected and concealed by a golden fly, which moved around a socket. There were also four golden vases, one of which was studded with gems.

In a second casket of gilded silver, placed at the left side, were found one hundred and fifty objects,—gold rings with engraved stones, earrings, brooches, necklaces, buttons, hair-pins, etc. covered with emeralds, pearls and sapphires; a golden nut, which opened in halves; a *bulla* which has been published in a special work by Mazzucchelli,[102] and an emerald engraved with the bust of Honorius, valued at five hundred ducats. Silver objects were scarce; of these we find mentioned only a hairpin and a buckle of répoussé work.

The letters and names engraved on some pieces prove that they formed the *mundus muliebris* (wedding gifts) and toilet articles of Maria, daughter of Stilicho and Serena, sister of Thermantia and Eucherius, and wife of the emperor Honorius. Besides the names of the four arch-angels—Raphael, Gabriel, Michael and Uriel—engraved on a band of gold, those of Domina Nostra Maria, and of Dominus Noster Honorius, were seen on other objects. The *bulla* was inscribed with the names of Honorius, Maria, Stilicho, Serena, Thermantia, and

Eucherius, radiating in the form of a double cross   with the exclamation "Vivatis!" between them. With the exception of this *bulla*, which was bought by Marchese Trivulzio of Milan, at the beginning of the present century, every article has disappeared. That the gold was melted, and that the precious stones were disposed of in various ways, so as to deprive them of their identity, is easy to understand, but where have the vases gone? Were it not for the rough sketches made at the time of discovery we should not be able to form an idea of their beauty and elegance of shape. They were not the work of goldsmiths of the fifth century, but were of classical origin; in fact they represent a portion of the imperial state jewels, which Honorius had inherited from his predecessors, and which he had offered to Maria on her wedding day. Claudianus, the court poet, described them expressly as having sparkled on the breast and forehead of empresses in bygone days.

We know from Paul Diaconus that Honorius was laid to rest by the side of his empress; his coffin, however, has never been found. It must still be concealed under the pavement of the modern church at the southern end of the transept, near the altar of the crucifixion of S. Peter.

An incident narrated by Flavius Josephus ("Antiqq." xvi., ii.) proves that even in this line of discoveries there is nothing new under the sun. Speaking of the financial troubles of King Herod, and of his urgent need of new resources for the royal treasury, he describes how Hircanus had rifled the sum of three thousand silver talents ($3,940,000) from the tomb of David. Herod, on being reminded of this experiment, decided to try it again, in the hope that other treasures might be concealed in the recesses of the royal vault. Precautions were taken to conceal the attempt from the people: the tomb was entered in the darkness of the night, and only a few intimate friends were admitted to the secret. Herod found no more silver in coin or bars, but a considerable quantity of vases and other objects beautifully chiselled in gold. With the help of his associates the booty was removed to the palace. But the more the king had, the more he wanted: and setting aside dignity, self-respect and reverence for the memory of his great predecessors, he ordered his guard to search the vaults, even to the very coffins of David and Solomon. The legend says that the profanation was prevented by an outburst of flames which killed two of the men. This event filled Herod with fear, and to expiate his sacrilege he raised a beautiful monument of white marble at the entrance of the tombs.

The reader must not believe that such discoveries are either of doubtful credibility or a matter of the past only. They have taken place in all centuries, the present included; they take place now.

In July, 1793, behind the choir of the nuns of S. Francesco di Paola, in the Via di S. Lucia in

Selci, a room of a private Roman house was discovered, and in a corner of it a magnificent silver service, which had once belonged to Projecta, wife of Turcius Asterius Secundus, who was prefect of the city in 362 A. D. The discovery was witnessed and described by Ennio Quirino Visconti and Filippo Aurelio Visconti. The objects were of pure silver, heavily gilded, and weighed one thousand and twenty-nine ounces. Besides plates and saucers, forks and spoons, candelabras of various sizes and shapes, there was a wedding-casket with bas-reliefs representing the bride and groom crowned with wreaths of myrtle; she, with braids of hair encircling her head many times, in the fashion of the age of the empress Helena; he, with the beard cut square, in the style worn by Julian the apostate, and Eugenius. The reliefs of the body of the casket represented love-scenes, Venus and the Nereids, the Muses and other pagan subjects; and just under them was engraved the salutation:—

Secundus and Proiecta, may you live in Christ."

The casket was filled with toilet articles and jewels. Later discoveries brought the total weight of the silver to fifteen hundred ounces.

In 1810 a peasant ploughing his field in the territory of Faleria, three miles from Civita Castellana, met with an obstacle which, on closer examination, proved to be a box filled with silver. He loaded himself with the precious spoils, as did many other peasants, whom the news of the discovery had attracted to the spot. There were plates, cups and saucers; a tureen weighing four pounds, wrought in enamelled répoussé, with birds, lizards, branches of ivy, berries, and other fruits and animals, and signed by the maker; a statue of a centaur; and a wine jug, which, after passing through many hands, became the property of the queen of Naples, Caroline Murat, at a cost of five thousand ducats.

Alessandro Visconti reported the treasure-trove at once to count Tournon, the French prefect; but he took no official notice of it, and the silver was melted in the mint of Rome, and by the silversmiths of Viterbo and Perugia. Visconti estimates the weight of the silver at *thirty thousand ounces*.[103]

In 1821, under the foundations of a house at Parma, precious objects were found to the value of several thousand scudi. The few bought for the Museo Parmense by its director, Pietro de Lama, comprise eight bracelets, four rings, a necklace, a chain to which is attached a medallion of Gallienus, a brooch, and thirty-four medals; all of pure gold, and weighing three pounds and four ounces.

On May 9, 1877, two earthen jars were discovered at Belinzago, near Milan, in a farm belonging to a man named Erba. They contained twenty-seven thousand bronze coins, with a total weight of three hundred and sixty pounds. Except a few pieces belonging to Romulus, Maximian, Chlorus, Galerius, Galeria Valeria, and Licinius, the great mass bear the effigy and name of Maxentius, with an astonishing variety of letters and symbols on the reverse.

My personal experience in the discovery of treasure, in the special significance of the word, is limited to the fragments of a bedstead (?) of gilt brass, studded with gems. This discovery took place in 1879, near the southwest corner of the Piazza Vittorio Emanuele, on the

Esquiline, in a room belonging to the Horti Lamiani, the favorite residence of Caligula and of Alexander Severus. The frame of the couch rested on four supports, most gracefully cut in rock-crystal; the frame itself was ornamented with bulls' heads and inlaid with cameos and gems, to the number of four hundred and thirty. There was also a "glass paste" representing the heads of Septimius Severus and his empress Julia Domna. It seems that parts of this rich piece of furniture must have been inlaid with agate incrustations, of which one hundred and sixty-eight pieces were discovered in the same room.

CHAPTER V.

PAPAL TOMBS.

Portraits of the early Popes.—Those of SS. Peter and Paul.—The tombs of the Popes.—Their interest for the student.—The tomb of Cornelius Martyr.—Inscriptions and other monuments found in his crypt.—The two Cornelii, pagan and Christian.—The pontifical crypt in the Cemetery of Callixtus.—The tomb of Gregory the Great.—S. Peter's as a burial-place for the Popes.—Gregory's several resting-places.—The stress of Rome in his time.—The legend of the angel.—Gregory's good works.—His house.—The tomb of the Saxon Ceadwalla.—That of Benedict VII.—The turbulent times in which he lived.—The Crescenzi.—The church of Santa Croce in Gerusalemme.—Pope Sylvester II.—The tradition about his death and tomb.—The vicissitudes of the Lateran basilica.—The Vassalletti.—Study of the antique by mediæval artists.—The stone-cutter's shop on the site of the Banca Nazionale.—The tomb of Innocent VIII.—The story of the holy lance.—The tomb of Paul III.—His services to art.—The tomb of Clement XIII.—Bracci and Canova.—The Jesuits in Clement's time.

Among the curiosities of the three principal basilicas of Rome,—the Lateran, the Vatican, and the Ostiensis (S. Paul's),—were collections of portrait heads of the Popes, which were painted above the colonnade on the three sides of the nave. In S. Peter's there were two sets, one on the frieze, above the capitals of the columns, the other on the walls of the nave, above the cornice; the first is marked with the letters "G H." in the drawing of Ciampini which is reproduced in chapter iii., p. 134; the second, with the letters "I L." The set of the Lateran was painted by order of Nicholas III. (1277-1280). Since his time the basilica has been burned to the ground twice—in 1308 and 1360—and restored three times. Its last disfigurement, by Innocent X. and Borromini in 1644, concealed whatever was left standing of the old building, and made it impossible for us to study its iconic pictures, if there were any still existing. We possess better information in regard to S. Peter's, thanks to Grimaldi, who described and copied both series of medallions before their destruction by Paul V. in 1607. The lower series, which was painted by order of Nicholas III., began with Pope Pius I. (142-157) and ended with Anastasius (397-401). Grimaldi remarks that the Popes of the times of the persecutions, from Pius to Sylvester, were bareheaded; those of a later age wore the tiara; all had the round halo, or nimbus, except Tiberius (352-366), who had a square one. This last particular would prove that the portraits were originally painted in the time of Tiberius, because the square nimbus is the symbol of living persons. The upper series above the cornice was the more important of the two, on account of the chronological inscriptions which accompanied and explained each medallion. These inscriptions, which were too small and faint to be read with the naked eye from below, were not copied before their destruction. Grimaldi could decipher but a few: Siricius . sedit ann(*is*) xv. m(*ensibus*) v. d(*iebus*) xx.— Felix . sedit ann(*o*) i. m(*ensibus*) ... etc. The heads were bare, and framed by a round halo. They seem to have been painted at the time of Pope Formosus (891-896), as were also the fresco-panels which appear in the above-mentioned drawing of Ciampini.

The guide-books of modern Rome describe the series of S. Paul's, restored in mosaic after the fire of 1823, as made up of imaginary likenesses except in the case of later Popes. This statement is not correct. The original medallions were painted on each side of the nave, and on the cross or end wall above the entrances. Those of the end wall disappeared long since, on the occasion of some repairs to this part of the basilica. Those of the left side perished in the fire of 1823; but those of the right side, beginning with S. Peter and ending with Innocent (401-417), were saved. They have since been detached from the wall, transferred first to canvas, then to stone, and are now exhibited in one of the corridors of the monastery.[104] As regards those which perished in the fire, they had already been copied, first in the seventeenth century by order of Cardinal Francesco Barberini, and again in 1751 by Marangoni. The new series in mosaic is therefore not all fanciful and imaginary, but follows the tradition of the likenesses as they were first produced in the fifth century. At that time the study of the pontifical succession was receiving considerable attention in Rome. There were written catalogues inserted in liturgical books, which were read to the congregation on certain days of the year, so that everybody could argue on the subject, and remember the order of succession of the bishops. To impress this more forcibly on the minds of the people, it was written on the walls of the newly erected basilica of S. Paul, and illustrated with portraits. The series must have struck the imagination of visitors and pilgrims. The idea of apostolic inheritance, of uninterrupted hierarchy, of the supremacy of the See of Rome, took a definite shape in the array of these busts of bishops, led by S. Peter, and congregated, as it were, around the grave of S. Paul.

The custom found imitators in other churches and in other cities. Speaking of the gallery of Popes in the duomo at Siena, Symonds remarks how the accumulated majesty of their busts, larger than life, with solemn faces, each leaning from his separate niche, brings the whole past history of the Church into the presence of its living members. A bishop walking up the nave of Siena must feel as a Roman felt among the waxen images of ancestors renowned in council or war. "Of course," Symonds concludes, "the portraits are imaginary for the most part, but the artists have contrived to vary their features and expressions with great skill." This statement may be correct in a general way, especially in regard to the Middle Ages, but is subject to important exceptions. There is no doubt, for instance, that the likenesses of SS. Peter and Paul have been carefully preserved in Rome ever since their lifetime, and that they were familiar to every one, even to school-children. These portraits have come down to us by scores. They are painted in the cubiculi of the catacombs, engraved in gold leaf in the so-called *vetri cemeteriali*, cast in bronze, hammered in silver or copper, and designed in mosaic.[105] The type never varies: S. Peter's face is full and strong, with short curly hair and beard, while S. Paul appears more wiry and thin, slightly bald, with a long pointed beard. The antiquity and the genuineness of both types cannot be doubted. After the peace of Constantine, when Sylvester, Mark, Damasus, Siricius, and Symmachus began to fill the city with their churches and memorial buildings, and as the habit of exhibiting in each of them portraits of the founders became general, it is evident that the author of the collection of portraits in S. Paul's, which dates from the fifth century, must have had plenty of authentic originals at his disposal. Next to these portraits, in the power of exciting the imagination and appealing to the sentiments of visitors and pilgrims, come the tombs of the Popes. I place them next to the images, because the tombs were of the most simple and modest character, and marked only by a name, or by an inscription which a few could read and decipher. But to us, passionate students of history and art, those graves are invaluable; they mark the various stages of the decline and fall of the great city from year to year, as well as of her glorious resurrection; they chronicle the leading events which have agitated Rome, Italy, and the world for the last sixteen centuries. To be sure, there are considerable breaks in the chain, due to the destruction of old S. Peter's, which contained eighty-seven graves; but the descriptions of Pietro Mallio, of Maffeo Vegio, and of Pietro Sabino, and the drawings of Grimaldi and Ciampini, help us to fill the gaps.

Ferdinand Gregorovius was inspired to write his book on the subject while in contemplation of the monument of Paul III., Farnese. He glanced around in the dim light of the evening and saw effigy after effigy of venerable men, seated on their marble thrones, with outstretched 214 hands, like an assembly of patriarchs intrusted with the guardianship of their church. He devoted many hours to the study of this class of monuments, so strikingly Roman, "for in Rome, more than in any other city of the world, does investigation lead one in the footsteps of Death." His volume,[106] however, seems to me more like an essay written in hours of depression than an exhaustive and satisfying treatise. The *materia prima* has greatly increased since he wrote, owing to the discoveries made in the catacombs, in libraries and archives, and to the reproduction by photography of the fragments collected in the sacred grottos of the Vatican. If any of our younger colleagues are willing and prepared to go over the work in a critical spirit, let them divide the subject into three periods. During the first, which begins with the entombment of S. Peter, June 29, A. D. 67, and ends with that of Melchiades, A. D. 314, the bishops of Rome were interred in the depths of the suburban cemeteries, and their loculi marked with a simple name. During the second period, which begins with the peace of Constantine and ends with the destruction of the Vatican basilica in 1506-1606, the pontifical graves were mostly ancient sarcophagi or bathing basins from the thermæ, accompanied by an inscription in verse, and, as the Renaissance was approached, by canopies of Gothic or Romanesque style. In the third period, which ends with our time, the new church of S. Peter is transformed into a papal mausoleum which is worthy of being compared in refinement of art, in splendor of decoration, in richness of material, in historical interest, with the Pantheons of ancient Rome. I shall select from each of the three periods a few representative specimens.

THE TOMB OF CORNELIUS, ON THE APPIAN WAY. In 1849, while de Rossi was exploring the 215 Vigna Molinari between the Via Appia and the Ardeatina, in his attempt to define the site and extent of the various cemeteries which undermine that region, he found a fragment of a marble slab with the letters ···· ELIVS MARTYR.

Excited by a discovery the capital importance of which he was able to foresee at once, he asked an audience of the Pope, Pius IX., and begged him to purchase the Vigna Molinari, and grant the funds necessary to discover the crypt to which this fragment of a tombstone belonged. After listening quietly to the arguments by which the young man was advocating his cause, the Pope answered only four disheartening words: "Sogni di un archeologo!" (dreams of an archæologist). At the same time he gave orders for the immediate purchase of the vigna (now called dei Palazzi Apostolici) and for the appropriation of an "exploration fund." In March, 1852, a crypt was discovered on the very border of the Appian Way; in the crypt was a tomb, and with it were the missing fragments of the epitaph of Cornelius.

Some weeks later the young discoverer escorted the Pope to the historical grave, and pointing to the epitaph exclaimed: "Sogni di un archeologo!" To judge of the importance of the discovery we must remember that the identification of the crypts of Lucina, and that of all the surrounding catacombs, depended mostly upon the identification of this one. The "Liber Pontificalis" says: "The emperor Decius gave judgment in the case of Cornelius: that he should be taken to the temple of Mars *extra muros*, and asked to perform an act of adoration: in case of a refusal that he should be beheaded. This was accordingly done, and Cornelius gave his life for his faith. Lucina, a noble matron, assisted by members of the clergy, collected his remains and buried them in a crypt on her own estate near the Cemetery of Callixtus, on the Appian Way; and this happened on September 14 (A. D. 253)." As the Cemetery of Callixtus was the recognized burial-place of the bishops of Rome, why was this exception made to the rule? The reason is evident: the estate of Lucina contained the family vault of the Cornelii, or at least of a branch of the Cornelian race. The victim of the persecution of Decius was the first Pope of noble and ancient lineage. Apparently his relatives wished to emphasize this fact in the place selected for his burial, and by proclaiming his illustrious descent on his gravestone through the use of the old and simple language of the republic,—"Cornelius Martyr." The use of Latin at this age constitutes another conspicuous exception to the rule, because the Greek language was not only fashionable in the third century, but had been adopted almost officially by the Church. The majority of liturgical words, such as hymn, psalm, liturgy, homily, catechism, baptism, eucharist, deacon, presbyter, pope, cemetery, diocese, are of Greek origin, and the names of the Popes in the pontifical crypt of this same cemetery are, likewise, written in Greek letters even when they are strictly Roman, as in the case of ΛΟΥΚΙΣ for LVCIVS.

The crypt of Cornelius contains other historical records. A metric inscription composed by Damasus and placed above the loculus says to the pilgrim: "Behold: a descent to the crypt has been built: darkness has been expelled: you can behold the memorial of Cornelius and his resting-place. The zeal of Damasus has enabled him, though careworn and ailing, to accomplish the work and make your pilgrimage easier and more efficacious. If you are prepared to pray to the Lord in purity of heart, entreat Him to restore Damasus to health; not that he is fond of life, but because the duties of his mission bind him still to this earth." These verses are, probably, the very last composed by the dying pontiff († 384). His work was finished by Siricius (A. D. 384-397), as proved by a second inscription below the loculus: "Siricius has completed the work and dressed the tomb of Cornelius in marble."

The paintings of the crypt, although they date from the Byzantine period, are of historical interest. On the right we see the images of Cornelius and Cyprian, bishop of Carthage. Their intimate connection in life, their martyrdom on the same day of the same month, made their memory inseparable. The church commemorates them on the same *natale* or anniversary, and their images stand side by side in this crypt. The artist who painted them prophesied the future; he saw that the time would come when, in their graves, the bodies of the two friends would be united as their souls had been while they lived. Their remains were removed to Compiègne in the reign of Charles the Bald, those of Cornelius from Rome, those of Cyprian from Carthage, never to part again.

A circular pedestal, like a section of a column, stands against the wall under the images. Such pedestals are not uncommon in the catacombs; and they were intended to support a large flat bowl not unlike the holy-water basins of modern churches. Several specimens have been found *in situ*, in the cemeteries of Saturninus, Alexander, Agnes, and Callixtus. They are of the same make, cut in marble so delicately as to be translucent, flat-bottomed, and very low. For what were they used? We cannot think of "holy water" in the modern sense, because in those days the faithful were wont to purify their hands, not in receptacles of stagnant water, but in springs or living fountains. It seems more in accordance with ancient rites to consider them as lamps, filled with scented oil or nard, on the surface of which wicks, secured to a piece of papyrus, floated like a *veilleuse*, to guide the footsteps of pilgrims in the darkness.

A papyrus in the archives or treasury of the cathedral at Monza contains a list of oils collected by John, abbot of Monza, in the cemeteries of Rome, and offered by him to Theodolinda, Queen of the Lombards. Special mention is made in the document of the oil from the tomb of S. Cornelius; and de Rossi asserts that the fragments of a diaphanous oil-basin found in the exploration of this crypt were soaked with an oleaginous substance.[107]

One cannot help being impressed by the coexistence on this same road, and within a mile of each other, of two family vaults of the Cornelii: one in the aristocratic burial-grounds between the viæ Appia and Latina, the other in the subterranean haunts of a despised and persecuted race. One need not be a deep thinker or a religious enthusiast to appreciate that each is worthy of the other; and that the Cornelius of the third century who chose to die the death of a criminal rather than betray his conscience, is a worthy descendant of the Scipios, the heroes of republican Rome. Whenever I happen to pay a visit to the hypogæum of the Cornelii Scipiones,[108] I try to finish my walk by way of that of their noble representative, the victim

219

of the persecution of Decius.

THE PONTIFICAL CRYPT. I have just mentioned the vault
of the Popes as belonging to the same Cemetery of
Callixtus. It was discovered in 1854. Its approaches
were inscribed with a great number of *graffiti*, which
marked the place as the most celebrated in the
cemetery, if not in the whole of underground Rome. A
pious hand had written near the entrance door:
GERVSALE[M] CIVITAS ET ORNAMENTVM
MARTYRVM DNI [*Domini*]: "This is the Jerusalem of
the martyrs of the Lord." The débris which obstructed
the chamber was removed as quickly as the narrowness
of the space would permit, and as it passed under the
eyes of de Rossi, he was able to detect the names of
Anteros, Fabianus, Lucius, and Eutychianus on the
broken marbles. There were, besides, one hundred and

Portrait of Pope Cornelius; from a fresco
near his grave.

twenty-five fragments of a metric inscription by Damasus, which gave the desired information,
in the following words:—

"Here lie together in great numbers the holy bodies you are seeking. These tombs contain
their remains, but their souls are in the heavenly kingdom. Here you see the companions of
Sixtus waving the trophies of victory; there the bishops [of Rome] who shielded the altar of
Christ; the pontiff who saw the first years of peace [Melchiades, A. D. 311-314]; the noble
confessors who came to us from Greece [Hippolytus, Hadrias, Maria, Neon, Paulina], and
others. I confess I wished most ardently to find my last resting place among these saints, but I
did not dare to disturb their remains."

Callixtus (218-223), the founder of the cemetery, does not lie in it. He perished in a popular
outbreak, having been thrown from the windows of his house into the square, the site of
which corresponds with the modern Piazza di Santa Maria in Trastevere, the *area Callisti* of
the fourth century. The Christians recovered his body, and buried it in the nearest cemetery at
hand,—that of Calepodius by the Via Aurelia (between the Villa Pamfili and the Casaletto di
Pio V.).

Urban, his successor (A. D. 223-230), opens the series in the episcopal crypt of the Appian
Way. His name, OYPBANOC E (πισχοπος), has been read on a fragment of a marble
sarcophagus. Then follow Anteros (A. D. 235-236), Fabianus (A. D. 236-251), Lucius (A. D.
252-253), and Eutychianos (A. D. 275-283),—in all, five bishops out of the eleven who are
known to have been buried in the crypt.

In looking at these humble graves we cannot help comparing them with the great mausolea of
contemporary emperors. A war was then raging between the builders of the catacombs and
the occupants of the imperial palace. It was a duel between principles and power, between

moral and material strength. In 296, bishop Gaius, one of the last victims of Diocletian's persecution, was interred by the side of his predecessors in the crypt; in 313, only seventeen years later, Sylvester took possession of the Lateran Palace, which had been offered to him by Constantine. Such is the history of Rome; such are the events which the study of her ruins recalls to our memory.

THE TOMB OF GREGORY THE GREAT. In the account of his life given in the "Liber Pontificalis," i. 312, two things especially attract our attention: the mission sent by him to the British Isles, and his entombment in the "Paradise" of S. Peter's. Beginning with the latter, we are told that he died on March 12 of the year 604, and that his remains were buried "in the basilica of the blessed Peter, in front of the secretarium, in one of the intercolumniations of the portico." This statement requires a few words of comment.

We have seen how the bishops of the age of persecutions were buried in the underground cemeteries, with a marked preference for those of the Via Appia and the Via Salaria. From the time of Sylvester (314-335) to that of Leo the Great (440-461) they still sought the proximity of martyrs, and obeyed the rule which forbade burial within the walls of the city. Sylvester raised a modest mausoleum for himself and his successors over the Cemetery of Priscilla, on the Via Salaria, the remains of which have just been discovered.[109] Anastasius and Innocent I. found their resting-place over the Cemetery of Pontianus, on the road to Porto; Zosimus and Sixtus in the church of S. Lorenzo; Boniface I. in that of S. Felicitas, on the Via Salaria.

The Vatican began to be the official mausoleum of the Popes with Leo I. in 461. The place selected is not the interior of the church, but the vestibule, and more exactly the space between the middle doorway (the *Porta argentea*) and the southwest corner, occupied by the *secretarium*, or sacristy, a hall of basilican shape in which the Popes donned their official robes before entering the church. The place can be easily identified by comparing the accompanying reproduction of Ciampini's drawing of the front of the old basilica of S. Peter's with the plan published in chapter iii., p. 127. For nearly two and a half centuries they were laid side by side, until every inch of space was occupied, the graves being under the floor, and marked by a plain slab inscribed with a few Latin distichs of semi-barbaric style. These short biographical poems have been transmitted to us, with a few exceptions, by the pilgrims of the seventh and ninth centuries, whose copies were afterwards collected in volumes, the most important of which is known as the Codex of Lauresheim. At the time of Gregory the Great there was but a small space left near the secretarium. This was occupied by Pelagius I., Johannes III., Benedict I., and a few others.

Sergius I. (687-701) was the first who dared to cross the threshold of the church, which he did, however, not for his own benefit, but to do honor to the memory of Leo I. The inscription in which he describes the event is too prolix to be given here. It tells us that the grave of Leo the Great was in the vestibule below the sacristy. There he lay "like the keeper of the temple, like a shepherd watching his flock." But other graves had crowded the place so that it was almost impossible to single them out, and read their epitaphs. Sergius therefore ordered the body of his predecessor to be removed to an oratory, or chapel, in the south transept of the church, and to be enclosed in a beautiful monument which he adorned with costly marbles, and with mosaics representing prophets and saints. The monument was destroyed by Paul V. on Saturday, May 26, 1607.

The remains of Gregory the Great have also been moved several times. His tombstone must have been worn by the feet of pilgrims, as only eighteen letters out of many hundred have been preserved to our time. These were discovered not many years ago, in a dark corner of the Grotte Vaticane. Two centuries after his death, his successor, Gregory IV. (827-844), carried his remains inside the church, to an oratory near the new sacristy, covered the tomb with panels of silver, and the back wall with golden mosaics. The body remained in this second place until the pontificate of Enea Silvio Piccolomini, Pius II. (1458-1464), who, having built a chapel to S. Andrew the apostle, removed Gregory's coffin to the new altar.

The coffin is described as a *conca ægyptiaca*, an ancient bathing-basin, of porphyry, which was protected by an iron grating. The chapel, the altar, and the tomb were again sacrificed to the renovation of the church in the time of Paul V. On December 28, 1605, the porphyry urn was opened, and the body of the great man transferred to a cypress case; on the eighth day of the following January a procession, headed by the college of cardinals and the aristocracy, accompanied the remains to their fourth and last resting-place, the Cappella Clementina, built by Clement VIII., near the entrance to the modern sacristy. There are now two inscriptions: one on the marble lid, "Here lies Saint Gregory the Great, first of his name, doctor of the church;" the other on the cypress case, "Evangelista Pallotta, cardinal of S. Lorenzo in Lucina, dean of this church, collected in this case the remains of Gregory the Great, and removed them from the altar of S. Andrew to this new chapel. Done by order of Paul V., in the first year of his pontificate, on Sunday, January 8, A. D. 1606." The altarpiece was not painted by Muziano, as stated in old guidebooks, but by Andrea Sacchi. The picture was removed to Paris, with many other masterpieces, at the time of Napoleon I.; but Canova obtained its restitution in 1815. It is now preserved in the Vatican Gallery; the copy in mosaic is the joint work of Alessandro Cocchi and Francesco Castellini.

The history of the pontificate of Gregory has been written and will shortly be published by my learned friend Professor H. Grisar. No better or greater subject could be found than this period when the city, abandoned by the Byzantine emperors, harassed, besieged, starved by the Lombards, found in her bishops her only chance of salvation. They never appear to greater advantage than in those eventful times, when Rome was sinking so low within, when her surroundings were changed into a lifeless desert. The queen who had ruled the world was trampled under the feet of her former slaves, and found assistance and sympathy nowhere. When Alboin overran the peninsula in 568, at the head of his Lombards, with whom warriors of several other races, especially Saxons, were intermixed, the emperor Justin could offer no other help to the Romans than the advice of bribing the Lombard chiefs, or of calling in the Franks. Barbarians for barbarians!

Statue of S. Gregory the Great.

"On the death of Pope John III. in 573, Rome was so closely pressed that it was impossible to send to Constantinople for the confirmation of Benedict I., who had been elected his successor, and the papal throne remained vacant for one year. The same appears to have been the case on the death of Benedict, in 578, when Rome was held in siege by Zoto, duke of Beneventum, for the Lombard power had been distributed among thirty-six duchies. The particulars of this siege are unknown, but it probably lasted two or three years. On withdrawing from Rome Zoto took and plundered the Benedictine convent on Montecassino. The monks retired to Rome and established themselves in a convent near the Lateran, which they named after S. John Baptist, whence the basilica of Constantine or the Saviour subsequently took its name.... The misery of the Romans was aggravated by some natural calamities. Towards the end of 589, several temples and other monuments were destroyed by the flooding of the Tiber, and the city was afterwards afflicted by a devastating pestilence.

"To the year 590, which is that of the election of Gregory, is referred the legend of the angel that was seen to hover over the Mausoleum of Hadrian, while Gregory was passing it in solemn procession, and to sheathe his flaming sword as a sign that the pestilence was about to cease. At the same time three angels were heard to sing the antiphony *Regina Cæli*, to which Gregory replied with the hymn *Ora pro nobis Deum alleluja!*[110]

This graceful story is the invention of a later century, but it is worth while to trace its origin. It was customary in the Middle Ages to consecrate the summits of hills and mountains to Michael, the archangel, from an association of ideas which needs no explanation. Similarly, in classical times, the Alpine passes had been placed under the protection of Jupiter the Thunderer, and lofty peaks crowned with his temples. Without citing the examples of Mont Saint Michel on the coast of Normandy, or of Monte Gargano on the coast of Apulia, we need only look around the neighborhood of Rome to find the figure of the angel wherever a solitary hill or a commanding ruin suggested the idea or the sensation of height. *Deus in altis habitat*. Here is the isolated cone of Castel Giubileo on the Via Salaria (a fortified outpost of Fidenæ); there the mountain of S. Angelo above Nomentum, and the convent of S. Michele on the peak of Corniculum. The highest point within the walls of Rome, now occupied by the Villa Aurelia (Heyland) was covered likewise by a church named S. Angelo in Janiculo. The two principal ruins in the valley of the Tiber—the Mausoleum of Augustus and that of Hadrian—were also shaded by the angel's wings. The shrine over the vault of the Julian emperors was called S. Angelo de Augusto, while that built by Boniface IV. (608-615) above Hadrian's tomb was called *inter nubes* (among the clouds), or *inter cœlos* (in the heavens). This shrine was replaced later by the figure of an angel. During the pestilence of 1348 the statue was reported by thirty witnesses to have bowed to the image of the Virgin which the panic-stricken people were carrying from the church of Ara Cœli to S. Peter's. In 1378 the ungrateful crowd destroyed it in their attempt to storm the castle. Nicholas V. (1447-1455) placed a new image on the top of the monument, which perished in the explosion of the powder-magazine in 1497. The shock was so violent that pieces of the statue were found beyond S. Maria Maggiore, a distance of a mile and a half. Alexander VI., Borgia, set up a statue for the third time, which was stolen by the hordes of Charles V. for the sake of its heavy gilding. The marble effigy by Raffaele di Montelupo was placed on the vacant base, and remained until Benedict XIV. (1740-1758) set up a fifth and last figure, which was cast in bronze by Wenschefeld.

It is remarkable that Gregory could think of the spiritual mission of the church in times so troubled, when the last hour of Rome and the civilized world seemed to have come. He saw that neither the condition of the world nor that of the Church was hopeless, and his ability, assisted by political circumstances, gave promise of more prosperous times. A great part of Europe accepted the Christian faith during his pontificate. Theolinda, queen of the Lombards, after the death of her husband Autharic, in 590, contributed greatly to the spreading of the gospel among her own people. The west Goths of Spain were converted through Reccared, their king. We need not repeat here the well-known story of the manner in which Gregory's sympathy for the Anglo-Saxon race was excited by seeing one of them in the slave-market of Rome. The mission to which he intrusted the conversion of the British Isles was composed of three holy men, Mellitus, Augustin, and John, who were accompanied by other devout followers. They left Rome in the spring of 596, but could not land on the shores of England until the middle of the following year. Mention of this fact is made in two documents only,—in the "Liber Pontificalis," vol. i. p. 312, and in a writing by Prosper of Aquitania in which the English nation is called *gens extremo oceano posita* (a people living at the end of the ocean).

Not less surprising in the career of this man is the institution of a school for religious music. It was established in one of the halls of the Lateran, and even the Carlovingian kings obtained from it skilful maestri and organists. It is still prosperous. To Gregory we owe the *canto fermo*, or Gregorian chant, which, if properly executed, imparts such a grave and solemn character to the ceremonies of our church.

Gregory's paternal house stood on the slope of the Cælian, facing the palace of the Cæsars, on a street named the Clivus Scauri, which corresponds very nearly to the modern Via dei SS. Giovanni e Paolo. Fond as he was of monastic life, he extended hospitality to men of his own sentiments and habit of thought; and transformed the old *lararium* into a chapel of S. Andrew. The place, which was governed by the rule of S. Benedict, became known as the "Monastery of S. Andrew in the street of Scaurus." The typical plan of a Roman palace was not altered; the atrium, accessible to the clients and guests of the monks, is described as having in the centre a "wonderful and most salubrious" spring, no doubt the "spring of Mercury" of classical times. It still exists, in a remote and hardly accessible corner of the garden, but its waters are no longer believed to be miracle-working, nor are they sought by crowds of ailing pilgrims as formerly. Time has brought other changes upon this cluster of buildings. In 1633 cardinal Scipione Borghese completed its modernization by raising the façade, which does so little honor to him and his architect, Giovanni Soria. But let us pause on the top of the staircase which leads to it, with our faces towards the Palatine; there is no more

230

impressive sight in the whole of Rome. Placed as we are between the Baths of Caracalla, the Circus Maximus, the dwelling of the emperors, and the Coliseum, with the Via Triumphalis at our feet, we can hardly realize the wonderful transformation of men and things. From the hill beyond us the generals who led the Roman armies to the conquest of the world took their departure; from this modest monastery went a handful of humble missionaries who were to preach the gospel and to bring civilization into countries far beyond the boundary line of the Roman empire. Of their success in the British Islands we have monumental evidence everywhere in Rome. Here in the vestibule of this very church is engraved the name of Sir Edward Carne, one of the Commissioners sent by Henry VIII. to obtain the opinion of foreign universities respecting his divorce from Catherine of Aragon; and, not far from it, that of Robert Pecham, who died in 1567, an exile for his faith, and left his substance to the poor.

These, however, are comparatively recent memories. In the vestibule of S. Peter's, not far from the original grave of Gregory the Great, we should have found that of a British king, reckoned among the saints in the old martyrologies, who had come in grateful acknowledgment of the double civilization which his native island had received from pagan and Christian Rome.[111] Under the date of 688 the Anglo-Saxon Chronicle records: "This year king Ceadwalla went to Rome and received baptism from Pope Sergius, and he gave him the name of Peter, and in about seven days afterwards, on the twelfth before the Kalends

of May (April 20), while he was yet in his baptismal garments, he died, and he was buried in S. Peter's." The fair-haired convert, who had met with a solemn and enthusiastic reception from Pope Sergius, the clergy, and the people, received after his death the greatest honor that the Church and the Romans could offer him: he was buried in the "Popes' Corner," or *porticus pontificum*, almost side by side with Gregory the Great. The verses engraved on the tomb of the latter—

"Ad Christum Anglos convertit pietate magistra
Sic fidei acquirens agmina gente nova,"

(by pious cares he converted the English to Christ, acquiring thereby for the true faith multitudes of a new race)—could not have found a more convincing witness to their truth than this grave of Ceadwalla, because with his conversion, which was due to the preaching of S. Wilfrid, the Christian religion spread rapidly among the Saxons of the West, and that part of the country which had most resisted the new faith was forever secured to Christian civilization. In fact Wessex became the most powerful member of the Heptarchy, till it attained absolute dominion over the whole island.

Ceadwalla's tomb, forgotten, and perhaps concealed by superstructures, was brought to light again towards the end of the sixteenth century. Giovanni de Deis, in a work published in 1588, says: "The epitaph[112] and the tomb on which it was engraved lay for a long time concealed from the eyes of visitors, and only in later years it was discovered by the masons engaged in rebuilding S. Peter's." Not a fragment of the monument has come down to us, and such was the contempt with which the learned men of the age looked upon these historical monuments, that none of them condescended to give us the details of the discovery. "It is deeply to be regretted," says cardinal Mai, "that such a notable trophy as the tomb of Ceadwalla, the royal catechumen, which was erected and inscribed by Sergius I., disappeared from the Vatican, and was irretrievably lost, together with innumerable monuments of ancient art and piety, owing to the calamities of the times, the avidity of the workmen, and the negligence of the superintendents."

"Ceadwalla's tomb," I quote from Tesoroni, "was not the only monument of Anglo-Saxon interest to be seen in old S. Pietro. William of Malmesbury and other chroniclers mention two other kings, Offa of Essex, and Coenred of Mercia, as having renounced their crowns and embraced the monastic life in one of the Vatican cloisters. They were also buried in the Paradise near the Popes' Corner. It is doubtful whether king Ina, who succeeded Ceadwalla, and his queen, Aethelburga, were buried in the same place, or in the Anglo-Saxon quarter by the church of S. Maria in Saxia, founded, probably, by Ina himself. It is certain, however, that at a later time king Burrhed of Mercia was entombed in the same quarter, and in the same church. The place is still named from the Anglo-Saxons, S. Spirito in Sassia."

The threshold of S. Peter's once crossed, we hear no more of Popes being buried outside, in the old atrium. The second aisle on the left—that entered by the Gate of Judgment—was intended to receive their mortal remains. Hence its name of *porticus pontificum* (the aisle of the pontiffs). On the day of his coronation the newly elected head of the church was asked to cross this aisle on his way from the chapel of S. Gregory to the high altar, that the sight of so many graves should impress on his mind the maxim, "The glory of the world vanisheth like the flame of a handful of straw;" and a handful of straw was actually burned before his eyes, while the dean of the church addressed to him the words, "My father, *sic transit gloria mundi*."

234

THE TOMB OF BENEDICT VII. (974-983). The basilica of S. Croce in Gerusalemme contains but one tomb, that of Benedict VII., whose career is described in a metric inscription of seventeen verses, inserted in the wall of the nave on the right of the entrance. I mention it because Gregorovius seems to have been unaware of its existence, in spite of its historical value.[113] It recalls to our mind one of the most turbulent and riotous periods in the annals of Rome and the papacy, the fight between the "independents" led by the Crescenzi, and the party of the Saxon emperors, represented by Popes Benedict VI. and VII. The Crescenzio mentioned in the epitaph of Benedict VII. was the son of John and Theodora, and one of the most active members of a family which has thrice attempted to reëstablish the republic of ancient Rome and shake off the yoke of German oppression. This one is known as Crescentius de Theodora, from the name of his mother; and also as Crescentius de Caballo, from his residence on the Quirinal, near the colossal statues of Castor and Pollux, which have given to the hill its modern name of Monte Cavallo. The Castel S. Angelo was the stronghold of the family. Under the shelter of its massive ramparts they were able to dictate the law to the Popes, and commit bloodshed and sacrilege with impunity. In 928 Marozia and her second husband Guido, marquis of Tuscany, with their partisans, fell on Pope John X., who was staying in the Lateran Palace, murdered his brother Pietro before his eyes, and dragged him through the streets of Rome to the castle. The unfortunate Pope lingered awhile in a dark

235

dungeon, and was ultimately killed by suffocation. Marozia, perhaps to dispel the suspicions of a violent death, allowed him to be buried with due honors near the middle door of the Lateran, at the foot of the nave. His gravestone was seen and described by Johannes Diaconus, but has long since disappeared. In 974 Crescenzio, son of Theodora, committed another sacrilegious murder, that of Benedict VI. Helped by a deacon named Franco he confined him in the same dungeon of Castel S. Angelo, while Franco placed himself on the chair of S. Peter, under the name of Boniface VII. The legal Pope was soon after strangled. Such crimes startled for a moment the apathy of the Romans, who besieged and stormed the castle, deposed the usurper, and named in his place Benedict VII., whose grave we are now visiting in S. Croce in Gerusalemme. Yet Crescenzio and Franco did not pay dearly for their crimes. Franco, after plundering the Vatican basilica of its valuables, migrated to Constantinople, a rich and free man. Crescenzio died peacefully in the monastery of S. Alessio on the Aventine in the year 984. His tomb, the tomb of a murderer, whose hands had been stained with the blood of a Pope, was allowed the honor of a laudatory inscription. It can still be seen in the cloisters of the monastery: "Here lies the body of Crescentius, the illustrious, the honorable citizen of Rome, the great leader, the great descendant of a great family," etc. "Christ the Saviour of our souls made him infirm and an invalid, so that, abandoning any further hope of worldly success, he entered this monastery, and spent his last years in prayer and retirement."

All these events are alluded to in the epitaph of Benedict VII., in S. Croce. This church has been so thoroughly deprived of its charm and interest by another Benedict (XIV., in the year 1744) that one cannot help paying attention to the few objects which have survived the "transformation," and especially to this humble stone hardly known to students.

Should any of my readers care to arrange their researches in Rome systematically, and study its monuments group by group, according to chronological and historical connections, they will find abundance of material in the period in which the murders of John X. and Benedict VI. took place. There is the tomb of Landolfo, brother of Crescenzio, at S. Lorenzo fuori le Mura; that of Crescenzio at S. Alessio; the house of Nicola di Crescenzio, near the Bocca della Verità, a fascinating subject for a day's work.

The church of S. Croce has seen another strange death of a Pope,—that of Sylvester II. (999-1003), a Frenchman, Gerbert by name. A legend, related first by cardinal Benno in 1099, describes him as deep in necromantic knowledge, which he had gathered during a journey through the Hispano-Arabic provinces. He is said to have carried in his travels a sort of a diabolical oracle, a brazen head which uttered prophetic answers. After his election, in 999, he inquired how long he should remain in power; the response was "as long as he avoided saying mass in Jerusalem." The prophecy was soon fulfilled. He expired in great agony on Quadragesima Sunday, 1003, while celebrating mass in this church, the classic name of which he seems not to have known. The legend asserts that his sins were pardoned by God, and that he was given an honorable burial in the church of S. John Lateran. A mysterious influence, however, hung over his grave. Whenever one of his successors was approaching the end of life, the bones of Sylvester would stir in their vault, and the marble lid would be moistened with drops of water, as stated in the epitaph, which is still visible in S. John Lateran, against one of the pillars of the first right aisle. It begins with the distich:—

ISTE LOCVS MVNDI SILVESTRI MEMBRA SEPVLTI
VENTVRO DOMINO CONFERET AD SONITVM.

We are ready to forgive the originators of the legend about the rattling of the bones; the verses are so bad and distorted that it is no wonder they were wrongly understood. Their author wanted to express the readiness of the deceased to appear before the Lord at His coming; but, not being particularly successful in the choice of his language, his simple-minded contemporaries, so inclined towards the supernatural, saw in the words *venturo domino* an allusion to the coming, not of the Sovereign Judge, but of the future Pope; and they thought the expression *ad sonitum* referred not to the trumpet of the last judgment, but to the rattling of the bones whenever a *dominus venturus* might appear on the scene.

This popular interpretation soon became official. John the Deacon has accepted it blindly in his description of the Lateran. "In the same aisle (the last on the left, near the Cappella Corsini) lies Gerbert, archbishop of Reims, who took the name of Sylvester after his election to the pontificate. His tomb, although in a dry place, sends forth drops of water even in clear and dry weather," etc. The tomb was opened and destroyed in 1648. Rasponi, an eye-witness, describes the event in his book "De Basilica et Patriarchio Lateranensi" (Rome, 1656, p. 76): "In the year 1648, while new foundations were being laid for the left wing of the church, the corpse of Sylvester II. was found in a marble sarcophagus, twelve feet below the ground. The body was well composed and dressed in state robes; the arms were crossed on the breast; the head crowned with the tiara. It fell into dust at the touch of our hands, while a pleasant odor filled the air, owing to the rare substances in which it had been embalmed. Nothing was saved but a silver cross and the signet ring."

The church of S. John Lateran has passed through the same vicissitudes as that of S. Croce in Gerusalemme, but with less detriment. Clement VIII., who reconstructed the transept; Sixtus V., who rebuilt the north portico; Innocent X., Pius IX., and Leo XIII. have all been more merciful than Benedict XIV. At all events, if the sight of the church itself in its present state is distasteful to the true lover of ancient and mediæval Rome, nothing could delight him more than the cloisters of Vassalectus which open at the south end of the transept. I speak of the building as well as of its contents. The cloisters have just been restored to their original appearance by Leo XIII. and by his architect, conte Francesco Vespignani, and a museum of works of art from the old basilica has been formed under its arcades.

238

There are three or four details regarding it which deserve notice. The design of this exquisite structure has been attributed, as usual, to one of the Cosmatis; but it belongs to Pietro Vassalletto and his son. In demolishing one of the clumsy buttresses, which were built two centuries ago against the colonnade of the south side, count Vespignani discovered (1887) the authentic signatures of both artists, in the inscription which is here reproduced. It is thus translated: "I, Vassalectus, a noble and skilful master in my profession, have finished alone this work which I began in company with my father."[114] Their school lasted for four generations, from 1153 to the middle of the following century, and ranks next in importance to that of the Cosmatis. Many of their productions are signed, as for example the episcopal chair in the church of S. Andrea at Anagni, dated 1263; a screen in the cathedral of Segni, dated 1185; the candelabra in S. Paolo fuori le Mura; the lion in the porch of SS. Apostoli; the canopy in SS. Cosma e Damiano, dated 1153; fragments of an inlaid screen in the studio of the illustrious artist, Señor Villegas, etc. We are in the habit of asserting that only the Renaissance masters studied and were inspired by the antique; but the fascination of ancient art was equally felt by their early precursors of the twelfth century. The archway in the middle of the south side of these cloisters (opposite the one represented in our illustration) rests on sphinxes, one of which is bearded. The human-headed monsters, wearing the *claft* or *nemes*, images of Egyptian

Inscription of Vassalectus.

239

240

Pharaohs, were obviously modelled in imitation of ancient originals. Nor is this the only case. The gate of S. Antonio on the Esquiline is also supported by crouching sphinxes (A. D. 1269). It has been suggested that such works were inspired by crusaders who had seen the wonders of Egypt. But if the reader remembers what I said about the Temple of Isis in the Campus Martius, in chapter ii., p. 92, he will at once perceive how the Vassalletti were able to draw their Egyptian models from a much nearer source. A fact mentioned by Winckelmann[115] proves that one of them owned and studied a statue of Æsculapius, in the plinth of which he actually engraved his own name, [V]ASSALECTVS. The statue was seen by Winckelmann in the Verospi palace, but I have not been able to ascertain its present location. In these same cloisters are some delightful figures of saints, in high relief, from an old ciborium. One of them, representing S. John the Baptist, is obviously modelled on the type of an Antinous, with the same abundance of curly hair, the same profile and characteristic eyebrows. In October, 1886, I actually saw a mediæval stonecutter's shop, dating perhaps from the eleventh or twelfth century, in which the place of honor was given to a statue of Antinous. The fact is so remarkable for an age in which statues were sought, not as models, but as material for the limekiln, that I beg leave to describe it.

The site of the Palazzo della Banca Nazionale, in the street of the same name, was occupied in old times by the house of Tiberius Julius Frugi, a member of the college of the Arvales. This house shared the fate of all ancient buildings: it was allowed to fall to ruin, and later became the property of whoever chose to occupy it. Among these mediæval occupants was a stonecutter who collected

Candelabrum in the Church of S. Paolo fuori le Mura.

in the half-ruined halls fragments, blocks of columns, and marbles of various kinds, some of which had already been re-cut for new uses. There was also a deposit of the fine sand which is even now employed for sawing stones. We can judge of the approximate age in which the stonecutter lived, by the fact that in his time the pavements of the Roman house were already covered with a stratum of rubbish six feet thick.

A statue of Antinous, the favorite of Hadrian, deified after his death and worshipped in the form of a Bacchus, was found standing against the rear wall of the workshop. It is cut in Greek marble, and the style of sculpture is excellent. None of the prominent portions of the body have been separated from the trunk, so that the only injuries wrought by time are slight, and confined to the nose and hands. A patient study of this figure has enabled me to reconstruct its story. First of all, we are sure that, from the knees down, the statue had been immersed in a stream of water for a very long period, because the surface of the marble is corroded and full of small holes, caused by the action of running water. It also bears visible traces of having been scraped with a piece of iron and scoured to get rid of the mud and calcareous carbonates with which it must have been incrusted when taken out of the stream. These facts concur to prove that the Antinous, having been thrown into the water, or having fallen in by accident, was found or bought after the lapse of centuries, by our stonecutter. An attempt was then made to clean the statue, and, with the intention of preserving it as a work of art and a model, it was placed in the best room of the workshop. Both were buried for a second time, to be brought to light again in 1886. The statue can now be seen in the vestibule of the Banca Nazionale.

As representative specimens of later art and later glories I venture to suggest the tombs of Innocent VIII. (1484-1492) by Antonio Pollaiuolo, of Paul III. (1524-1549) by Guglielmo della Porta, and of Clement XIII. (1758-1769) by Antonio Canova.

The Antinous of the Banca Nazionale.

THE TOMB OF INNOCENT VIII. This noble work, by Antonio Pollaiuolo, is set against the second pilaster of the nave of S. Peter's on the left side, opposite the "Porta dei Musici." If we reflect that, besides its importance in the history of art, this monument brings back to our memory the fall of Constantinople and Granada, the discovery of the new world, the figures of Bayazid, Ferdinand, and Christopher Columbus, we have a subject for meditation, as well as æsthetic enjoyment. Innocent VIII., Giovanni Battista Cibo, of Genoa, is represented on his sarcophagus sleeping the sleep of the just, while above it he appears again in the full power of life, seated on the pontifical throne, with the right hand raised in the act of blessing the multitude, and the left holding the lance with which Longinus had pierced the side of the Saviour on the cross. This holy relic was a gift from the infidels, who had just taken possession of the capital of the Greek empire, and had raised the crescent on the pinnacles of S. Sophia. It seems that while Bayazid II. was besieging Broussa, his rebellious brother Zem or Zizim, who had already been defeated in the battle of June 20, 1481, succeeded in making his escape to Egypt, and ultimately to the island of Rhodes. The grand master of the Knights of S. John, d'Aubusson, received him cordially and sent him first to France, and later to Rome. Here he was received with royal honors; he rode through the streets on a charger, escorted by Francesco Cibo, a relative of the Pope, and count d'Aubusson, brother of the grand master. He is described as a man fond of sight-seeing, about forty years old, of a fierce and cruel countenance, tall, erect, well proportioned, with shaggy eyebrows, and aquiline nose. His brother Bayazid, fearing that he might be induced to try another rebellion with the help of the knights, the Pope, and the Venetians, treated him generously with a yearly allowance of forty thousand scudi; and secured the good grace of Innocent VIII. with the present of the holy lance.[116]

To this extraordinary gift of Bayazid we owe one of the masterpieces of the Renaissance, the *ciborio della santa lancia*, begun by Innocent VIII. and finished by the executors of his will, Lorenzo Cibo and Antoniotto Pallavicino, in 1495. Unfortunately we have now only a drawing of it by the unskilful hand of Giacomo Grimaldi;[117] it was taken to pieces in 1606, and a few of its panels, medallions, and statues, which were of the school of Mino da Fiesole, were removed to the Sacred Grottos, where no one is allowed to see them. Grimaldi, who wrote the procès-verbal of the demolition of the ciborium, says that the desecration and the removal of the relics took place on Septuagesima Sunday, January 22, about seven in the evening; at nine o'clock lightning struck the unfinished roof of the basilica; heavy pieces of masonry fell with a crash; mosaics were wrenched from their sockets, and fissures and rents produced in various parts of the building. In the same night the Tiber overflowed its banks, and the turbulent waters rushed as far as the palace of Cardinal Rusticucci in the direction of the Vatican.

The inscription on the tomb of Innocent VIII. mentions, among the glories of his pontificate, the discovery of a new world. Thirty years before his election Constantinople had been taken by the infidels; but the conquests made in the West brought a compensation for the losses sustained on the shores of the Bosphorus. Innocent lived to hear of the capture of Granada and of the conquest of Ferdinand of Aragon, in the Moorish provinces of southern Spain; and just at that time the Hispano-Portuguese branch of the great Latin family seems to have burst forth with renewed vitality and religious enthusiasm, destined to give Rome new victories and new worlds. Bartolomeo Diaz had already doubled the Cape of Good Hope; the sea route to India was opened. The Pope could once again consider himself the master of the world, and was able to present John II. of Portugal with "the lands of Africa, whether known or unknown." Death overtook the gentle and peaceful pontiff on July 26, 1492. Eight days after his demise another Genoese,[118] another worthy representative of the strong Ligurian race, set sail from the harbor of Palos to discover another continent, and begin a third era in the history of mankind.

THE TOMB OF PAUL III. Historians and artists alike agree in placing the monument of Paul III.

at the head of this class of artistic creations. In a niche on the left of the high altar of S. Peter's the figure of the noble old pontiff is seated on a bronze throne. With his head bent upon his breast, he seems absorbed in thought. Great events, to be sure, had taken place during his administration, which were more or less connected with the affairs of his own family: such as the foundation of the duchy of Parma in favor of his son, Pierluigi, the marriage of his grandson Ottavio to Marguerite, daughter of Charles V., and the creation of the order of the Jesuits; and as some of these events had resulted differently from what he had expected, no wonder his countenance betrays a feeling of disappointment. Two female figures of marble are seen reclining against the sarcophagus: one old, representing Prudence, the other young, representing Justice; the one holds a mirror, the other a bundle of rods. It seems that Guglielmo della Porta modelled them according to a sketch proposed by Michelangelo; in fact, they bear a strong resemblance to the figures of Night and Day on the tomb of Lorenzo de' Medici, at Florence. The Prudence is said to be a portrait of Giovannella Caetani da Sermoneta, the mother of the Pope, while Justice represents his sister-in-law, Giulia Farnese, according to Martinelli, or his daughter Constance, the wife of Bosio Sforza, according to Rotti. The elder woman's profile is exactly that of Dante,—so much so that Maes speaks of her as the "Dantessa di S. Pietro." Her younger companion is, or rather was, of marvellous beauty, before Bernini draped her form with a leaden tunic. During my lifetime, this has been removed once, for the benefit of a Frenchman who was collecting materials for the life of della Porta; but I have not been able to obtain a copy of the photograph taken at the time. Formerly the statue was miscalled Truth, which gave rise to the saying that, although Truth as a rule is not pleasing, this pleased too much. The strange infatuation of a Spanish gentleman for her is described by Sprenger, Caylus, and Cancellieri.[119]

The original design of the monument required four statues, because it was intended to stand alone in the middle of the church, and not half concealed in a niche. The other two statues were actually modelled, one as Abundance, the other Tenderness; they are now preserved in one of the halls of the Farnese palace.

Paul III., Alessandro Farnese, was the first Roman elevated to the supreme pontificate after Martin V., Colonna (1417-1424). Pomponio Leto, his preceptor, had imbued him with the spirit of the humanists. His conversation was gay and spirituelle; he seemed to bring back with him the fine old times of Leo III. He died beloved and worshipped by his subjects. We may well share a little of these sentiments, if we remember how much art is indebted to him.

247

The Palazzo Madama, now used as the Senate-house, and the Villa Madama, on the eastern slope of Monte Mario, still belonging to the descendants of the Farnese family, were given by him to Marguerite of Spain, after her marriage with his grandson Ottavio. The Farnesina, which he bought at auction in 1586, associates his memory with that of the Chigis, of Raphael, Michelangelo, and Baldassarre Peruzzi. Then comes his share in the construction of S. Peter's; in the painting of the "Last Judgment," and in the finishing of the "Sala Regia," the richest hall in the Vatican. But no other work, in my estimation, gives us as true an idea of his taste and delicate sentiment as the apartments which he caused to be built and decorated, on the summit of Hadrian's Mole. I am writing these lines in the loggia or vestibule which opens from the great hall. Paul himself placed on the lintel a record of his work, of which Raffaello da Montelupo and Antonio da Sangallo were the architects; Marco da Siena, Pierin del Vaga, and Giulio Romano, the decorators. The ceilings of the bedroom and dining-hall, carved in wood, and those of the reception-room, in gilt and painted stucco, are things of beauty which no visitor to Rome should fail to see. The bath-room, a work of his predecessor, Clement VII., is copied from the antique. In 1538, while the building of this artistic gem was in progress, Benvenuto Cellini was thrown into one of the dungeons below, as a prisoner of state. He was accused of having stolen jewels belonging to the apostolic treasury; but the true reason seems to have been an offence against the Pope, which he had committed in 1527, while the hosts of the constable de Bourbon were besieging the castle. The offence is described by Benvenuto himself in the following words:— 248

"While I was performing this duty [of keeping guard on the ramparts] some of the cardinals who were in the castle used to come up to see me, and most of all cardinal Ravenna and cardinal de' Gaddi, to whom I often said that I wished they would not come any more, because their red caps could be seen a long way off, and made it mighty dangerous for both them and me from those palaces which were near by, like the Torre de' Bini; so that, finally, I shut them out altogether, and gained thereby their ill-will quite decidedly. Signor Orazio Baglioni, who was my very good friend, also used to come and chat with me. While he was talking with me one day, he noticed a kind of a demonstration in a certain tavern, which was outside the Porta di Castello, at a place called Baccanello. This tavern had for a sign a red sun, painted between two windows. The windows being closed, Signor Orazio guessed that just behind the sun between them, there was a company of soldiers having a good time. So he said to me, 'Benvenuto, if you had a mind to fire your cannon near that sun, I believe you would do a good piece of work, because there is a good deal of noise there, and they must be men of importance.' I replied to the gentleman, 'It is enough for me to see that sun to be able to fire into the middle of it; but if I do, the noise of the gun and the shock it will make will knock over that barrel of stones which is standing near its mouth.' To which the gentleman answered, 'Don't wait to talk about it, Benvenuto, for, in the first place, in the way in which the barrel is standing, the shock of the cannon could not knock it over; but even if it did, and the Pope himself were under it, it would not be as bad as you think; so shoot, shoot!' So I, thinking no more about it, fired right into the middle of the sun, exactly as I had promised I would. The barrel fell, just as I said, and struck the ground between cardinal Farnese and messer Jacopo Salviati. It would have crushed both of them had it not happened that they were quarrelling, because the cardinal had just accused messer Jacopo of being the cause of the sacking of Rome, and had separated to give more room to the insults they were flinging at each other.'[120] The cardinal never forgot his narrow escape. 249

From the point of view of archæological interests Paul III. will always be remembered as long as the Museo Nazionale of Naples and the Baths of Caracalla of Rome continue to hold the admiration of students. In reading the account of his excavation of the Baths, we seem to be transported to dreamland. No one before him had laid hands on the immeasurable treasures which the building contained. Statues were found in their niches or lying in front of them; the columns were standing on their pedestals; the walls were still incrusted with rare marbles and richly carved panels; the swimming-basins were still ready for use. Pietro Sante Bartoli says: "The excavation of the Baths of Caracalla, which took place in the time of Paul III. (1546) is the most successful ever accomplished. It yielded such a mass of statues, columns, bas-reliefs, marbles, cameos, intaglios, bronze figures, medals, and lamps, that no more room could be found for them in the Farnese palace." The collection comprises the Farnese Bull, the two statues of Herakles, the Flora, the Athletes, the Venus Callipyge, the Diana, the "Atreus and Thyestes," the so-called "Tuccia," and a hundred more masterpieces, which were, unfortunately, removed to Naples towards the end of the last century.

THE TOMB OF CLEMENT XIII. From the golden age of Guglielmo della Porta to the barocco art of the eighteenth century, from the tomb of Alessandro Farnese to that of Prospero Lambertini (Benedict XIV., 1740-1758), we can follow, stage by stage, the pernicious influence exercised on Roman art by the school of Bernini. The richness and magnificence of papal mausolea increased in proportion to the decline in taste. The sculptors seem to have had but one ambition, to produce a theatrical effect; their abuse of polychromy is incredible; the grouping of their figures conventional; the contortions to which they submit their Hopes and Charities, their Liberalities and Benevolences, their Justices and Prudences are simply absurd.

Pietro Bracci, the artist of the monument of Benedict XIV., by pushing mannerism to the extreme point, caused a wholesome reaction in art. The tomb of Clement XIII., Carlo Rezzonico of Venice (1758-1769), was intrusted to Canova. There is the difference of a few years only between the two, but it seems as if there were centuries. This monument, which marks a prodigious reaction towards the pure ideals of classical art, was uncovered on April 4, 1795, before an immense assembly of people. The whole of Rome was there, and the defeat of the partisans of Bernini's style could not have been more complete.

Disguised in ecclesiastical robes, Canova mixed with the crowd, and was able to hear for himself that the reign of a false taste in art was once more over, so unanimous was the admiration and approval of the multitudes for his bold attempt. The tomb of Clement XIII. rests on a high basement of grayish marble, in the middle of which opens a door of the Doric style, giving access to the vault. The two world-renowned marble lions crouch upon the steps, watching the sarcophagus; Religion stands on the left, holding a cross in the right hand; while the Genius of Death, with an inverted torch, is seen reclining on the opposite side. It is a graceful, but slightly conventional figure. One can easily perceive the influence of the study of the antique in the head of this Genius, which Canova considered one of his best productions. It is the Apollo Belvedere of modern times, the "Catholic Apollo," as Forsyth calls the archangel of Guido in the church of the Capuchins. The Pope is represented kneeling and praying, with hands clasped, and a face full of sentiment and thought. When, seated before this monument, we turn our eyes towards the tombs of Clement X. and Benedict XIV., and other similar productions of the eighteenth century, we can hardly realize that Canova was a contemporary of Pietro Bracci and Carlo Monaldi.

The tomb is also historically interesting. It was under Clement XIII. that the order of the Jesuits was tried before the tribunal of Europe. The kingdom of Portugal, where they had made their first advance towards greatness and fame, was the first to attack them. The marquess of Pombal, prime minister of Joseph I., taking advantage of the uneasiness caused by the earthquake of 1755 and by a murderous attempt against the king, expelled the order from the country and the colonies (January 9-September 3, 1759). One hundred and twenty-four were put in irons; one, named Malagrida, executed; thirty-seven allowed to die in prison; and the rest were embarked on seven ships and transported to foreign lands. Charles III. of Spain, and his minister, count d'Aranda, followed the example of Portugal. The Jesuits were banished from Spain, February 28, 1767; and in the night between April 2 and 3, they were put, five thousand in number, on transport vessels, and sent to Rome. King Louis XV. and the duc de Choiseul used the same process in France. The attempt of Damiens, January 5, 1757, and an alleged scandal in the administration of the property of the order at la Martinique were taken up as pretexts for punishment, and the order was banished in 1764. King Ferdinand IV. of Naples, the grand master of Malta, the duke of Parma, and other potentates took their share also in the crusade. Whatever may be the sentiment which we personally feel towards this brotherhood, the figures of Lorenzo Ricci, the general who so bravely contested every inch of the battlefield, and of Clement XIII., who died before signing the decree of suppression so loudly demanded by Portugal, Spain, France, Parma, Naples and Malta, will always be remembered with respect. The pressure brought on the old Pope by half the kingdoms of Europe, which were governed directly or indirectly by the Bourbons, was not merely that of diplomacy. He was deprived of Avignon and the comté Venoisin in France, of Benevento in southern Italy; but to no purpose. The decree suppressing the order was only signed by his successor Clement XIV., Ganganelli, on July 21, 1773. Lorenzo Ricci died the following year, a state prisoner in the castle of S. Angelo.

CHAPTER VI.

PAGAN CEMETERIES.

Various modes of burial in Rome.—Inhumation and cremation.—Gradual predominance of the latter.—Columbaria.—Inscription describing the organization of one of these, on the Via Latina.—The extent of the pagan cemeteries outside of Rome, and the number of graves they contained.—Curiosities of the epitaphs.—The excavations in the garden of La Farnesina.—The Roman house discovered there.—The tomb of Sulpicius Platorinus.—Its

interesting contents.—The "divine crows."—The cemetery in the Villa Pamfili.
—Tombs on the Via Triumphalis.—That of Helius, the shoemaker.—The
tombs of the Via Salaria.—That of the Licinii Calpurnii.—The unhappy history
of this family.—The tomb of the precocious boy.—Improvvisatori of later
times.—The tomb of Lucilia Polla and her brother.—Its history.—The Valle
della Caffarella.—Its associations with Herodes Atticus.—His fortune and its
origin.—His monuments to his wife.—The remarkable discovery of the corpse
of a young woman, in 1485.—Various contemporary accounts of it.—Its
ultimate fate.—Discovery of a similar nature in 1889.

Inhumation seems to have been more common than cremation in prehistoric Rome; hence,
certain families, to give material evidence of their ancient lineage, would never submit to
cremation. Such were the Cornelii Scipiones, whose sarcophagi were discovered during the
last century in the Vigna Sassi. Sulla is the first Cornelius whose body was burned; but this he
ordered done to avoid retaliation, that is to say, for fear of its being treated as he had treated
the corpse of Marius. Both systems are mentioned in the law of the twelve tables: *hominem
mortuum in urbe ne sepelito neve urito*, a statement which shows that each had an equal
number of partisans, at the time of the promulgation of the law.

This theory is confirmed by discoveries in the prehistoric cemeteries of the Viminal and
Esquiline hills, which contain coffins as well as cineraria, or ash-urns. The discoveries have
been published only in a fragmentary way, so that we cannot yet follow their development
stage by stage, and determine at what periods and within what limits the influence of more
civilized neighbors was felt by the primitive dwellers upon the Seven Hills. One thing is
certain; the race that first colonized the Campagna was buried in trunks of trees, hollowed
inside and cut to measure, as is the custom among some Indian tribes of the present day. In
March, 1889, the engineers who were attending to the drainage of the Lago di Castiglione—
the ancient Regillus—discovered a trunk of *quercus robur*, sawn lengthways into two halves,
with a human skeleton inside, and fragments of objects in amber and ivory lying by it. The
coffin, roughly cut and shaped, was buried at a depth of fourteen feet, in a trench a trifle
longer and larger than itself, and the space between the coffin and the sides of the trench was
filled with archaic pottery, of the type found in our own Roman necropolis of the Via dello
Statuto. There were also specimens of imported pottery, and a bronze cup. The tomb and its
contents are now exhibited in the Villa di Papa Giulio, outside the Porta del Popolo.

When Rome was founded, this semi-barbaric fashion of burial was by no means forgotten or
abandoned by its inhabitants. We have not yet discovered coffins actually dug out of a tree,
but we have found rude imitations of them in clay. These belong to the interval of time
between the foundation of the city and the fortifications of Servius Tullius, having been found
at the considerable depth of forty-two feet below the embankment of the Servian wall, in the
Vigna Spithoever. They are now exhibited in the Capitoline Museum (Palazzo dei
Conservatori), together with the skeletons, pottery, and bronze *suppellex* they contained.

Nearly every type of tomb known in Etruria, Magna Græcia, and the prehistoric Italic stations has a representative in the old cemeteries of the Viminal and the Esquiline. There are caves hewn out of the natural rock, with the entrance sealed by a block of the same material; in these are skeletons lying on the funeral beds on either side of the cave, or even on the floor between them, with the feet turned towards the door, and Italo-Greek pottery, together with objects in bronze, amber, and gold. There are also artificial caves, formed by horizontal courses of stones which project one beyond another, from both sides, till they meet at the top. Then there are bodies protected by a circle of uncut stones; others lying at the bottom of wells, and finally regular sarcophagi in the shape of square huts, and cineraria like those described on page 29 of my "Ancient Rome."

Comparing these data we reach the conclusion that inhumation was abandoned, with a few exceptions, towards the end of the fifth century of Rome, to be resumed only towards the middle of the second century after Christ, under the influence of Eastern doctrines and customs. For the student of Roman archæology these facts have not merely a speculative interest; a knowledge of them is necessary for the chronological classification of the material found in cemeteries and represented so abundantly in public and private collections.

The acceptance of cremation as a national, exclusive system brought as a consequence the institution of the *ustrina*, the sacred enclosures in which pyres were built to convert the corpses into ashes. Several specimens of *ustrina* have been found near the city, and one of them is still to be seen in good preservation. It is built in the shape of a military camp, on the right of the Appian Way, five and a half miles from the gate. When Fabretti first saw it in 1699, it was intact, save a breach or gap on the north side. He describes it as a rectangle three hundred and forty feet long, and two hundred feet wide, enclosed by a wall thirteen feet high. Its masonry is irregular both in the shape and size of the blocks of stone, and may well be assigned to the fifth century of Rome, when the necessity for popular *ustrina* was first felt. When Nibby and Gell visited the spot in 1822 they found that the noble owner of the farm had just destroyed the western side and a portion of the eastern, to build with their materials a *maceria*, or dry wall.

The *ustrina* which were connected with the Mausoleum of Augustus and the ara of the Antonines have already been described in chapter iv. Another institution, that of *columbaria*, or *ossaria*, as they would more properly be called, owes its origin to the same cause. Columbaria are a specialty of Rome and the Campagna, and are found nowhere else, not even in the colonies or settlements originating directly from the city. They begin to appear some twenty years before Christ, under the rule of Augustus and the premiership of Mæcenas. Inasmuch as the Campus Esquilinus, which, up to their time, had been used for the burial of artisans, laborers, servants, slaves, and freedmen, was suppressed in consequence of the sanitary reforms described by Horace,[121] and was buried under an embankment of pure earth, and converted into a public park; as, moreover, the disappearance of the said cemetery was followed closely by the appearance of columbaria, I believe one fact to be a consequence of the other, and both to be part of the same hygienic reform. No cleaner, healthier, or more respectable substitute for the old *puticoli* could have been contrived by those enlightened statesmen. Any one, no matter how low in social position, could secure a decent place of rest for a paltry sum of money. The following inscription, still to be seen in the columbarium discovered in 1838, in the Villa Pamfili,—

has been interpreted by Hülsen to mean that Paciæcus Isargyros had sold to Pinaria Murtinis a place for one *as*. Tombstones often mention transactions of this kind, and state the cost of purchase for one or more loculi, or for the whole tomb. Friedländer, in a Königsberg Programm for October, 1881,[122] has collected thirty-eight documents concerning the cost of tombs; they vary from a minimum of two hundred sestertii ($8.25) to a maximum of one hundred and ninety-two thousand ($8,000).

There were three kinds of columbaria: first, those built by one man or one family either for their own private use, or for their servants and freedmen; second, those built by one or more individuals for speculation, in which any one could secure a place by purchase; third, those built by a company for the personal use of shareholders and contributors.

As a good specimen of the columbaria of the second kind we can cite one built on the Via Latina, by a company of thirty-six shareholders. It was discovered in 1599, not far from the gate, and its records were scattered all over the city. As a proof of the negligence with which excavations were conducted in former times, we may state that, the same place having been searched again in 1854 by a man named Luigi Arduini, other inscriptions of great value were discovered, from which we learn how these burial companies were organized and operated. The first document, a marble inscription above the door of the crypt, states that in the year 6 B. C. thirty-six citizens formed a company for the building of a columbarium, each subscribing for an equal number of shares, and that they selected two of the stockholders to act as administrators. Their names are Marcus Æmilius, and Marcus Fabius Felix, and their official title is *curatores ædificii xxxvi. sociorum*. They collected the contributions, bought the land, built the columbarium, approved and paid the contractors' bills, and having thus fulfilled their duty convened a general meeting for September 30. Their report was approved, and a deed was drawn up and duly signed by all present, declaring that the administrators had discharged their duty according to the statute. They then proceeded to the distribution of the loculi in equal lots, the loculi representing, as it were, the dividend of the company. The tomb contained one hundred and eighty loculi for cinerary urns, and each of the shareholders was consequently entitled to five. The distribution, however, was not so easy a matter as the number would make it appear. We know that it was made by drawing lots, *per sortitionem ollarum*, and we know also that in some cases the shareholders, as a remuneration to their chairmen, administrators, and auditors of accounts, voted them exemption from the rule, by giving them the right of selecting their loculi without drawing (*sine sorte*). Evidently some places were more desirable than others, and if we remember how columbaria are built, it is not difficult to see which loculi must have been most in demand.

The pious devotion of the Romans towards the dead caused them to pay frequent visits to their tombs, especially on anniversaries, when the urns were decorated with flowers, libations were offered, and other ceremonies performed. These *inferiæ*, or rites, could be celebrated easily if the loculus and the cinerary urn were near the ground, while ladders were required to reach the upper tiers. The same difficulty was experienced when cinerary urns had to be placed in their niches; and the funeral tablets and memorials containing the name, age, condition, etc., of the deceased, which were either written in ink or charcoal, or else engraved on marble, could not be read if too high above the pavement. For these reasons, and to avoid any suspicion of partiality in the distribution of lots, the shareholders trusted to chance. The crypt discovered in the Via Latina contained five rows of niches of thirty-six each. The rows were called *sortes*, the niches *loci*. Now, as each shareholder was entitled to five *loci*, one on each row, lots were drawn only in regard to the *locus*, not to the row. The inscriptions discovered in 1599 and 1854 are therefore all worded with the formula:—"Of Caius Rabirius Faustus, second tier, twenty-eighth locus;" "Of Caius Julius Æschinus, fourth tier, thirty-fourth locus;" "Of Lucius Scribonius Sosus, first tier, twenty-third locus;"—in all, nine names out of thirty-six. The allotment of Rabirius Faustus is the only one known entirely. He had drawn No. 30 in the first row, No. 28 in the second, No. 6 in the third, No. 8 in the fourth, No. 31 in the fifth.

It took at least thirty-one years for the members of the company to gain the full benefit of their investment; the last interment mentioned in the tablets having taken place A. D. 25. This late comer is not an obscure man; he is the famous charioteer, or *auriga circensis*, Scirtus, who began his career A. D. 13, enlisting in the white squadron. In the lapse of thirteen years he won the first prize seven times, the second thirty-nine times, the third forty times, besides other honors minutely specified on his tombstone.[123]

The theory that Roman tombs were built along the high roads in two or three rows only, so that they could all be seen by those passing, has been shown by modern excavations to be unfounded. The space allotted for burial purposes was more extensive than that. Sometimes it extended over the whole stretch of land from one high-road to the next. Such is the case with the spaces between the Via Appia and the Via Latina, the Labicana and Prænestina, and the Salaria and Nomentana, each of which contains hundreds of acres densely packed with tombs. In the triangle formed by the Via Appia, the Via Latina, and the walls of Aurelian, one thousand five hundred and fifty-nine tombs have been discovered in modern times, not including the family vault of the Scipios.[124] Nine hundred and ninety-four have been found on the Via Labicana, near the Porta Maggiore, in a space sixty yards long by fifty wide. The number of pagan tombstones registered in volume vi. of the "Corpus" is 28,180, exclusive of the *additamenta*, which will bring the grand total to thirty thousand. As hardly one tombstone out of ten has escaped destruction, we may assume as a certainty that Rome was surrounded by a belt of at least three hundred thousand tombs.

The reader may easily imagine what a mass of information is to be gathered from this source. In this respect, the perusal of parts II., III., and IV. of the sixth volume of the "Corpus" is more useful to the student than all the handbooks and "Sittengeschichten" in the world; and besides, the reading is not dry and tiresome, as one might suppose. Many epitaphs give an account of the life of the deceased; of his rank in the army, and the campaigns in which he fought; of the name of the man-of-war to which he belonged, if he had served in the navy; of the branch of trade he was engaged in; the address of his place of business; his success in the equestrian or senatorial career, or in the circus or the theatre; his "état civil," his age, place of birth, and so on. Sometimes tombstones display a remarkable eloquence, and even a sense of humor.

Here is an expression of overpowering grief, written on a sarcophagus between the images of a boy and a girl: "O cruel, impious mother that I am: to the memory of my sweetest children. Publilius who lived 13 years 55 days, and Æria Theodora who lived 27 years 12 days. Oh, miserable mother, who hast seen the most cruel end of thy children! If God had been merciful, thou hadst been buried by them." Another woman writes on the urn of her son Marius Exoriens: "The preposterous laws of death have torn him from my arms! As I have the advantage of years, so ought death to have reaped me first."

The following words were dictated by a young widow for the grave of her departed companion: "To the adorable, blessed soul of L. Sempronius Firmus. We knew, we loved each other from childhood: married, an impious hand separated us at once. Oh, infernal Gods, do be kind and merciful to him, and let him appear to me in the silent hours of the night. And also let me share his fate, that we may be reunited *dulcius et celerius*." I have left the two adverbs in their original form; their exquisite feeling defies translation.

The following sentence is copied from the grave of a freedman: "Erected to the memory of Memmius Clarus by his co-servant Memmius Urbanus. I know that there never was the shade of a disagreement between thee and me: never a cloud passed over our common happiness. I swear to the gods of Heaven and Hell, that we worked faithfully and lovingly together, that we were set free from servitude on the same day and in the same house: nothing would ever have separated us, except this fatal hour."

A remarkable feature of ancient funeral eloquence is found in the imprecations addressed to the passer, to insure the safety of the tomb and its contents:[125]—

"Any one who injures my tomb or steals its ornaments, may he see the death of all his relatives."

"Whoever steals the nails from this structure, may he thrust them into his eyes."

A grumbler wrote on a gravestone found in the Vigna Codini:—

"Lawyers and the evil-eyed keep away from my tomb."

It is manifestly impossible to make the reader acquainted with all the discoveries in this department of Roman archæology since 1870. The following specimens from the viæ Aurelia, Triumphalis, Salaria, and Appia seem to me to represent fairly well what is of average interest in this class of monuments.

Via Aurelia. Under this head I record the tomb of Platorinus, which was found in 1880 on the banks of the Tiber, near La Farnesina, although, strictly speaking, it belongs to a side road running from the Via Aurelia to the Vatican quarters, parallel with the stream. The discovery was made in the following circumstances:—

A strip of land four hundred metres long by eighty broad was bought by the state in 1876 and cut away from the gardens of la Farnesina, to widen the bed of the Tiber. It was found to contain several ancient edifices, which have since become famous in topographical books. I refer more particularly to the patrician house discovered near the church of S. Giacomo in Settimiana, the paintings of which are now exhibited in Michelangelo's cloisters, adjoining the Baths of Diocletian.

These paintings have been admirably reproduced in color and outline by the German Archæological Institute,[126] but they have not yet been illustrated from the point of view of the subjects they represent. They are divided into panels by pilasters and colored columns, each half being distinguished by a different color: white (Nos. 1, 5, 6, of the plan), red (Nos. 2, 4), or black (No. 3). The frieze of the "black" series represents the trying of a criminal case by a magistrate, very likely the owner of the palace, with curious details concerning the evidence asked and freely given to him.

Near the frieze, the artist has drawn pictures as though hung to the wall, with folding shutters, some wide open, some

Ancient house in the Farnesina Gardens.

half-closed. They are genre subjects, such as a school of declamation, a wedding, a banquet; and though the figures are not five inches long, they are so wonderfully executed that even the eyebrows are discernible.

The pictures in the centre of the panels are of larger size. Those of the "white" room are painted in the style of the Attic lekythoi, or oil-jugs. The figures are drawn in outline with a dark, subtle color, each space within the outline being filled in with the proper tint; though a few only are drawn without the colors. One of these remarkable pictures represents two women,—one sitting, the other standing, and both looking at a winged Cupid. Another represents a lady playing on the seven-stringed lyre, each of the strings being marked by a sign which, perhaps, corresponds to the notes of the scale. In one of the panels from room No. 4 is still visible what we suppose to be the signature of the artist: CEΛEYKOC EΠOEI (*sic*). It seems as if Baldassarre Peruzzi, Raphael, Giulio Romano, il Sodoma, il Fattore, and Gaudenzio Ferrari, to whom we owe the wonders of the Farnesina dei Chigi, must have unconsciously felt the influence of the wonders of this Roman house which was buried under their feet. It is a great pity that the two could not have been left standing together. What a subject for study and comparison these two sets of masterpieces of the golden ages of Augustus and Leo X. would have offered to the lover of art!

DETAIL FROM THE CEILING OF THE HOUSE DISCOVERED IN THE FARNESINA GARDENS

The ceiling of the room No. 2, carved in stucco, is worthy of the paintings. The reliefs are so flat that the prominent points do not stand out more than three millimetres. The artist might have modelled them by breathing over the stucco, they are so light and delicate. One of the scenes represents the borders of a river, with villas, temples, shrines, and pastoral huts scattered under the shade of palm or sycamore trees, the foliage of which is waving gently in the breeze. The people are variously occupied,—some are fishing with the rod, some bathing, some carrying water-jars on their heads. The gem of the reliefs is a group of oxen, grazing in the meadow, of such exquisite beauty as to cast into shade the best engravings of Italo-Greek or Sicilian coins.

Next in importance to the Roman house comes the tomb of Sulpicius Platorinus, discovered in May, 1880, at the opposite end of the Farnesina Gardens, near the walls of Aurelian. A corner of this tomb had been exposed to view for a couple of years, nobody paying attention to it, because, as a rule, tombs within the walls, having been exposed for centuries to the thieving instincts of the populace in general, and of treasure-hunters in particular, are always found plundered and barren of contents. In this instance, however, it was our fortune to meet with a welcome exception to the rule.

From an inscription engraved on marble above the entrance door, we learn that the mausoleum was raised in memory of Caius Sulpicius Platorinus, a magistrate of the time of Augustus, and of his sister Sulpicia Platorina, the wife of Cornelius Priscus. The room contained nine niches, and each niche a cinerary urn, of which six were still untouched. These urns are of the most elaborate kind, carved in white marble, with festoons hanging from bulls' heads, and birds of various kinds eating fruit. Some of the urns are round, some square, the motive of the decoration being the same for all of them. The cover of the round ones is in the shape of a *tholus*, a building shaped something like a beehive, the tiles being represented by acanthus leaves, and the pinnacle by a bunch of flowers.

The covers of these urns were fastened with molten lead. The unsealing of them was an event of great excitement; it was performed in the coffee-house of the Farnesina, in the presence of a large and distinguished assembly. I remember the date, May 3, 1880. They were found to be half full of water from the last flood of the Tiber, with a layer of ashes and bones at the bottom. The contents were emptied on a sheet of white linen. Those of the first had no value; the second contained a gold ring without its stone,—which was found, however, in the third cinerarium; a most extraordinary circumstance. It can be explained by supposing that both bodies were cremated at the same time, and that their ashes were somehow mixed together. The stone, probably an onyx, was injured by the action of the fire, and its engraving nearly effaced. It seems to represent a lion in repose. Nothing was found in the fourth; the fifth furnished two heavy gold rings with cameos representing respectively a mask and a bear-hunt. The last urn, inscribed with the name of Minasia Polla,—a girl of about sixteen, as shown by the teeth and the size of some fragments of bone,—contained a plain hair-pin of brass.

Having thus finished with the cineraria and their contents, the exploration of the tomb itself was resumed. Inscriptions engraved on other parts of the frieze gave us a full list of the personages who had found their last resting-place within, besides the two Platorini, and the girl Minasia Polla, just mentioned. They are: Aulus Crispinius Cæpio, who played an important part in court intrigues at the time of Tiberius; Antonia Furnilla; and her daughter, Marcia Furnilla, the second wife of Titus. She was repudiated by him A. D. 64, as described by Suetonius.[127] Historians have inquired why, and found no clew, considering what a model man Titus is known to have been. If the marble statue found in this tomb, and reproduced in our illustration, is really that of Marcia Furnilla, and a good likeness, the reason for the divorce is easily found,—she looks hopelessly disagreeable.

The bust represented in the same plate, one of the most refined and carefully executed portraits found in Rome, is probably that of Minasia Polla, and gives a good idea of the appearance of a young noble Roman lady of the first half of the first century. Another statue, that of the emperor Tiberius, in the so-called "heroic" style, was found lying on the mosaic floor. Although crushed by the falling of the vaulted ceiling, no important piece was missing.

Both statues, the bust, the cinerary urns, and the inscriptions, are now exhibited in Michelangelo's cloisters in the Museo delle Terme.

It is difficult to explain how this rich tomb escaped plunder and destruction, plainly visible as it was for many centuries, in one of the most populous and unscrupulous quarters of the city. Perhaps when Aurelian built his wall, which ran close to it, and raised the level of Trastevere, the tomb itself was buried, and its treasures left untouched.

Beginning now the ascent of the Janiculum, on our way towards the Porta S. Pancrazio and the Villa Pamfili, I must mention a curious discovery made three centuries ago near the church of S. Pietro in Montorio; that of a platform, lined with terminal stones inscribed with the legend: DEVAS CORNISCAS SACRVM ("this area is sacred to the divine crows"). The place is described by Festus (Ep. 64). It is a remarkable fact that in Rome not only men but animals should remain faithful to old habits and traditions. Some of my readers may have noticed how regularly every day, towards sunset, flights of crows are seen crossing the skies on their way to their night lodgings in the pine-trees of the Villa Borghese. They have two or three favorite halting-places, for instance the campanile of S. Andrea delle Fratte, the towers of the Trinità de' Monti, where they hold noisy meetings which last until the first stroke of the Ave-Maria. This sound is interpreted by them as a call to rest. Whether the area of the sacred crows described by Festus was planted with pines, and used as a rest at night, or simply as a halting-place, the fact of their daily migration to and from the swamps of the Maremma, and of their evening meetings, dates from classical times.

And now, leaving on our right the Villa Heyland, the Villa Aurelia, formerly Savorelli, which is built on the remains of the mediæval monastery of SS. John and Paul, and the Villa del Vascello, which marks the western end of the gardens of Geta, let us enter the Villa Pamfili-Doria, interesting equally for the beauty of its scenery and its archæological recollections. We are told by Pietro Sante Bartoli that when he first came to Rome, towards 1660, Olimpia Maidalchini and Camillo Pamfili, who were then laying the foundations of the casino, discovered "several tombs decorated with paintings, stucco-carvings, and *nobilissimi* mosaics." There were also glass urns, with remains of golden cloths, and the figures of a lion

269

and a tigress, which were bought by the Viceroy of Naples, the marchese di Leve. Some years later, when Monsignor Lorenzo Corsini began the construction of the Casino dei Quattro Venti (since added to the Villa Pamfili and transformed into a sort of monumental archway), thirty-four exquisite tombs were found and destroyed for the sake of their building-materials. One cannot read Bartoli's account[128] and examine the twenty-two plates with which he illustrates his text, without feeling a sense of horror at the deeds which those enlightened personages were capable of perpetrating in cold blood.

He says that the thirty-four tombs formed, as it were, a small village, with streets, sidewalks, and squares; that they were built of red and yellow brick, exquisitely carved, like those of the Via Latina. Each retained its funeral *suppellex* and decorations almost intact: paintings, bas-reliefs, mosaics, inscriptions, lamps, jewelry, statues, busts, cinerary urns, and sarcophagi. Some were still closed, the doors being made not of wood or bronze, but of marble; and inscriptions were carved on the lintels or pediments, giving an account of each tomb. These records tell us that in Roman times this portion of the Villa Pamfili was called *Ager Fonteianus*, and that the inclined tract of the Via Aurelia, which runs close by, was called *Clivus Rutarius*. Bartoli attributes the extraordinary preservation of this cemetery to its having been buried purposely under an embankment of earth, before the fall of the empire. Since the seventeenth century many hundreds of tombs have been found and destroyed in the villa, especially in April, 1859. The only one still visible was discovered in 1838, and is remarkable for its *painted* inscriptions, and for its frescoes.[129] There were originally one hundred and seventy-five panels, but scarcely half that number are now to be seen. They represent animals, landscapes, caricatures, scenes from daily life, and mythological and dramatic subjects. One only is historical, and, according to Petersen, represents the Judgment of Solomon (see p. 271). This subject, although exceedingly rare, is by no means unique in classical art, having already been found painted on the walls of a Pompeian house.

VIA TRIUMPHALIS. The necropolis which lined the Via Triumphalis, from Nero's bridge near S. Spirito, to the top of the Monte Mario, has absolutely disappeared, although some of its monuments equalled in size and magnificence those of the viæ Ostiensis, Appia, and Labicana. Such were the two pyramids, on the site of S. Maria Trasportina, called, in the Middle Ages, the "Meta di Borgo" and the "Terebinth of Nero." Both are shown in the bas-reliefs of Filarete's bronze door in S. Peter's (see p. 272), in the ciborium of Sixtus IV. (now in the Grotte Vaticane), and in other mediæval and Renaissance representations of the crucifixion of the apostle. The pyramid is described by Ruccellai and Pietro Mallio as standing in the middle of a square which is paved with slabs of travertine, and towering to the height of forty metres above the road. It was coated with marble, like the one of Caius Cestius by the Porta S. Paolo. Pope Donnus I. dismantled it A. D. 675, and made use of its materials to build the steps of S. Peter's. The pyramid itself, built of solid concrete, was levelled to the ground by Pope Alexander VI., when he opened the Borgo Nuovo in 1495.

The "Terebinth of Nero" is described as a round marble structure, as high as Hadrian's tomb. It was also dismantled by Pope Donnus, and its materials were used in the restoration and embellishment of the "Paradisus" or quadriportico of S. Peter's.

Panel from the bronze door of S. Peter's, by Filarete.

Next to the "terebinth" was the tomb of the favorite horse of Lucius Verus. This wonderful racer, belonging to the squadron of the Greens, was named Volucris, the Flyer, and the emperor's admiration for his exploits was such that, after honoring him with statues of gilt-bronze in his lifetime, he raised a mausoleum to his memory in the Vatican grounds, after his career had been brought to a close. The selection of the site was not made at random, as we know that the Greens themselves had their burial-ground on this Via Triumphalis.

Proceeding on our pilgrimage towards the Clivus Cinnæ, the ascent to the Monte Mario, we have to record a line of tombs discovered by Sangallo in building the fortifications or "Bastione di Belvedere." One of them is thus described by Pirro Ligorio on p. 139 of the Bodleian MSS. "This tomb [of which he gives the design] was discovered with many others in the foundations of the Bastione di Belvedere, on the side facing the Castle of S. Angelo. It is square in shape, with two recesses for cinerary urns on each side, and three in the front wall. It was gracefully decorated with stucco-work and frescoes. Next to it was an *ustrinum* where corpses were cremated, and on the other side a second tomb, also decorated with painted stucco-work. Here was found a piece of agate in the shape of a nut, so beautifully carved that it was mistaken for a real nutshell. There was also a skeleton, the skull of which was found between the legs, and in its place there was a mask or plaster cast of the head, reproducing most vividly the features of the dead man. The cast is now preserved in the Pope's wardrobe."[130]

Finally, I shall mention the tomb of a boot and shoe maker, which was discovered February 5, 1887, in the foundations of one of the new houses at the foot of the Belvedere. This excellent work of art, cut in Carrara marble, shows the bust of the owner in a square niche, above which is a round pediment. The portrait is extremely characteristic: the forehead is bald, with a few locks of short curled hair behind the ears; and the face shaven, except that on the left of the mouth there is a mole covered with hair. The man appears to be of mature age, but healthy, robust, and of rather stern expression.

Above the niche, two "forms" or lasts are represented, one of them inside a *caliga*. They are evidently the signs of the trade carried on by the owner of the tomb, which is announced in his epitaph: "Caius Julius Helius, shoemaker at the Porta Pontinalis, built this tomb during his lifetime for himself, his daughter Julia Flaccilla, his freedman Caius Julius Onesimus and his other servants."

Julius Helius was therefore a shoe-merchant with a retail shop near the modern Piazza di Magnanapoli on the Quirinal. Although the qualification of *sutor* is rather indefinite and can be applied indifferently to the *solearii, sandaliarii, crepidarii, baxearii* (makers of slippers, sandals, Greek shoes), etc., as well as to the *sutores veteramentarii* or menders of old boots, yet Julius Helius, as shown by the specimen represented on his tomb, was a *caligarius*, or maker of *caligæ*, which were used chiefly by military men. Boot and shoe makers and purveyors of leather and lacings (*comparatores mercis sutoriæ*) seem to have been rather proud men in their day, and liked to be represented on their tombs with the tools of their trade. A bas-relief in the Museo di Brera represents Caius Atilius Justus, one of the fraternity, seated at his bench, in the act of adjusting a *caliga* to the wooden last. A sarcophagus inscribed with the name of Atilius Artemas, a local shoemaker, was discovered at Ostia in 1877, with a representation of a number of tools. The reader is probably familiar with the fresco from Herculaneum representing two Genii seated at a bench; one of them is forcing a last into a shoe, while his companion is busy mending another. Class XVI. of the Museo Cristiano at the Lateran contains several tombstones of Christian *sutores* with various emblems of their calling.

The shoemakers formed a powerful corporation from the time of the kings; their club called the *Atrium sutorium* was the scene of a religious ceremony called *Tubilustrium*, which took place every year on March 23. They seem to have been also an irritable and violent set. Ulpianus[131] speaks of an action for damages brought before the magistrate by a boy whose parents had placed him in a boot-shop to learn the trade, and who, having misunderstood the directions of his master, was struck by him so heavily on the head with a wooden form that he lost the sight of one eye.

Tomb of Helius, the shoemaker.

VIA SALARIA. Visitors who remember the Rome of past days will be unpleasantly impressed by the change which the suburban quarters crossed by the viæ Salaria, Pinciana and Nomentana have undergone in the last ten years. In driving outside the gates the stranger was formerly surprised by the sudden appearance of a region of villas and gardens. The villas Albani, Patrizi, Alberoni, and Torlonia, not to speak of minor pleasure-grounds, merged as they were into one great forest of venerable trees, with the blue Sabine range in the background, gave him a true impression of the aspect of the Roman Campagna in the imperial times.

The scene is now changed, and not for the better. Still, if any one has no right to grumble, it is the archæologist, because the building of these suburban quarters has placed more knowledge at his disposal than could have been gathered before in the lapse of a century. I quote only one instance. Famous in the annals of Roman excavations are those made between 1695 and 1741 in the vineyard of the Naro family, between the Salaria and the Pinciana, back of the Casino di Villa Borghese. It took forty-six years to dig out the contents of that small property, which included twenty-six graves of prætorians and one hundred and forty-one of civilians.

In 1887, in cutting open the Corso d' Italia, which connects the Porta Pinciana with the Salaria, eight hundred and fifty-five tombs were discovered in nine months. The cemetery extends from the Villa Borghese to the prætorian camp, from the walls of Servius Tullius to the first milestone. The gardens of Sallust were surrounded by it on two sides; a striking contrast between the silent city of death on the one hand, and the merriest and noisiest meeting-place of the living on the other.

Although the cemetery was mostly occupied by military men, the high-roads which cross it were lined with mausolea belonging to historical families. Such is the tomb of the Licinii Calpurnii, discovered in 1884, in the foundations of the house No. 29, Via di Porta Salaria, the richest and most important of those found in Rome in my lifetime.[132] Its history is connected with one of the worst crimes of Messalina.

There lived in Rome in her time a nobleman, Marcus Licinius Crassus Frugi, ex-prætor, ex-consul (A. D. 27) ex-governor of Mauritania, the husband of Scribonia, by whom he had three sons. There was never a more unlucky family than this. The origin of their misfortunes is curious enough. Licinius Crassus, whom Seneca calls "stupid enough to be made emperor," committed, among other fatuities, that of naming his eldest son Pompeius Magnus, after his great-grandfather on the maternal side: a useless display of pride, as the boy had titles enough of his own to place him at the head of the Roman aristocracy. Caligula, jealous of the high-sounding name, was the first to threaten his life; but spared it at the expense of the name. Claudius restored the title to him, as a wedding-present, on the day of his marriage with Antonia, daughter of the emperor himself by Ælia Pætina. His splendid career, his nobility and grace of manners, and his alliance with the imperial family, excited the hatred of Messalina, a foe far more dangerous than Caligula. She extorted from her weak husband the sentence of death against Pompeius and his father and mother. The execution took place in the spring of 47.

The second son, Licinius Crassus, was murdered by Nero in 67.

The third son, Lucius Calpurnius Piso Frugi Licinianus, who was only eleven at the time of the executions of 47, spent many years in banishment, while the extermination of his family was slowly progressing. Being left alone in the world, at last Galba took mercy upon him, adopted him as a son, and heir to the Sulpician estates, and lastly, in January, 69, named him successor to the throne. If he had but spared him this honor! Only four days later he was murdered, together with Galba, by the prætorian rebels; and his head, severed from his body, was given to his young widow, Verania Gemina.

History speaks of a fifth unfortunate member of the family, who died a violent death even under the mild and just rule of Hadrian. His name was Calpurnius Licinianus, ex-consul A. D. 87. Having conspired against Nerva, he, and his wife, Agedia Quintina, were banished to Tarentum. A second conspiracy against Trajan brought upon him banishment to a solitary island, and an attempt to escape from it was the cause of his death.

Such was the fate of the seven occupants of this sepulchral chamber. When I first descended into it, in November, 1884, and found myself surrounded by those great historical names of murdered men and women, I felt more than ever the vast difference between reading Roman history in books, and studying it from its monuments, in the presence of its leading actors; and I realized once more what a privilege it is to live in a city where discoveries of such importance occur frequently.

I wish I could tell my readers that my hands did actually touch the bones of those murdered patricians, and the contents of their cinerary urns. They did not, however, because the spell of adversity seems to have pursued the Calpurnii even into their tombs, and there is reason to believe that their last repose was troubled by persecutors, who followed them to their graves. Their cippi were found broken into fragments, their names half erased, and their ashes scattered to the four winds.

The inscriptions, silent on the main point at issue, that of their violent death, are worded with marvellous dignity, coupled with a sad touch of irony. That engraved on the urn of Pompeius Magnus says:— 279

CN · POMP*eius*
CRASSI F · MEN
MAGNVS
PONTIF · QVAEST
TI · CLAVDI · CAESARIS · AVG
GERMANICI
SOCERI · SVI

"[Here lies] Cnæus Pompeius Magnus, son of Crassus, etc., quæstor of the Emperor Claudius, *his father-in-law.*" When we remember that it was precisely the alliance with the imperial family that caused the death of the youth; that his death sentence was signed by Claudius, who was his father-in-law, we cannot help thinking that the names of the murdered man and his murderer were coupled purposely in this short epitaph.

In a second and much larger chamber ten marble sarcophagi were discovered, precious as works of art, but devoid of historical interest, because no name is engraved upon them. Perhaps the experience of their ancestors warned the Calpurnii of later generations not to tempt obnoxious fate again, but to adhere to obscurity and retirement, even in the secrecy of the family vault. As a work of art, each of the coffins is a choice specimen of Roman funeral sculpture of the second century of our era. Some are simply decorated with festoons, winged genii, scenic masks, or chimeras; others with scenes relating to the Bacchic cycle, such as the infancy of the god, his triumphal return from India, and his desertion of Ariadne in the island of Naxos. The finest sarcophagus, of which we give an illustration, represents the rape of the daughters of Leukippos by Castor and Pollux. 280

The collection of sarcophagi, inscriptions, urns, portrait-heads, coins, and other objects belonging to the tombs, and the tombs themselves, ought to have become public property, and to have been kept together as a monument of national interest. Until recently the marbles were to be seen on the ground floor of the Palazzo Maraini in the Via Agostino Depretis, but some of them have now been removed to No. 9 Via della Mercede.

Proceeding two hundred yards farther, on the same side of the Via Salaria, we find the base of the tomb of the precocious boy Quintus Sulpicius Maximus, the tomb itself having been discovered in 1871, in the interior of the right tower of the Porta Salaria, while this was being rebuilt after the bombardment of September 20, 1870.[133] The tomb had formed the core of the tower, just as that of Eurysaces, the baker, found in 1833, had been imbedded in the left tower of the Porta Praenestina.

The tomb is composed of a pedestal, built of blocks of travertine, with a marble cippus upon it, ornamented with a statue of the youth, and the story of his life told in Greek and Latin verse. The story is simple and sad.

On September 14, A. D. 95, the anniversary of his accession to the throne, Domitian opened for the third time the *certamen quinquennale*, a competition for the world's championship in gymnastics, equestrian sports, music, and poetry, which he had instituted at the beginning of his reign.[134] Fifty-two competitors in Greek poetry were present. The subject, drawn by lot, was: "The words which Jupiter made use of in reproving Apollo for having trusted his chariot to Phaeton." Quintus Sulpicius Maximus improvised, on this rather poor theme, forty-three *versus extemporales*. The meaning of the adjective is doubtful. We are not certain whether the boy spoke his verses extemporaneously, his words being taken down by shorthand; or

281

whether he and his fifty-one colleagues were allowed some time to consider the subject and write the composition, as is now the practice in literary examinations. Ancient writers speak of "improvvisatori" who manifested their wonderful gift at a premature age;[135] still, it seems almost impossible that fifty-two such prodigies could have been brought together at one competition. Sulpicius Maximus was crowned by the emperor with the Capitoline laurels and awarded the championship of the world. The verses by which he won the competition are really very good, and show a thorough knowledge of Greek prosody. The victory, however, cost him dearly; in fact, he paid for it with his life. The following inscription was engraved on his tomb:—

"To Q. Sulpicius Maximus, son of Quintus, born in Rome, and lived eleven years, five months, twelve days. He won the competition, among fifty-two Greek poets, at the third celebration of the Capitoline games. His most unhappy parents, Quintus Sulpicius Eugramus and Licinia Januaria, have caused his extemporized poem to be engraved on this tomb, to prove that in praising his talents they have not been inspired solely by their deep love for him (*ne adfectibus suis indulsisse videantur*)."

Let the fate of this boy be a warning to those parents who, discovering in their children a precocious inclination for some branch of human learning, encourage and force this fatal cleverness for the gratification of their own pride, instead of moderating it in accordance with the physical power and development of youth.

The world's competition, instituted by Domitian, had a long and successful career, and we can follow its celebration for many centuries, to the age of Petrarca and Tasso. An inscription discovered at Vasto, the ancient Histonium, describes the one which took place A. D. 107 in these words: "To Lucius Valerius Pudens, son of Lucius. Being only thirteen years old, he took part in the sixth *certamen sacrum*, near the temple of Jupiter Capitolinus; and won the championship among the Latin poets by the unanimous vote of the judges." These last words show that special jurors were appointed by the emperor for each section of the competitions. In the year 319 Constantine the Great and Licinius Cæsar celebrated with great solemnity the fifty-eighth *certamen*. Ausonius of Burdigala, the great poet of the fourth century, speaks of an Attius Delfidius, an infant prodigy (*pæne ab incunabulis poeta*), who gained the prize under Valentinian I. The mediæval and Renaissance custom of "laureating" poets on the Capitol was certainly derived from Domitian's institution.

The race of the "improvvisatori" has never died out in central and southern Italy. One of the most celebrated in the sixteenth century, named Silvio Antoniano, at the age of eleven could sing to the accompaniment of his lute on any argument proposed to him, the poetry being as graceful and pleasing as the music. One day, while sitting at a state banquet in the Palazzo di Venezia, Giovanni Angelo de' Medici, one of the cardinals present, asked him if he could improvise "on the praises of the clock," the sound of which, from the belfry of the palace, had just struck his ears. The melodious song of Silvio, on such an extraordinary theme, was received with loud applause; and when Giovanni Angelo de' Medici was elected Pope in 1559, under the name of Pius IV., he raised the young poet to the rank of a cardinal in recognition of his extraordinary talent.

The mausoleum of Lucilia Polla and her brother Lucilius Pætus was discovered in May, 1885, in the Villa Bertone, opposite the Villa Albani, at a distance of seven hundred metres from the gate. It is the largest sepulchral structure discovered in my time, and worthy of being compared in size to the mausoleum of Metella on the Appian Way, and the so-called Torrione on the Labicana. It was originally composed of two parts: a basement, one hundred and ten feet in diameter, built of travertine and marble, which is the only part that remains; and a cone of earth fifty-two feet high, covered with trees, in imitation of the Mausoleum of Augustus, with which it was contemporary. The cone has disappeared. The inscription, sixteen feet long, is engraved on the side facing the Via Salaria, in letters of the most exquisite form to be found in Rome. It states that Marcus Lucilius Pætus, an officer who had the command of the cavalry and the military engineers in one or more campaigns, in the time of Augustus, had built the tomb for his sister Lucilia Polla, already deceased, and for himself.

284

The fate of the monument has been truly remarkable. I believe there is no other in the necropolis of the Via Salaria which has undergone so many changes in the course of centuries. The first took place in the reign of Trajan, when the monument was buried under a prodigious mass of earth, together with a large section of an adjoining cemetery. In fact, columbaria dating from the time of Hadrian have been found built against the beautiful inscription of Lucilia Polla; and the inscription itself was disfigured by a coating of red paint, to make it harmonize with the color of the three other walls of the crypt. The whole tract between the Salaria and the Pinciana was raised in the same manner twenty-five feet; and contains, therefore, two layers of tombs,—the lower belonging to the republican or early imperial epoch, the upper to the time of Hadrian and later.

Where did this enormous mass of earth come from?

A clew to the answer is given on page 87 of my "Ancient Rome," where, in describing the construction of Trajan's forum, and the column which stands in the middle of it, "to show to posterity how high rose the mountain levelled by the emperor" (ad declarandum quantæ altitudinis mons et locus sit egestus), I stated that I had been able to estimate the amount of earth and rock removed to make room for the forum at 24,000,000 cubic feet, and concluded, "I have made investigations over the Campagna to discover the place where the twenty-four million cubic feet were carted and dumped, but my efforts have not, as yet, been crowned with success." The place is now discovered. None but an emperor would have dared to bury a cemetery so important as that which I am now describing; and if we

285

remember that it was the open space which was nearest of all to Trajan's excavations, easy of access, that the burying of a cemetery for a necessity of state could be justified by the proceedings of Mæcenas and Augustus, described on page 67 of the same book, and that the change must have taken place at the beginning of the second century, as proved by the dates, and by the construction and type of tombs belonging respectively to the lower and upper strata, I think that my surmise may be accepted as an established fact.

Thus vanished the mausoleum of the Lucilii from the eyes and from the memory of the Romans of the second century. Towards the end of the fourth century the Christians, while tunnelling the ground near it, for one of their smaller catacombs, discovered the crypt by accident, and occupied it. The shape of this crypt may be compared to that of Hadrian's mausoleum; that is, it was a hall in the form of a Greek cross, in the centre of the circular structure, and was reached by means of a corridor. The Christians scattered the relics of the first occupants, knocked down their busts, built arcosolia in the three recesses of the Greek cross, and honeycombed with loculi the side walls of the corridor. The transformation was so complete that, when we first entered the corridor, in July, 1886, we thought we had found a wing of the catacombs of S. Saturninus. Some of the loculi were closed with tiles, others with pagan inscriptions which the *fossores* had found by chance in tunnelling their way into the crypt. Two loculi, excavated near the entrance outside the corridor, contained bodies of infants with magic circlets around their necks. They are most extraordinary objects in both material and variety of shape. The pendants are cut in bone, ivory, rock crystal, onyx, jasper, amethyst, amber, touch-stone, metal, glass, and enamel; and they represent elephants, bells, doves, pastoral flutes, hares, knives, rabbits, poniards, rats, Fortuna, jelly-fish, human arms, hammers, symbols of fecundity, helms, marbles, boar's tusks, loaves of bread, and so on.

The vicissitudes of the mausoleum did not end with this change of religion and ownership. Two or three centuries ago, when the fever of discovering and ransacking the catacombs of the Via Salaria was at its height, some one found his way to the crypt, and committed purely wanton destruction. The arcosolia were dismantled, and the loculi violated one by one. We found the bones of the Christians of the fourth century scattered over the floor, and, among them, the marble busts of Lucilius Pætus and Lucilia Polla, which the Christians of the fourth century had knocked from their pedestals. Such is the history of Rome.

Via Appia. A delightful afternoon excursion in the vicinity of the city can be made to the Valle della Caffarella from the so-called "Tempio del Dio Redicolo" to the "Sacred Grove" by S. Urbano. Leaving Rome by the Porta S. Sebastiano, and turning to the left directly after passing the chapel of Domine quo vadis, we descend to the valley of the river Almo, now called the Valle della Caffarella, from the ducal family who owned it before the Torlonias. The path is full of charm, running, as it does, along the banks of the historical stream, and between hillsides which are covered with evergreens, and scented with the perfume of wild flowers. The place is secluded and quiet, and the solitary rambler is unconsciously reminded of Horace's stanza (Epod. II.):—

287

> "Beatus ille, qui procul negotiis,
> Ut prisca gens mortalium,
> Paterna rura bobus exercet suis,
> Solutus omni fœnore,
>
> .   .   .
>
> Forumque vitat, et superba civium
> Potentiorum limina."

In no other capital of the present day can the sentiment expressed by Horace be felt and enjoyed more than in Rome, where it is so easy to forget the worries and frivolities of city life by walking a few steps outside the gates. The Val d'Inferno and the Via del Casaletto, outside the Porta Angelica, the Vigne Nuove outside the Porta Pia, and the Valle della Caffarella, to which I am now leading my readers, all are dreamy wildernesses, made purposely to give to our thoughts fresher and healthier inspirations. Sometimes indistinct sounds from the city yonder are borne to our ears by the wind, to increase, by contrast, the happiness of the moment. And it is not only the natural beauty of these secluded spots that fascinates the stranger: there are associations special to each which increase its interest tenfold. At the Vigne Nuove one can locate within a hundred feet the spot in which Nero's suicide took place. The Val d'Inferno brings back to our memory the two Domitiæ Lucillæ, their clay-quarries and brick-kilns, of which the products were shipped even to Africa; the Valle della Caffarella is full of souvenirs of Herodes Atticus and Annia Regilla, who are brought to mind by their tombs, by the sacred grove, by the so-called Grotto of Egeria, and by the remains of their beautiful villa.

Herodes Atticus, born at Marathon A. D. 104, of noble Athenian parents, became one of the 288 most distinguished men of his time. Philostratos, the biographer of the Sophists, gives a detailed account of his life and fortunes at the beginning of Book II. Inscriptions relating to his career have been found in Rome, on the borders of the Appian Way, the best-known being the *Iscrizioni greche triopee ora Borghesiane*, edited by Ennio Quirino Visconti in 1794.[136] His father, Tiberius Claudius Atticus Herodes, lost his fortune by confiscation for reasons of state, and was therefore obliged, at the beginning of his career, to depend upon the fortune of his wife, Vibullia Alcia, for his support. Suddenly he became the richest man in Greece, and probably in the world. Many writers have given accounts of his extraordinary discovery of treasure, which was made in the foundations of a small house which he owned at the foot of the Akropolis, near the Dionysiac Theatre. He seems to have been more frightened than pleased at the amount found, knowing how complicated was the jurisprudence on this subject, and how greedy provincial magistrates were. He addressed himself in general terms to the emperor Nerva, asking what he should do with his discovery. The answer was that he could make use of it as he pleased. Even then he was not reassured, and wrote again to the emperor declaring that the fortune was far beyond his condition in life. Nerva's answer 289 confirmed him emphatically in the full possession of this wealth. Herodes did much good with it, as a noble revenge for the persecutions which he had undergone in his younger days; and at his death his son inherited, with the fortune, his generous instincts and kindliness.

Curiosity leads us to inquire where this amount of gold and treasure came from, who it was that concealed it in the rock of the Akropolis, and when, and for what reason. Visconti's surmise that it was hidden there by a wealthy Roman, during the civic wars, and the proscriptions which followed them towards the end of the Republic, is obviously incorrect. No Roman general, magistrate, or merchant of republican times could have collected such a fortune in impoverished Greece. I have a more probable suggestion to make. When Xerxes engaged his fleet against the Greek allies in the straits of Salamis, he was so confident of gaining the day that he established himself comfortably on a lofty throne on the slope of Mount Ægaleos to witness the fight. And when he saw Fortune turn against his forces, and was obliged to retire in hot haste, trusting his own safety to flight, I suppose that the funds of war, which were kept by the treasurer of the army at headquarters, may have been buried in a cleft of the Akropolis, in the hope of a speedy and more successful return. The amount of money carried by Xerxes' treasury officials for purposes of war must have been enormous, when we consider that 2,641,000 men were counted at the review held in the plains of Doriskos.

Whatever may have been the origin of the wealth of Atticus it could not have fallen into better hands. His liberality towards men of letters, and needy friends; his works of general utility executed in Greece, Asia Minor, and Italy; his exhibitions of games and entertainments in the Circus and in the Amphitheatre, did not prevent him from cultivating science to such an extent that, on his arrival in Rome, he was selected as tutor of the two adopted sons of Antoninus Pius,—Marcus Aurelius and Lucius Verus. Here he married Annia Regilla, one of the wealthiest ladies of the day, by whom he had six children. She died in childbirth, and Herodes was accused, we do not know on what ground, of having accelerated or caused her death by ill-treatment or violence. Regilla's brother, Appius Annius Bradua, consul A. D. 160, brought an action of uxoricide against Herodes, but failed to prove his case. Still, the calumny remained in the mind of the public. To dispel it, and to regain his position in society, Herodes, although stricken with grief, made himself conspicuous almost to excess in honoring the memory of his departed wife. Her jewels were offered to Ceres and Proserpina; and the land which she had owned between the Via Appia and the valley of the Almo was covered with memorial buildings, and also consecrated to the gods. On the boundary line of the property, columns were raised bearing the inscription in Greek and Latin:—

"To the memory of Annia Regilla, wife of Herodes, the light and soul of the house, to whom these lands once belonged."[137]

The lands are described in other epigraphic documents as containing a village named Triopium, wheat-fields, vineyards, olive-groves, pastures, a temple dedicated to Faustina the younger under the title of the New Ceres, a burialspace for the family, placed under the protection of Minerva and Nemesis, and lastly a grove sacred to the memory of Regilla.

Many of these monuments are still in existence. The first structure we meet with is a tomb of considerable size built in the shape of a temple, the lowest steps of which are watered by the Almo. Its popular name of "Temple of the God Rediculus" is derived from a tradition which points to this spot as the one at which Hannibal turned back before the gates of Rome, and where a shrine to the "God of Retreat" was subsequently raised by the Romans. The Campagna abounds in sepulchral monuments of a similar design, but none can be compared with this in the elegance of its terra-cotta carvings, which give it the appearance and lightness of lace. The polychrome effect produced by the alternate use of dark red and yellow bricks is particularly fine.

Although no inscription has been found within or near this heroön, there are reasons to prove that it was the family tomb of Regilla, Herodes, and their six children. A more beautiful and interesting structure is hardly to be found in the Campagna, and I wonder why so few visit it. Perhaps it is better that it should be so, because its present owner has just rented it for a pig-pen.

Higher up the valley, on a spur of the hill above the springs of Egeria, stands the Temple of Ceres and Faustina, now called S. Urbano alla Caffarella. It belongs to the Barberinis, who take good care of it, as well as of the sacred grove of ilexes which covers the slope to the south of the springs. The vestibule is supported by four marble pillars, but, the intercolumniations having been filled up by Urban VIII. in 1634, the picturesqueness of the effect is destroyed. Here Herodes dedicated to the memory of his wife a statue, minutely described in the second Triopian inscription, alluded to above. Early Christians took possession of the temple and consecrated it to the memory of Pope Urbanus, the martyr, whose remains were buried close by, in the *crypta magna* of the Catacombs of Prætextatus. Pope Paschal I. caused the Confession of the church to be decorated with frescoes representing the saint from whom it was named, with the Virgin Mary, and S. John. In the year 1011 the panels between the pilasters of the cella were covered with paintings illustrating the lives and martyrdoms of Cæcilia, Tiburtius, Valerianus and Urbanus, and, although injured by restorations, these paintings form the most important contribution to the history of Italian art in the eleventh century. We have therefore under one roof, and within the four walls of this temple, the names of Ceres, Faustina, Herodes and Annia Regilla, coupled with those of S. Cæcilia and S. Valerianus, of Paschal I., and Pope Barberini; decorations in stucco and brick of the time of Marcus Aurelius; paintings of the ninth and eleventh centuries; and all this variety of wealth intrusted to the care of a good old hermit, whose dreams are surely not troubled by the conflicting souvenirs of so many events.

I need not remind the reader that the name of Egeria, given to the nymphæum below the temple, is of Renaissance origin. The grotto in which, according to the legend, and to Juvenal's description, Numa held his secret meetings with the nymph Egeria, was situated within the line of the walls of Aurelian, and in the lower grounds of the Villa Fonseca, that is to say, at the foot of the Cælian Hill, near the Via della Ferratella. I saw it first in 1868, and again in 1880 when collecting materials for my volume on the "Aqueducts and Springs of Ancient Rome."[138] In 1887 it was buried by the military engineers, while they were building their new hospital near Santo Stefano Rotondo. The springs still make their way through the newly-made ground, and appear again in the beautiful nymphæum of the Villa Mattei (von Hoffmann) at the corner of the Via delle Mole di S. Sisto and the Via di Porta S. Sebastiano.

As regards the Sacred Grove, there is no doubt that its present beautiful ilexes continue the tradition, and flourish on the very spot of the old grove, sacred to the memory of Annia Regilla, CVIVS HAEC PRAEDIA FVERVNT.

The Sacred Grove and the Temple of Ceres; now S. Urbano alla Caffarella.

To come back, however, to the "Queen of the Roads:" among the many discoveries that have taken place in the cemeteries which line it, that made on April 16, 1485, during the pontificate of Innocent VIII., remains unrivalled.

There have been so many accounts published by modern writers[139] in reference to this extraordinary event that it may interest my readers to learn the truth by reviewing the evidence as it stands in its original simplicity. I shall only quote such authorities as enable us to ascertain what really took place on that memorable day. The case is in itself so unique that it does not need amplification or the addition of imaginary details. Let us first consult the diary of Antonio di Vaseli:—

(f. 48.) "To-day, April 19, 1485, the news came into Rome, that a body buried a thousand years ago had been found in a farm of Santa Maria Nova, in the Campagna, near the Casale Rotondo.... (f. 49.) The Conservatori of Rome despatched a coffin to Santa Maria Nova elaborately made, and a company of men for the transportation of the body into the city. The body has been placed for exhibition in the Conservatori palace, and large crowds of citizens and noblemen have gone to see it. The body seems to be covered with a glutinous substance, a mixture of myrrh and other precious ointments, which attract swarms of bees. The said body is intact. The hair is long and thick; the eyelashes, eyes, nose, and ears are spotless, as well as the nails. It appears to be the body of a woman, of good size; and her head is covered with a light cap of woven gold thread, very beautiful. The teeth are white and perfect; the flesh and the tongue retain their natural color; but if the glutinous substance is washed off, the flesh blackens in less than an hour. Much care has been taken in searching the tomb in which the corpse was found, in the hope of discovering the epitaph, with her name; it must be an illustrious one, because none but a noble and wealthy person could afford to be buried in such a costly sarcophagus thus filled with precious ointments."

Translation of a letter of messer Daniele da San Sebastiano, dated MCCCCLXXXV:—

"In the course of excavations which were made on the Appian Way, to find stones and marbles, three marble tombs have been discovered during these last days, sunk twelve feet below the ground. One was of Terentia Tulliola, daughter of Cicero; the other had no epitaph. One of them contained a young girl, intact in all her members, covered from head to foot with a coating of aromatic paste, one inch thick. On the removal of this coating, which we believe to be composed of myrrh, frankincense, aloe, and other priceless drugs, a face appeared, so lovely, so pleasing, so attractive, that, although the girl had certainly been dead fifteen hundred years, she appeared to have been laid to rest that very day. The thick masses of hair, collected on the top of the head in the old style, seemed to have been combed then and there. The eyelids could be opened and shut; the ears and the nose were so well preserved that, after being bent to one side or the other, they instantly resumed their original shape. By pressing the flesh of the cheeks the color would disappear as in a living body. The tongue could be seen through the pink lips; the articulations of the hands and feet still retained their elasticity. The whole of Rome, men and women, to the number of twenty thousand, visited the marvel of Santa Maria Nova that day. I hasten to inform you of this event, because I want you to understand how the ancients took care to prepare not only their souls but also their bodies for immortality. I am sure that if you had had the privilege of beholding that lovely young face, your pleasure would have equalled your astonishment."

Translation of a letter, dated Rome, April 15, 1485, among Schedel's papers in Cod. 716 of the Munich library:

"Knowing your eagerness for novelties, I send you the news of a discovery just made on the Appian Way, five miles from the gate, at a place called Statuario (the same as S. Maria Nova). Some workmen engaged in searching for stones and marbles have discovered there a marble coffin of great beauty, with a female body in it, wearing a knot of hair on the back of her head, in the fashion now popular among the Hungarians. It was covered with a cap of woven gold, and tied with golden strings. Cap and strings were stolen at the moment of the discovery, together with a ring which she wore on the second finger of the left hand. The eyes were open, and the body preserved such elasticity that the flesh would yield to pressure, and regain its natural shape immediately. The form of the body was beautiful in the extreme; the appearance was that of a girl of twenty-five. Many identify her with Tulliola, daughter of Cicero, and I am ready to believe so, because I have seen, close by there, a tombstone with the name of Marcus Tullius; and because Cicero is known to have owned lands in the neighborhood. Never mind whose daughter she was; she was certainly noble and rich by birth. The body owed its preservation to a coating of ointment two inches thick, composed of myrrh, balm, and oil of cedar. The skin was white, soft, and perfumed. Words cannot describe the number and the excitement of the multitudes who rushed to admire this marvel. To make matters easy, the Conservatori have agreed to remove the beautiful body to the Capitol. One would think there is some great indulgence and remission of sins to be gained by climbing that hill, so great is the crowd, especially of women, attracted by the sight.

"The marble coffin has not yet been removed to the city; but I am told that the following letters are engraved on it: 'Here lies Julia Prisca Secunda. She lived twenty-six years and one month. She has committed no fault, except to die.' It seems that another name is engraved on the same coffin, that of a Claudius Hilarus, who died at forty-six. If we are to believe current rumors, the discoverers of the body have fled, taking with them great treasures."

And now let the reader gaze at the mysterious lady. The accompanying cut represents her body as it was exhibited in the Conservatori palace, and is taken from an original sketch in the Ashburnham Codex, 1174, f. 134.

The body of a girl found in 1485.

Celio Rodigino, Leandro Alberti, Alexander ab Alexandro and Corona give other particulars of some interest:—

The excavations were undertaken by the monks of Santa Maria Nuova (now S. Francesca Romana), five miles from the gate. The tomb stood on the left or east side of the road, high above the ground. The sarcophagus was imbedded in the walls of the foundation, and its cover was sealed with molten lead. As soon as the lid was removed, a strong odor of turpentine and myrrh was remarked by those present. The body is described as well arranged in the coffin, with arms and legs still flexible. The hair was blonde, and bound by a fillet (*infula*) woven of gold. The color of the flesh was absolutely lifelike. The eyes and mouth were partly open, and if one drew the tongue out slightly it would go back to its place of itself.

During the first days of the exhibition on the Capitol this wonderful relic showed no signs of decay; but after a time the action of the air began to tell upon it, and the face and hands turned black. The coffin seems to have been placed near the cistern of the Conservatori palace, so as to allow the crowd of visitors to move around and behold the wonder with more ease. Celio Rodigino says that the first symptoms of putrefaction were noticed on the third day; and he attributes the decay more to the removal of the coating of ointments than to the action of the air. Alexander ab Alexandro describes the ointment which filled the bottom of the coffin as having the appearance and scent of a fresh perfume.

These various accounts are no doubt written under the excitement of the moment, and by men naturally inclined to exaggeration; still, they all agree in the main details of the discovery,—in the date, the place of discovery, and the description of the corpse. Who was, then, the girl for the preservation of whose remains so much care had been taken?

Pomponio Leto, the leading archæologist of the age, expressed the opinion that she might have been either Tulliola, daughter of Cicero, or Priscilla, wife of Abascantus, whose tomb on the Appian Way is described by Statius (Sylv. V. i. 22). Either supposition is wrong. The first is invalidated by the fact that the body was of a young and tender girl, while Tulliola is known to have died in childbirth at the age of thirty-two. Moreover, there is no document to prove that Cicero had a family vault at the sixth milestone of the Appian Way. The tomb of Priscilla, wife of Abascantus, a favorite freedman of Domitian, is placed by Statius near the bridge of the Almo (Fiume Almone, Acquataccio) four and a half miles nearer the gate; where, in front of the Chapel of Domine quo vadis, it has been found and twice excavated: the first time in 1773 by Amaduzzi; the second in 1887, under my supervision. The only clew worth following is that given in Pehem's letter of April 15, now in the Munich library; but even this leads to no result. The inscription, which was said to mention the name and age of the girl, is perfectly genuine, and duly registered in the "Corpus Inscriptionum," No. 20,634. It is as follows:—

300

D · M

IVLIA · L · L · PRISCA

VIX · ANN · XXVI · M · I · D · I

Q · CLODIVS · HILARVS

VIX · ANN · XXXXVI

NIHIL · VNQVAM · PECCAVIT

NISI · QVOD · MORTVA · EST

"To the infernal gods. [Here lie] Julia Prisca, freedwoman of Lucius Julius, who lived twenty-six years one month, one day; [and also] Q. Clodius Hilarus, who lived forty-six years. She never did any wrong except to die." Pehem, Malaguy, Fantaguzzi, Waelscapple and all the rest of them, assert unanimously that the inscription was found with the body on April 16, 1485, and they are all mistaken. It had been seen and copied, *at least twenty-two years before*, by Felix Felicianus of Verona, and is to be found in the MSS. collection of ancient epitaphs, which he dedicated to Andrea Mantegna in 1463. The number of spurious inscriptions concocted for the occasion is truly remarkable. Georges of Spalato (1484-1545)

301

gives the following version of this one in his MSS. diary, now in Weimar: "Here lies my only daughter Tulliola, who has committed no offence, except to die. Marcus Tullius Cicero, her unhappy father, has raised this memorial."

The poor girl, whose name and condition in life will never be known, and whose body for twelve centuries had so wonderfully escaped destruction, was most abominably treated by her discoverers in 1485. There are two versions as to her ultimate fate. According to one, Pope Innocent VIII., to stop the excitement and the superstitions of the citizens, caused the *conservatori* to remove the body at night outside the Porta Salaria, and bury it secretly at the foot of the city walls. According to the second it was thrown into the Tiber. One is just about as probable as the other.

How differently we treat these discoveries in our days! In the early morning of May 12, 1889, I was called to witness the opening of a marble coffin which had been discovered two days before, under the foundations of the new Halls of Justice, on the right bank of the Tiber, near Hadrian's Mausoleum. As a rule, the ceremony of cutting the brass clamps which fasten the lids of urns and sarcophagi is performed in one of our archæological repositories, where the contents can be quietly and carefully examined, away from an excited and sometimes dangerous crowd. In the present case this plan was found impracticable, because the coffin was ascertained to be filled with water which had, in the course of centuries, filtered in, drop by drop, through the interstices of the lid. The removal to the Capitol was therefore abandoned, not only on account of the excessive weight of the coffin, but also because the shaking of the water would have damaged and disordered the skeleton and the objects which, perchance, were buried inside.

302

The marble sarcophagus was embedded in a stratum of blue clay, at a depth of twenty-five feet below the level of the city, that is, only four or five feet above the level of the Tiber, which runs close by. It was inscribed simply with the name CREPEREIA TRYPHAENA, and decorated with bas-reliefs representing the scene of her death. No sooner had the seals been broken, and the lid put aside, than my assistants, myself, and the whole crowd of workmen from the Halls of Justice, were almost horrified at the sight before us. Gazing at the skeleton through the veil of the clear water, we saw the skull covered, as it were, with long masses of brown hair, which were floating in the liquid crystal. The comments made by the simple and excited crowd by which we were surrounded were almost as interesting as the discovery itself. The news concerning the prodigious hair spread like wild-fire among the populace of the district; and so the exhumation of Crepereia Tryphæna was accomplished with unexpected solemnity, and its remembrance will last for many years in the popular traditions of the new quarter of the Prati di Castello. The mystery of the hair is easily explained. Together with the spring-water, germs or seeds of an aquatic plant had entered the sarcophagus, settled on the convex surface of the skull, and developed into long glossy threads of a dark shade.

The skull was inclined slightly towards the left shoulder and towards an exquisite little doll, carved of oak, which was lying on the scapula, or shoulder-blade. On each side of the head were gold earrings with pearl drops. Mingled with the vertebræ of the neck and back were a gold necklace, woven as a chain, with thirty-seven pendants of green jasper, and a brooch with an amethyst intaglio of Greek workmanship, representing the fight of a griffin and a deer. Where the left hand had been lying, we found four rings of solid gold. One is an engagement-ring, with an engraving in red jasper representing two hands clasped together. The second has the name PHILETVS engraved on the stone; the third and fourth are plain gold bands. Proceeding further with our exploration, we discovered, close to the right hip, a box containing toilet articles. The box was made of thin pieces of hard wood, inlaid *alla Certosina*, with lines, squares, circles, triangles, and diamonds, of bone, ivory, and wood of various kinds and colors. The box, however, had been completely disjointed by the action of the water. Inside there were two fine combs in excellent preservation, with the teeth larger on one side than on the other: a small mirror of polished steel, a silver box for cosmetics, an amber hairpin, an oblong piece of soft leather, and a few fragments of a sponge.[140] The most impressive discovery was made after the removal of the water, and the drying of the coffin. The woman had been buried in a shroud of fine white linen, pieces of which were still encrusted and cemented against the bottom and sides of the case, and she had been laid with a wreath of myrtle fastened with a silver clasp about the forehead. The preservation of the leaves is truly remarkable.

Who was this woman, whose sudden and unexpected reappearance among us on the twelfth 304 of May, 1889, created such a sensation? When did she live? At what age did she die? What caused her death? What was her condition in life? Was she beautiful? Why was she buried with her doll? The careful examination of the tomb and its contents enable us to answer all these questions satisfactorily.

Crepereia Tryphæna lived at the beginning of the third century after Christ, during the reigns of Septimius Severus and Caracalla, as is shown by the form of the letters and the style of the bas-reliefs engraved on the sarcophagus. She was not noble by birth; her Greek surname *Tryphæna* shows that she belonged to a family of freedmen, former servants of the noble family of the Creperei. We know nothing about her features, except that she had a strong and fine set of teeth. Her figure, however, seems to have been rather defective, on account of a deformity in the ribs, probably caused by scrofula. Scrofula, in fact, seems to have been the cause of her death. In spite of this deformity, however, there is no doubt that she was betrothed to the young man Philetus, whose name is engraved on the stone of the second ring, and that the two happy lovers had exchanged the oath of fidelity and mutual devotion for life, which is expressed by the symbol of the clasped hands. The story of her sad death, and of the sudden grief which overtook her family on the eve of a joyful wedding, is plainly told by the presence in the coffin of the doll and the myrtle wreath, which is a *corona nuptialis*. I believe, in fact, that the girl was buried in her full bridal costume, and then covered with the linen shroud, because there are fragments of clothes of various textures and qualities mixed with those of the white linen.

And now let us turn our attention to the doll. This exquisite *pupa*, a work of art in itself, is of 305 oak, to which the combined action of time and water has given the hardness of metal. It is modelled in perfect imitation of a woman's form, and ranks amongst the finest of its kind yet found in Roman excavations. The hands and feet are carved with the utmost skill. The arrangement of the hair is characteristic of the age of the Antonines, and differs but little from the coiffure of Faustina the elder. The doll was probably dressed, because in the thumb of her right hand are inserted two gold keyrings like those carried by housewives. This charming little figure, the joints of which at the hips, knees, shoulders, and elbows are still in good order, is nearly a foot high. Dolls and playthings are not peculiar to children's tombs. It was customary for young ladies to offer their dolls to Venus or Diana on their wedding-day. But this was not the end reserved for Crepereia's doll. She was doomed to share the sad fate of her young mistress, and to be placed with her corpse, before the marriage ceremony could be performed.

CHAPTER VII.

CHRISTIAN CEMETERIES.[141]

Sanctity of tombs guaranteed to all creeds alike.—The Christians' preference for underground cemeteries not due to fear at first.—Origin and cause of the first persecutions.—The attitude of Trajan towards the Christians, and its results.—The persecution of Diocletian.—The history of the early Christians illustrated by their graves.—The tombs of the first century.—The catacombs.—How they were named.—The security they offered against attack.—Their enormous extent.—Their gradual abandonment in the fourth century.—Open-air cemeteries developed in proportion.—The Goths in Rome.—Their pillage of the catacombs.—Thereafter burial within the city walls became common.—The translation of the bodies of martyrs.—Pilgrims and their itineraries.—The catacombs neglected from the ninth to the sixteenth century.—Their discovery in 1578.—Their wanton treatment by scholars of that time.—Artistic treasures found in them.—The catacombs of Generosa.—The story of Simplicius, Faustina and Viatrix.—The cemetery of Domitilla.—The Christian Flavii buried there.—The basilica of Nereus, Achilleus and Petronilla.—The tomb of Ampliatus.—Was this S. Paul's friend?—The cemetery "ad catacumbas."—The translation of the bodies of SS. Peter and Paul.—The types of the Saviour in early art.—The cemetery of Cyriaca.—Discoveries made there.—Inscriptions and works of art.—The cemetery "ad duas Lauros."—Frescoes in it.—The symbolic supper.—The discoveries of Monsignor Wilpert.—The Academy of Pomponio Leto.

The Roman law which established the inviolability of tombs did not make exceptions either of persons or creeds. Whether the deceased had been pious or impious, a worshipper of Roman or foreign gods, or a follower of Eastern or barbaric religions, his burial-place was considered by law a *locus religiosus*, as inviolable as a temple. In this respect there was no distinction between Christians, pagans, and Jews; all enjoyed the same privileges, and were subject to the same rules. It is not easy to decide whether this condition of things was an advantage to the faithful. It was certainly advantageous to the Church that her cemeteries should be considered sacred by the law, and that the State itself should enforce and guarantee the observance of the rules (*lex monumenti*) made by the deceased in connection with his interment, and tomb; but as the police of cemeteries, and the enforcement of the *leges monumentorum*, was intrusted to the college of high priests, who were stern champions of paganism, the church was liable to be embarrassed in many ways. When, for instance, a body had to be transferred from its temporary repository to the tomb, it was necessary to obtain the consent of the *pontifices*; which was also required in case of subsequent removals, and even of simple repairs to the building. Roman epitaphs constantly refer to this authority of the pontiffs, and one of them, discovered by Ficoroni in July, 1730, near the Porta Metronia, contains the correspondence exchanged on the subject between the two parties. The petitioner, Arrius Alphius, a favorite freedman of the mother of Antoninus Pius, writes to the high priests: "Having lost at the same time wife and son, I buried them temporarily in a terra-cotta coffin. I have since purchased a burial lot on the left side of the Via Flaminia, between the second and the third milestones, and near the mausoleum of Silius Orcilus, and furnished it with marble sarcophagi. I beg permission of you, my Lords, to transfer the said bodies to the new family vault, so that when my hour shall come, I may be laid to rest beside the dear ones." The answer was: "Granted (*fieri placet*). Signed by me, Juventius Celsus, vice-president [of the college of pontiffs], on the 3d day of November [A. D. 155]."

308

The greatest difficulty with which the Christians had to deal was the obligation to perform expiatory sacrifices in given circumstances; as, for instance, when a corpse was removed from one place to another, or when a coffin, damaged by any accidental cause, such as lightning, inundation, fire, earthquake, or violence, had to be opened and the bones exposed to view. But these were exceptional cases; and there is no doubt that the magistrates of Rome were naturally lenient and forbearing in religious matters, except in time of persecution. The partiality shown by early Christians for underground cemeteries is due to two causes: the influence which Eastern customs and the example of the burial of Christ must necessarily have exercised on them, and the security and freedom which they enjoyed in the darkness and solitude of their crypts. Catacombs, however, could not be excavated everywhere, the presence of veins or beds of soft volcanic stone being a condition *sine qua non* of their existence. Cities and villages built on alluvial or marshy soil, or on hills of limestone and lava, were obliged to resort to open-air cemeteries. In Rome itself these were not uncommon. Certainly there was no reason why Christians should object to the authority of the pontiffs in hygienic and civic matters. This authority was so deeply rooted and respected, that the emperor Constans (346-350), although a stanch Christian and anxious to abolish idolatry, left the pontiffs full jurisdiction over Christian and pagan cemeteries, by a constitution issued in 349.[142]

309

From apostolic times to the persecution of Domitian, the faithful were buried, separately or collectively, in private tombs which did not have the character of a Church institution. These early tombs, whether above or below ground, display a sense of perfect security, and an absence of all fear or solicitude. This feeling arose from two facts: the small extent of the cemeteries, which secured to them the rights of private property, and the protection and freedom which the Jewish colony in Rome enjoyed from time immemorial. The Romans of the first century, populace as well as government officials, made no distinction between the proselytes of the Old Testament and those of the New.

Julius Cæsar and Augustus treated the Jews with kindness, and when S. Paul arrived in Rome the colony was living in peace and prosperity, practising religion openly in its Transtiberine synagogues.[143] The same state of things prevailed throughout the peninsula. Thus the rabbi or archon of the synagogue at Pompeii called the *Synagoga Libertinorum* (the existence of which was discovered in September, 1764), could take, in virtue of his office, an active part in city politics and petty municipal quarrels, and in his official capacity could sign a document recommending the election of a candidate for political honors, as is shown by one of the Pompeian inscriptions:—

Cuspium Pansam Æd[*ilem fieri rogat*] Fabius Eupor
Princeps Libertinorum.[144]

The persecution which took place under Claudius was really the first connected with the preaching of the gospel. According to Suetonius (Claud. 25) the Jews themselves were the cause of it, having suddenly become uneasy, troublesome, and offensive, *impulsore Chresto*, that is to say, on account of Christ's doctrine, which was beginning to be preached in their synagogues. The expression used by Suetonius shows how very little was known at the time about the new religion. Although Christ's name was not unknown to him, he speaks of this outbreak under Claudius as having been stirred up personally by a certain Chrestus, as though he were a living member of the Jewish colony. At that early stage the converts to the gospel were identified by the Romans with the Jews, not by mistake or error of judgment, but because they were legally and actually Jews, or rather one Jewish sect which was carrying on a dogmatic war against the others, on a point which had no interest whatever in the eyes of the Romans,—that is, the advent of the Messiah. This statement is corroborated by many passages in the Acts, such as xviii. 15; xxiii. 29; xxv. 9; xxvi. 28, 32; xxviii. 31. Claudius Lysias writes to the governor of Judæa that Paul was accused by his fellow-citizens, not of crimes deserving punishment, but on some controversial point concerning their law. In Rome itself the apostle could preach the gospel with freedom, even when in custody, or under police supervision.[145] And as it was lawful for a Roman citizen to embrace the Jewish persuasion, and give up the religion of his fathers, he was equally free to embrace the Evangelic faith, which was considered by the pagans a Jewish sect, not a new belief.

The pagans despised them both, and mixed themselves up with their affairs only from a fiscal point of view, because the Jews were subject to a tax of two drachms per head, and the treasury officials were obliged to keep themselves acquainted with the statistics of the colony.

This state of things did not last very long, it being of vital importance for the Jews to separate their cause from that of the new-comers. The responsibility for the persecutions which took place in the first century must be attributed to them, not to the Romans, whose tolerance in religious matters had become almost a state rule. The first attempt, made under Claudius, was not a success: it ended, in fact, with the banishment from the capital of every Jew, no matter whether he believed in the Old or the New Testament. *Judæos, impulsore Chresto assidue tumultuantes, Claudius Romæ expulit* (Suetonius: Claud. 25). It was, however, a passing cloud. As soon as they were allowed to come back to their Transtiberine haunts, the Jews set to work again, exciting the feelings of the populace, and denouncing the Christians as conspiring against the State and the gods, under the protection of the law which guaranteed to the Jews the free exercise of their religion. The populace, impressed by the conquests made by the gospel among all classes of citizens, was only too ready to believe the calumny. The Church, repudiated by her mother the Synagogue, could no longer share the privileges of the Jewish community. As for the State, it became a necessity either to recognize Christianity as a new legal religion, or to proscribe and condemn it. The great fire, which destroyed half of Rome under Nero, and which was purposely attributed to the Christians, brought the situation to a crisis. The first persecution began. Had the magistrate who conducted the inquiry been able to prove the indictment of arson, perhaps the storm would have been short, and confined to Rome; but as the Christians could easily exculpate themselves, the trial was changed from a criminal into a politico-religious one. The Christians were convicted not so much of arson (*non tam crimine incendii*) as of a hatred of mankind (*odio generis humani*); a formula which includes anarchism, atheism, and high treason. This monstrous accusation once admitted, the persecution could not be limited to Rome; it necessarily became general, and more violent in one place or another, according to the impulse of the magistrate who investigated this entirely unprecedented case.

Was the hope of a legal existence lost forever to the Church? After Nero's death, and the condemnation of his acts and memory, the Christians enjoyed thirty years of peace. Domitian broke it, first, by claiming with unprecedented severity the tribute from the Jews and those "living a Jewish life;"[146] secondly, by putting the "atheists," that is, the Christians, to the alternative of giving up their faith or their life. These measures were abolished shortly after by Nerva, who sanctioned the rule that in future no one should be brought to justice under the plea of impiety or Judaism. The answer given by Trajan to Pliny the younger, when governor of Bithynia, is famous in the annals of persecutions. To the inquiries made by the governor, as to the best way of dealing with those "adoring Christ for their God," Trajan replied, that the magistrate should not molest them at his own initiative; but if others should bring them to justice, and convict them of impiety and atheism, they deserved punishment.[147] These words contain the solemn recognition of the illegality of Christian worship; they make persecution a rule of state. The faithful were doomed to have no respite for the next two centuries, except what they could obtain at intervals from the personal kindness and tolerance of emperors and magistrates. Those of the Jewish religion continued to enjoy protection and privileges, but Christianity was either persecuted or tolerated, as it happened; so that, even under emperors who abhorred severity and bloodshed, the faithful were at the mercy of the first vagrant who chanced to accuse them of impiety.

Strange to say, more clemency was shown towards them by emperors whom we are accustomed to call tyrants, than by those who are considered models of virtue. The author of the "Philosophumena" (book ix., ch. 11) says that Commodus granted to Pope Victor the liberation of the Christians who had been condemned to the mines of Sardinia by Marcus

Aurelius. Thus that profligate emperor was really more merciful to the Church than the philosophic author of the "Meditations," who, in the year 174, had witnessed the miracle of the Thundering Legion. The reason is evident. The wise rulers foresaw the destructive effect of the new doctrines on pagan society, and indirectly on the empire itself; whereas those who were given over to dissipation were indifferent to the danger; "after them, the deluge!"

At the beginning of the third century, under the rule of Caracalla and Elagabalus, the Church enjoyed nearly thirty years of peace, interrupted only by the short persecution of Maximus, and by occasional outbreaks of popular hostility here and there.[148]

In 249 the "days of terror" returned, and continued fiercer than ever under the rules of Decius, Gallus, and Valerianus. The last persecution, that of Diocletian and his colleagues, was the longest and most cruel of all. For the space of ten years not a day of mercy shone over the *ecclesia fidelium*. The historian Eusebius, an eye-witness, says that when the persecutors became tired of bloodshed, they contrived a new form of cruelty. They put out the right eyes of the confessors, cut the tendon of their left legs, and then sent them to the mines, lame, half blind, half starved, and flogged nearly to death. In book VIII., chapter 12, the historian says that the number of sufferers was so great that no account could be kept of them in the archives of the Church. The memory of this decade of horrors has never died out in Rome. We have still a local tradition, not altogether unfounded, of ten thousand Christians who were condemned to quarry materials for Diocletian's Baths, and who were put to death after the dedication of the building.

Towards the end of 306, Maxentius stopped the persecution, but the true era of peace did not begin before 312, which is the date of Constantine's famous "edict of Milan," granting to the Church liberty and free possession of her places of worship and cemeteries forever.

The events of which I have given a summary sketch are beautifully illustrated by the discoveries which have been made in early Christian cemeteries, from May 31, 1578, which is the date of the discovery of the first catacomb, to the present day.

From the time of the apostles to the first persecution of Domitian, Christian tombs, whether above or below ground, were built with perfect impunity and in defiance of public opinion. We have been accustomed to consider the catacombs of Rome as crypts plunged in total darkness, and penetrating the bowels of the earth at unfathomable depths. This is, in a certain measure, the case with those catacombs, or sections of catacombs, which were excavated in times of persecution; but not with those belonging to the first century. The cemetery of these members of Domitian's family who had embraced the gospel—such as Flavius Clemens, Flavia Domitilla, Plautilla, Petronilla, and others—reveals a bold example of publicity.

The entrance to the crypt, discovered in 1714 and again in 1865, near the farmhouse of Tor Marancia, at the first milestone of the Via Ardeatina, is hewn out of a perpendicular cliff, which is conspicuous from the high road (the modern Via delle Sette Chiese). The crypt is approached through a vestibule, which was richly decorated with terra-cotta carvings, and, on the frieze, a monumental inscription enclosed by an elaborate frame. No pagan mausolea of the Via Appia or the Via Latina show a greater sense of security or are placed more conspicuously than this early Christian tomb. The frescoes on the ceiling of the vestibule, representing biblical scenes, such as Daniel in the lions' den, the history of Jonah, etc., were exposed to daylight, and through the open door could be seen by the passer. No precaution was taken to conceal these symbolic scenes from profane or hostile eyes. We regret the loss of the inscription above the entrance, which, besides the name of the owner of the crypt, probably contained the *lex monumenti*, and a formula specifying the religion of those buried within. In this very catacomb, a few steps from the vestibule, an inscription has been found, in which a Marcus Aurelius Restitutus declares that he has built a tomb for himself and his relatives (*sibi et suis*), provided they were believers in Christ (*fidentes in Domino*). Another tombstone, discovered in 1864, in the Villa Patrizi, near the catacombs of Nicomedes, states that none might be buried in the tomb to which it was attached except those who belonged to the creed (*pertinentes ad religionem*) of the founder.

Entrance to the Crypt of the Flavians.

The time soon came when these frank avowals of Christianity were either impossible or extremely hazardous; and although legally a tomb continued to be a *locus religiosus*, no matter what the creed of the deceased had been, a vague sense of anxiety was felt by the Church, lest even these last refuges should be violated by the mob and its leaders. Hence the extraordinary development which underground cemeteries underwent towards the end of the first and the beginning of the second century. These catacombs were considered by the law to be the property of the citizen who owned the ground above, and who either excavated them at his own cost, or gave the privilege of doing so to the Church. This is the reason why the names of our oldest suburban cemeteries are derived, not from the illustrious saints buried in them, but from the owner of the property under which the catacomb was first excavated. Balbina, Callixtus, Domitilla were never laid to rest in the catacombs which bear their names. Prætextatus, Apronianus, the Jordans, Novella, Pontianus, and Maximus, after whom other cemeteries were named, are all totally unknown persons. When these cemeteries became places of worship and pilgrimage, after the Peace of Constantine, the old names which had sheltered them from the violence of persecutors were abandoned, and replaced by those of local martyrs. Thus the catacomb of Domitilla became that of Nereus and Achilleus; that of Balbina was named for S. Mark; that of Callixtus for SS. Sixtus and Cæcilia; and that of Maximus for S. Felicitas.

One characteristic of Christian epigraphy shows what a comparatively safe place the catacombs were. Inscriptions belonging to them never contain those requests to the passer to respect the tomb, which are so frequent in sepulchral inscriptions from tombs above-ground, and which sometimes, on Christian as well as pagan graves, take the form of an imprecation. An epitaph discovered by Hamilton near Eumenia, Phrygia, contains this rather violent formula: "May the passer who damages my tomb bury all his children at the same time." In another, found near the church of S. Valeria, in Milan, the imprecation runs: "May the wrath of God and of his Christ fall on the one who dares to disturb the peace of our sleep."

318

The safety of the catacombs was not due to the fact that their existence was known only to the proselytes of Christ. The magistrates possessed a thorough knowledge of their location, number, and extent; and we have evidence of raids and descents by the police on extraordinary occasions, as, for instance, during the persecutions of Valerian and Diocletian. The ordinary entrances to the catacombs, which were known to the police, were sometimes walled up or otherwise concealed, and new secret outlets opened through abandoned pozzolana quarries (arenariæ). Some of these outlets have been discovered, or are to be seen, in the cemeteries of Agnes, Thrason, Callixtus, and Castulus. In May, 1867, while excavating on the southern boundary line of the Cemetery of Callixtus, de Rossi found himself suddenly confronted with sandpits, the galleries of which came in contact with those of the cemetery several times. The passage from one to the other had been most ingeniously disguised by the fossores, as those who dug the catacombs were called.[149]

The defence of these cemeteries in troubled times must have caused great anxiety to the Church. Tertullian tells how the population of Carthage, excited against the Christians, sought to obtain from Hilarianus, governor of Africa, the destruction of their graves. "Let them have no burial-ground!" (areæ eorum non sint) was the rallying cry of the mob.

The catacombs are unfit for men to live in, or to stay in even for a few days. The tradition that Antonio Bosio spent seventy or eighty consecutive hours in their depths is unfounded. When we hear of Popes, priests, or their followers seeking refuge in catacombs, we must understand that they repaired to the buildings connected with them, such as the lodgings of the keepers, undertakers, and local clergymen. Pope Boniface I., when molested by Symmachus

319

and Eulalius, found shelter in the house connected with the Cemetery of Maximus on the Via Salaria. The crypts themselves were sought as a refuge only in case of extreme emergency. Thus Barbatianus, a priest from Antiochia, concealed himself in the Catacombs of Callixtus to escape the wrath of Galla Placidia.

Many attempts have been made to estimate the extent of our catacombs, the length of their galleries, and the number of tombs which they contain. Michele Stefano de Rossi, brother of the archæologist, gives the following results for the belt of catacombs within three miles of the gates of Servius:[150]—

(A) Surface of tufa beds, capable of being excavated into catacombs, 67,000,000 square feet.

(B) Surface actually excavated into catacombs, from one to four stories deep, 22,500,000 square feet,—more than a square mile.

(C) Aggregate length of galleries, calculated on the average construction of six different catacombs, 866 kilometres, equal to 587 geographical miles.

The sides of the galleries contain several rows of loculi, sometimes six or eight. Some bodies are buried under the floor, or in the cubiculi which open right and left at short intervals. Assuming these galleries to be capable of containing two bodies per metre, the number of Christians buried in the catacombs, within three miles from the gates of Servius, may be estimated at a minimum of 1,752,000.

The construction of this prodigious labyrinth required the excavation and removal of 96,000,000 cubic feet of solid rock.

With regard to the number of inscriptions, I quote the following passage from Northcote's "Epitaphs," page 3: "Of Christian inscriptions in Rome, during the first six centuries, de Rossi has studied more than fifteen thousand, the immense majority of which were taken from the catacombs; and he tells us there is still an average yearly addition of about five hundred, derived from the same source. This number, vast as it is, is but a poor remnant of what once existed. From the collections made in the eighth and ninth centuries it appears that there were once at least one hundred and seventy ancient Christian inscriptions in Rome, which had an historical or monumental character; written generally in metre, and to be seen at that time in the places which they were intended to illustrate. Of these only twenty-six remain, either whole or in parts. In the Roman topographies of the seventh century, one hundred and forty sepulchres of famous martyrs and confessors are enumerated; we have recovered only twenty inscribed memorials, to assist us in the identification of these. Only nine epitaphs have come to light belonging to the bishops of Rome during the same six centuries; and yet, during that period, there were certainly buried in the suburbs of the city upwards of sixty. Thus, whatever facts we take as the basis of our calculation, it would seem that scarcely a seventh part of the original wealth of the Roman church in memorials of this kind has survived the wreck of ages; and de Rossi gives it as his conviction that there were once *more than one hundred thousand* of them."

320

When the catacombs began to be better known to the general public, and were visited by crowds of the devout or curious, they became one of the marvels of Rome. Travellers who so admired the *syringes* or crypts of the kings of Thebes, calling them τα θαυματα (the wonders), could not help being struck with awe at the great work accomplished by our Christian community in less than three centuries. An inscription found by Deville at Thebes, in one of the royal crypts, and published in the "Archives des missions scientifiques," 1866, vol. ii. p. 484, thus refers to the parallel wonders of Roman and Egyptian catacombs: "Antonius Theodorus, intendant of Egypt and Phœnicia, who has spent many years in the Queen-city of Rome, has seen the wonders (τα θαυματα) both there and here." The allusion to the catacombs in comparison with the *syringes* is evident. The inscription dates from the second half of the fourth century.

To the edict of Milan, and to the peace which it gave to the Church, we must attribute the origin of the decadence of underground cemeteries. Burial in open-air cemeteries having become secure once more, there was no reason why the faithful should give preference to the unhealthy and overcrowded crypts below. The example of desertion was set by the Popes themselves. Melchiades (311-314), who was the first to occupy the Lateran palace after the victory of the Church, was the last Pope buried near his predecessors *in cœmeteris Callisti in cripta*. Sylvester, his successor, was buried in a chapel built expressly, above the crypt of Priscilla, Mark above the crypts of Balbina, Julius above those of Calepodius, and so on. Still, the desire of securing a grave in proximity to the shrine of a martyr was so intense that the use of the catacombs lasted for a century longer, although in diminishing proportions. When a gallery is discovered which contains more graves than usual, and has been excavated even in the narrow ledges of rock which separated the original loculi, or else at the corners of the crossings, which were usually left untouched, as protection against the caving-in of the earth, we may be sure we are approaching a martyr's altar-tomb. Sometimes the paintings which decorate a martyr's *cubiculum* have been disfigured and their inscriptions effaced by an overzealous devotee. The accompanying cut shows the damage inflicted on a picture of the Good Shepherd in the cubiculum of S. Januarius, in the Catacombs of Prætextatus, by an unscrupulous disciple who wished to be buried as near as possible to his patron-saint.

By the end of the fourth century burials in catacombs became rare, and still more between 400 and 410. They were apparently given up altogether after 410. The development of open-air cemeteries increased in proportion, those of S. Lorenzo and S. Paolo fuori le Mura being among the most popular. In 1863, when the entrance-gate to the modern Camposanto adjoining S. Lorenzo was built, fifty tombs, mostly unopened, were found in a space ninety feet long by forty feet wide. Since that time five hundred tombstones have been gathered in the neighborhood of that favorite church. As regards S. Paul's cemetery, more than one thousand inscriptions, whole or in fragments, were found in rebuilding the basilica and its portico, after the fire of 1823;[151] two hundred in the excavations of S. Valentine's basilica, outside the Porta del Popolo. These last excavations are the only ones illustrating a Christian cemetery which are left visible; but their importance is limited. The cemeteries of Arles and Pola, alluded to by Dante, have disappeared; and so has the magnificent one of the officers and men employed in the Roman arsenal at Concordia Sagittaria, which was discovered in 1873, near Portogruaro, by Perulli and Bartolini. This cemetery, which contains, in the section already explored, nearly two hundred sarcophagi, cut in limestone, in the shape of Petrarch's coffin, at Arquà, or Antenor's at Padua, was wrecked by Attila in 452, and buried soon after by an inundation of the river Tagliamento, which spread masses of mud and sand over the district, and raised its level five feet. The accompanying plate is from a photograph taken at the time of the discovery.

I have just stated that burial in catacombs seems to have been abandoned in 410, because no inscription of a later date has yet been found. The reader will easily perceive the reason for the abandonment. On August 10, 410, Rome was stormed by Alaric, and the suburbs devastated. This fatal year marks the end of a great and glorious era in Christian epigraphy, and in the history of catacombs the end of the work of the *fossores*. More fatal still was the barbaric invasion of 457. The actual destruction began in 537, during the siege of Rome by Vitiges. The biographer of Pope Silverius expressly says: "Churches and tombs of martyrs have been destroyed by the Goths" (*ecclesiæ et corpora sanctorum martyrum exterminata sunt a Gothis*). It is difficult to explain why the Goths, confessed and even bigoted Christians (Arians) as they were, and full of respect for the basilicas of S. Peter and S. Paul, as Procopius declares, should have ransacked the catacombs, violated the tombs of martyrs, and broken their historical inscriptions. Perhaps it was because none of the barbarians could read Latin or Greek epitaphs, and make the distinction between pagan and Christian cemeteries; or perhaps they were moved by the desire of finding hidden treasures, or securing relics of saints. Whatever may have been the reason of their behavior, we must remember that two encampments, at least, of the Goths were just over catacombs and around their entrances; one on the Via Salaria, over those of Thrason; the other on the Via Labicana, above those of Peter and Marcellinus. The barbarians could not resist the temptation of exploring those subterranean wonders; indeed they were obliged to do so by the most elementary rules of precaution in order to insure the safety of their intrenchments against surprises. Here I have to record a remarkable coincidence. In each of these two catacombs the following memorial tablet has been seen or found, written in distichs by Pope Virgilius:—

CHRISTIAN MILITARY CEMETERY OF CONCORDIA SAGITTARIA

"When the Goths pitched their camps under the walls of Rome, they declared an impious war against the Saints:

"And destroyed in their sacrilegious attack the tombs dedicated to the memory of martyrs:

"Whose epitaphs, composed by Pope Damasus, have been destroyed.

"Pope Virgilius, having witnessed the destruction, has repaired the tombs, the inscriptions, and the underground sanctuaries after the retreat of the Goths."

The repairs must have been made in haste, between March, 537, the date of the flight of Vitiges, and the following November, the date of the journey of Virgilius to Constantinople, from which he never returned. Traces of this Pope's restorations have been found in other catacombs. In those of Callixtus the fragments of a tablet, dedicated by Damasus to S. Eusebius, have been found, dispersed over a large area, and also a copy set up by Virgilius in the place of the original. In those of Hippolytus, on the Via Tiburtina, an inscription was discovered in 1881, which stated that the "sacred caverns" had been restored *præsule Virgilio*. The example of Virgilius and his successors in the See of Rome was followed by private individuals. The tomb of Crysanthus and Daria on the Via Salaria was restored, after the retreat of the barbarians, *pauperis ex censu*, that is to say, with the modest means of a devotee.

Nibby has attributed the origin of cemeteries within the walls to the invasion of Vitiges, burial within the city limits having been strictly forbidden by the laws of Rome. But the law seems to have been practically disregarded even before the Gothic wars. Christians were buried in the Prætorian camp, and in the gardens of Mæcenas, during the reign of Theodoric (493-526). I have mentioned this particular because it marks another step towards the abandonment of suburban cemeteries. The country around Rome having become insecure and deserted, it was deemed necessary to place within the protection of the city walls the bodies of martyrs who had been buried at a great distance from the gates. The first translation took place in 648: the second in 682, when the bodies of Primus and Felicianus were removed from Nomentum, and those of Viatrix, Faustinus and Simplicius from the *Lucus Arvalium* (Monte delle Piche, by la Magliana). The last blow to the catacombs was given by Paschal I. (817-824). Contemporary documents mention innumerable transferences of bodies. The mosaic legend of the apse of S. Prassede says that Pope Paschal buried the bodies of many saints within its walls.[152]

The official catalogue of the remains removed on July 20, 817, which was compiled by the Pope's notary and engraved on marble, has come down to us. It speaks of the translation of twenty-three hundred bodies, most of which were buried under the chapel of S. Zeno, which Paschal I. had built as a memorial to his mother, Theodora Episcopa. The legend in the apse of S. Cæcilia speaks, likewise, of the transference to her church of bodies "which had formerly reposed in crypts" (*quæ primum in cryptis pausabant*): among them those of Cæcilia herself, Valerianus, Tiburtius, and Maximus. The finding and removal of Cæcilia's remains from the Catacombs of Callixtus is one of the most graceful episodes in the life of Paschal I. He describes it at length in a letter addressed to the people of Rome.

After many unsuccessful attempts to discover the coffin of the saint, he had come to the conclusion that it must have been stolen by the Lombards, when they were besieging the city in 755. S. Cæcilia, however, told him in a vision where her grave was; and hurrying to the catacombs of the Appian Way he at last discovered her crypt and coffin, together with those of fourteen Popes, from Zephyrinus to Melchiades. It is only fair to say that the discoveries made in this very crypt, between 1850 and 1853, confirm the account of Paschal in its minutest details.

The first half of the ninth century thus marks the final abandonment of the catacombs, and the cessation of divine worship in their historical crypts. In later times we find little or no mention of them in Church annals. When we read of Nicholas I. (858-867) and of Paschal II. (1099-1118) visiting the cemeteries, we must believe that their visits were to the basilicas erected over the catacombs, and to their special crypts, not to the catacombs themselves. In the chronicle of the monastery of S. Michael ad Mosam we read of a pilgrim of the eleventh century who obtained relics of saints "from the keeper of a certain cemetery, in which lamps are always burning." He refers to the basilica of S. Valentine and the small hypogæum attached to it (discovered in 1887), not to catacombs in the true sense of the word. The very last account referring directly to them dates from the time of Pope Nicholas I. (858-867) who is said to have restored the crypt of Mark on the Via Ardeatina, and of Felix, Abdon, and Sennen on the Via Portuensis. At this time also the visits of pilgrims, to whose itineraries, or guidebooks, we are indebted for so much knowledge of the topography of suburban cemeteries, come to an end. The best itineraries are those of Einsiedeln, Salzburg, Wurzburg, and William of Malmesbury; and the list of the oils from the lamps burning before the tombs of martyrs, which were collected by John, abbot of Monza, at the request of queen Theodolinda. The pilgrims left many records of their visits scratched on the walls of the sanctuaries; and to these *graffiti* also we are indebted for much information, since they contain formulas of devotion addressed to the saint of the place. They are very interesting in their simplicity of thought and diction, as are generally the memoirs of early pilgrims and pilgrimages. I shall mention one, discovered not many years ago in the cemetery of Mustiola at Chiusi. It is a plain tombstone, inscribed with the words:—

HIC · POSITUS · EST · PEREGRINUS · CICONIAS · CUIUS ·
NOMEN · DEUS · SCIT

"Here is buried a pilgrim from Thrace, whose name is known only to God." The tale is simple and touching. A pilgrim on his way to Rome, or back to his country, was overtaken by death at Chiusi, before he could make himself known to those who had come to his help. They could only suppose he had come from Thrace, the country of the Cicones, possibly from the language he spoke, or from the costume he wore.

On May 31, 1578, a workman, while digging a sandpit in the vineyard of Bartolomeo Sanchez at the second milestone of the Via Salaria, came upon a Christian cemetery containing frescoes, sarcophagi, and inscriptions. This unexpected discovery created a great sensation,[153] and the report was circulated that an underground city had been found. The leading men of the age hastened to the spot; among them Baronius, who speaks of these wondrous crypts three or four times in his annals.[154] It seems that the network of galleries, crossing one another at various angles, the skylights, the wells, the symmetry of the cubiculi and arcosolia, the number of loculi with which the sides of the galleries were honeycombed, affected the imagination of visitors even more than the pictures, the sarcophagi, and the epitaphs. The subjects of the frescoes were so varied as to contain almost the whole cycle of early Christian symbolism. There were the Good Shepherd and the Praying Soul, Noah and the ark, Daniel and the lions, Moses striking the rock, the story of Jonah, the sacrifice of Isaac, the three men in the fiery furnace, the resurrection of Lazarus, etc. The bas-reliefs of the marble coffins represented Christian love-feasts and pastoral scenes. The epitaphs contained simply names, except one, which was raised by a girl "to her sweet nurse Paulina, who dwells in Christ among the blessed." These pious memorials of the primitive church led the learned visitors to investigate their meaning and value, as well as the history and name of those mysterious labyrinths. The origin of Christian archæology, therefore, really dates from May 1, 1578. Antonio Bosio, the Columbus of subterranean Rome, was but three years old at that time, but he seems to have developed his marvellous instinct on the strength of what he saw in the Vigna Sanchez in his boyhood. The crypts, however, had but a short life: the quarry-men damaged and robbed them to such an extent that, when Bosio began his career in 1593, every trace of them had disappeared. They have never been found since. We can only point out to the lover of these studies the site of the Vigna Sanchez. It is marked by a monumental gate, on the right side of the Via Salaria, crowned by the well-known coat-of-arms of the della Rovere family, to whom the property was sold towards the end of the sixteenth century. The gate is a little more than a mile from the Porta Salaria.

From that time to the first quarter of the present century, we have to tell the same long tale of destruction. And who were responsible for this wholesale pillage? The very men—Aringhi, Boldetti, Marangoni, Bottari—who devoted their lives, energies and talents to the study of the catacombs, and to whom we are indebted for many standard works on Christian archæology. Such was the spirit of the age. Whether an historical inscription came out of one cemetery or another did not matter to them; the topographical importance of discoveries was not appreciated. Written or engraved memorials were sought, not for the sake of the history of the place to which they belonged, but to ornament houses, museums, villas, churches and monasteries. In 1863, de Rossi found a portion of the Cemetery of Callixtus, near the tombs of the Popes, in incredible confusion and disorder: loculi ransacked, their contents stolen, their inscriptions broken and scattered far and wide, and the bones themselves taken out of their graves. The perpetrators of the outrage had taken care to leave their names written in charcoal or with the smoke of tallow candles; they were men employed by Boldetti in his explorations of the catacombs, between 1713 and 1717. Some of the tombstones were removed by him to S. Maria in Trastevere, and inserted in the floor of the nave. Benedict XIV. took away the best, and placed them in the Vatican Library. They have now migrated again to the Museo Epigrafico of the Lateran Palace. Those left in the floor of S. Maria in Trastevere were removed to the vestibule of the church in 1865.

In 1714, some beautiful paintings of the first century were discovered in the crypt of the Flavian family (Domitilla) at Torre Marancia. They were examined by well-known archæologists and churchmen, whose names are scratched or written on the walls: Boldetti, Marangoni, Bottari, Leonardo da Porto Maurizio, and G.B. de Rossi (the last two since canonized by the Church), and by hundreds of priests, nuns, missionaries, and pilgrims. No mention is made of this beautiful discovery in contemporary books; but an attempt was made to steal the frescoes, which resulted, as usual, in their total destruction.[155] The catacombs owe their sad fate to the riches which they contained. In times of persecution, when the *fossores* were pressed by too much work and memorial tablets could not be secured in time, it was customary for the survivors to mark the graves of the dear ones either with a symbol, a word, or a date scratched in the fresh cement; or with some object of identification, such as glass cups, medallions, cameos, intaglios, objects cut in rock crystal, coral, etc. If the work of exploration has been carried on actively in the last three centuries, it is on account of the rich harvest which searching parties were sure to reap whenever they chanced to come across a catacomb or part of a catacomb, yet unexplored, with these signs of recognition untouched.

The best works of the glyptic art, the rarest gems, coins, and medallions of European cabinets have come to light in this way. Pietro Sante Bartoli, who chronicled the discoveries made in Rome in the second half of the seventeenth century, speaks several times of treasure-trove in catacombs.[156]

"In a Christian cemetery discovered outside the Porta Portese, in the vineyard of a priest named degli Effetti, many relics of martyrs have been found, a beautiful set of the rarest medallions (*bellissima serie di medaglioni rarissimi*), works in metal and crystal, engraved stones, jewels, and other curios and interesting objects, many of which were sold by the workmen at low prices." And again: "The opening of a catacomb was discovered by accident under the Casaletto of Pius V., outside the Porta S. Pancrazio. Although the crypt had never been entered, and promised to be very rich, no excavations were attempted, owing to the dangerous condition of the rock. One object only was extracted from the ruinous cavern; a polychrome cameo of marvellous beauty (*di meravigliosa bellezza*) representing a Bacchanalian. The stone measured sixteen inches in length by ten in width. It was given to cardinal Massimi."[157]

The number of catacombs has been greatly exaggerated. Panvinius and Baronius stated it as forty-three; Aringhi and his followers raised this number to sixty. De Rossi, however, in vol. i., p. 206, of the "Roma sotterranea" proves that the number of catacombs excavated during the first three centuries, within a radius of three miles from the walls of Servius Tullius, is but twenty-six; besides eleven of much less importance, and five which were excavated after the Peace of Constantine.

It would be impossible to give even a summary description of these forty-two cemeteries, within the limits of the present chapter. De Rossi's account of Lucina's crypts in the Cemetery of Callixtus occupies one hundred and thirty-two folio pages, and has required thirty-five plates of illustration. I must confine myself to the mention of the few discoveries, connected with the history and topography of underground Rome, which have come within my personal experience, or which I have had occasion to study.

THE CATACOMBS OF GENEROSA. In 1867, while watching with my friend commendatore Visconti (the present director of the Vatican Museum) the excavations of the Sacred Grove of the Arvales, on the Via Campana, five miles outside the Porta Portese, I witnessed for the first time the discovery of a catacomb. The experience could not have been more pleasant, nor the history of the first occupants of these crypts more interesting.

In the persecution of Diocletian two brothers, Simplicius and Faustinus, were tortured and put to death for their faith, and their bodies were thrown into the Tiber from the bridge of Æmilius Lepidus. The stream carried them to a considerable distance, and their young sister Beatrix, who was anxiously watching the banks of the river for the recovery of their dear remains, discovered them lying in the shallows of la Magliana, near the grove of the Arvales. She buried them in a small Christian cemetery which a certain Generosa had excavated close by, under the boundary line of the grove itself. Beatrix, left alone in the world, found shelter in the house of one of the Lucinas; but the persecutors, to whom her pious action had evidently been reported, discovered her retreat, and killed her by suffocation, seven months after the execution of Simplicius and Faustinus. Lucina laid her to rest in the same cemetery of Generosa, by the side of her brothers. This touching story is related in contemporary documents.

Pope Damasus, who in his younger days had been notary and stenographer of the church of Rome, and was acquainted with every detail of the last persecution, raised a small oratory to the memory of the three martyrs, and sanctified the ground which for eleven centuries had been the seat of the worship of the Dea Dia. The chapel lasted until the pontificate of Leo II., when it became evident that the only way of saving the remains of Beatrix, Simplicius, and Faustinus from profanation and robbery, was to remove them from a place so conspicuous for many miles around, and directly in the path of pirates and invaders from the sea, and to place them under the protection of the city walls. The translation took place in 682; the bodies were removed to the church of Santa Biviana, or the Bibiana, on the Esquiline, and placed in a sarcophagus, with the record: "Here lie in peace Simplicius and Faustinus, martyrs, drowned in the Tiber and buried in the cemetery of Generosa, above the landing-place called ad Sextum Philippi." Sarcophagus and inscription are still in existence. The discovery of the oratory of Pope Damasus and the cemetery of Generosa took place, as already stated, in the spring of 1867, when a fragment of the architrave of the altar was found in front of the apse, inscribed with the names, ······ STINO · VIATRICI, engraved in the best Damasian calligraphy. The spelling of the second name deserves attention, because it is certainly intentional, as Damasus and his engraver Furius Dionysius Philocalus are distinguished for absolute epigraphic correctness. *Viatrix*, the feminine of *Viator*, is altogether different from *Beatrix*, and has its own Christian meaning, as an allusion to the eventful journey of human life. Must we take the word *Beatrix* as a new form, more or less connected with the adjective *beatus*, or as a corruption of the genuine name? No doubt it is a corruption, as the oldest martyrologies and liturgies have the genuine spelling. The substitution of the B instead of the V took place in the eighth or ninth century, and appears for the first time in the Codex of Berne. The grammarian who wrote it was evidently of the opinion that *Viatrix* was not the right spelling; and so the true and beautiful name of the sister of Faustinas and Simplicius became corrupted.

The accompanying illustration represents the portrait of Viatrix discovered in the Catacomb of Generosa in the spring of 1868.

THE CEMETERY OF DOMITILLA. The farm of Torre Marancia, at the crossing of the Via Ardeatina and the Via delle Sette Chiese, is familiar to archæologists on account of the successful excavations which the duchess of Chablais made there in the spring of the years 1817 and 1822. Bartolomeo Borghesi, who first visited them in April, 1817, describes the remains of a noble villa of the first century, with mosaic pavements, fountains,

Sancta Viatrix.

statuary, candelabra, and frescos. The pictures of Pasiphae, Canace, Phædra, Myrrha, and Scylla, which are now in the Cabinet of the Aldobrandini Marriage, in the Vatican Library, were discovered in one of the bedrooms of the villa. Other works of art, now exhibited in the third compartment of the Galleria dei Candelabri, were found in the peristyle. An exact description of these discoveries, with maps and illustrations, is given by Marchese Biondi in a volume called "Monumenti Amaranziani," published in Rome in 1825.

The Villa Amaranthiana, from which the modern name of Torre Marancia is derived, belonged to two ladies, one of imperial descent, Flavia Domitilla, a relative of Domitian and Titus, the other of patrician birth, Munatia Procula, the daughter of Marcus. Domitilla's name appears twice in documents attesting her ownership of the ground; the first is the grant of a sepulchral area, measuring thirty-five feet by forty, to Sergius Cornelius Julianus *ex indulgentia Flaviæ Domitillæ*; the other mentions the construction of another tomb, *Flaviæ Domitillæ divi Vespasiani neptis beneficio.*[158] These concessions refer to burial-plots above ground, on the Via Ardeatina. Much more important was the permission given by Domitilla for the excavation of a catacomb in the service of the Church, which had just been established in Rome by the apostles. The catacomb consisted originally of two sections; one for the use of those members of the imperial Flavian family who had been converted to the gospel, and one for common use. I have already given a brief account of the first (see p. 10). The entrance to the crypts was built in a conspicuous place, under the safeguard of the law which guaranteed the inviolability of private tombs. The place can still be visited. On each side of the entrance are apartments for the celebration of anniversary banquets, the αγαπαι or love-feasts of the early Church. Those on the left are decorated in the so-called Pompeian style, with birds and festoons on a red ground. Here is the well, the drinking-fountain, the washing-trough, and the wardrobe. On the opposite side is the *schola*, or banqueting-room, with benches on three sides. There is no doubt that the builders and owners of these crypts were Christians; because the graves within were arranged for the interment of bodies, not for cremation; that is, for sarcophagi and coffins, not for cinerary urns; and, as I stated at the beginning of the previous chapter, the pagans of the first century, and of the first half of the second, were never interred. The Domitilla after whom the catacombs were named was a niece of Vespasian, *Divi Vespasiani neptis*. The reader will remember that in chapter i. I quoted Xiphilinus as saying that in the year 95 some members of the imperial family were condemned by Domitian on the charge of atheism, together with other leading personages, who had adopted "the customs and persuasion of the Jews,"—an expression which means the Christian faith. Among those condemned he mentions Clemens and Domitilla, whose genealogy is still subject to some uncertainty. 337

A tombstone discovered in 1741, by Marangoni, in these very catacombs, mentions two names, Flavius Sabinus and Flavia Titiana. They are descendants, perhaps grandchildren, of Flavius Sabinus, the brother of Vespasian. Sabinus was prefect of Rome during the persecution of Nero; but Tacitus[159] describes him as a gentle man, who hated violence (*mitem virum abhorrentem a sanguine et cædibus*). His second son, Titus Flavius Clemens, consul A. D. 82, was executed in 95 on account of his Christian faith; and Flavia Domitilla, his daughter-in-law, was banished for the same cause to the island Pandataria. There is a record of the banishment of another Flavia Domitilla to the island of Pontia; but her genealogy and relationship with the former have not been yet clearly established. Some writers, however, have identified her with the niece of Vespasian, mentioned in the inscription referred to above, as owner of the villa of Torre Marancia and founder of the catacombs. The small island, where she spent many years in solitary confinement, is described by S. Jerome as one of the leading places of pilgrimage in the fourth century of our era.

The "Acta Martyrum" state that Flavia Domitilla, niece of Flavius Clemens, was buried at Terracina, with her attendants, Theodora and Euphrosyne; and that her body-servants, or *cubicularii*, Nereus and Achilleus, who were executed for the same reason, were laid to rest in the crypts of the Villa Amaranthiana, half a mile from Rome, near the tomb of Petronilla, the so-called daughter of S. Peter. In the early itineraries the place is also indicated as the "cemetery of Domitilla, Nereus, and Achilleus, near Santa Petronilla." Bosio discovered it towards the end of the sixteenth century, and mistook it for the Cemetery of Callixtus. The discoveries made in 1873 leave no doubt as to its identification with the famous burial-place 338 of the Flavians; they brought to light, not a crypt of ordinary dimensions, but a basilica equal in size to the one dedicated to S. Lorenzo by Constantine.

Basilica of Nereus, Achilleus and Petronilla.

The pavement of the basilica is sunk to the level of the second floor of the catacombs, in order that the graves of Nereus, Achilleus, and Petronilla could be enclosed in the altar, without being raised, or touched at all. The body of the church is divided into nave and aisles by two rows of columns, mostly of *cipollino*, some of which were stolen in 1871 by the farmer; the others were found in 1876 lying on the floor, in parallel lines from northeast to southwest, as if they had been overthrown by an earthquake.

A fragment of one of the four columns which supported the ciborium above the high altar has been found in the apse. This fragment contains a bas-relief representing the execution of a martyr. The young man is tied to a stake, which is surmounted by a cross-beam, like a T, the true shape of the *patibulum cruciforme*. A soldier, dressed in a tunic and mantle, seizes the prisoner with the right hand, and stabs him in the neck with the left. The weapon used is not a lictor's axe, nor the sword of a legionary, but a sort of cutlass, which would be more likely to cut the throat than to sever the head from the body. The cross is crowned by a triumphal wreath, as a symbol of the immortal recompense which awaits the confessor of the Faith. The historical value of this rare sculpture is determined by the name, ACILLEVS, engraved above it.

The character of the letters and the style of the bas-relief are those of the second half of the fourth century. Of the sister column, with the name and martyrdom of NEREVS, only a small bit has been found. Another monument of equal value is a broken slab containing, in the first line, the letters ····RVM; in the second, the letters ····ORVM; and below these, the cross-shaped anchor, the mysterious but certain emblem of Christian hope. As the position of the symbol determines the middle point of the inscription, it is easy to reconstruct the whole text, by a careful calculation of the size of each letter:—

The Execution of Acilleus.

"the tomb of the Flavian family," namely, of those relatives of Domitilla who had embraced the Christian faith.

Under the pavement of the nave, aisles, and presbytery, are numberless graves, some of which belong to the original catacombs, before they were cut and disarranged by the building of the basilica; others are built in accordance with the architectural lines of the basilica itself. A grave belonging to the first series, that is, to a gallery of the catacombs which had been blocked by the foundations of the left aisle, bears the date of the year 390; while a sarcophagus placed at the foot of the altar is dated Monday, May 12, 395. It is evident, therefore, that the basilica was built between 390 and 395, during the pontificate of Siricius.

No memorial of Petronilla, the third saint for whom the building was named, has been found within the sacred enclosure,—a fact not wholly unexpected, because the coffin in which her remains were placed is known to have been removed to the Vatican by Paul I. (755-756), at the request of the king of France. In November, 1875, a cubiculum was found at the back of the apse, connected with it by a corridor which opens near the episcopal chair. The walls of this passage are covered with *graffiti* and other records of pilgrims. The cubiculum contains two graves: one empty, in the arcosolium, the place of honor; the other, in front of it, of a much later date. The front of the arcosolium is closed by a wall, on the surface of which is an interesting fresco, which is here reproduced.

Petronilla and Veneranda.

The younger figure, on the right, is Petronilla Martyr; the elder is a matron named Veneranda, buried January 7 (DEP*osita* VI. IDVS. IANVARIAS), in the sarcophagus below the picture. There is no doubt that Petronilla was buried in close proximity to this cubiculum. The story of her relationship to S. Peter has no foundation whatever; it rests on an etymological mistake, by which the name Petronilla is treated as a diminutive of Petrus, as is Plautilla of Plautius or Plautia, and Domitilla of Domitius or Domitia. Petrus is not a Latin name; it came into use with the spreading of the gospel, and only in rare and exceptional cases. The young martyr was named after a member of the same Flavian family to which this cemetery belonged, Titus Flavius Petron, an uncle of Vespasian. Her kinship with the apostle must consequently be taken in a spiritual sense.

Towards the end of 1881 another remarkable discovery took place in these catacombs: that of a cubiculum which in style of decoration is unique. It looks more like the room of a Pompeian house than a Christian crypt. Its architectural paintings with groups of frail columns supporting fantastic friezes, and enclosing pastoral landscapes, might be compared to the frescoes of the Golden House of Nero, or those of the house of Germanicus on the Palatine; but they find no parallel in "subterranean Rome."

The name of the owner of this conspicuous tomb is engraved above the arcosolium: AMPLIATI. The size and the beauty of the letters, the peculiarity of a single cognomen in a possessive case, the fact that a man of inferior condition[160] should own such a tomb; that at a later period, a staircase had been cut through the rock, to provide a direct communication between the Via Ardeatina and the tomb, for the accommodation of pilgrims; the care used to keep the tomb in good order, as shown by later restorations,—all these circumstances make us believe that Ampliatus was a prominent leader of our early Christian community.

Such being the case, the mind runs at once to the paragraph of S. Paul's Epistle to the Romans (xvi. 8): "Salute Ampliatus my beloved in the Lord," and one feels inclined to kneel before the tomb of the dear friend of the apostle. However, when discoveries of this kind happen, it is wise to proceed with caution, and examine every detail from a sceptical point of view. Doubtless the cubiculum of Ampliatus was made and painted in the first century of our era. The type of the letters engraved above the tomb is peculiar to painted or written inscriptions of the beginning of the second century. It is possible, therefore, that the name was at first painted on the white plaster, and engraved on marble many years after the deposition of Ampliatus. As regards Ampliatus himself, it is true that according to Greek tradition he died when Bishop of Mœsia,[161] but the tradition is derived from an apocryphal source. There are those who doubt whether all the salutations contained in S. Paul's epistle are really addressed to the faithful residing in Rome and belonging to the Roman community.[162] Another difficulty arises from the fact that in the same cubiculum a tombstone has been found, inserted in the wall above the arcosolium, between two painted peacocks, with this inscription: "Aurelius Ampliatus and his son Gordianus have placed this memorial to Aurelia Bonifatia, wife and mother incomparable, and truly chaste, who lived 25 years, 2 months, 4 days, and 2 hours." Although the name Aurelius is not uncommon on tombstones of the first century in this very Cemetery of Domitilla, there is no doubt that the tablet of Aurelia Bonifatia belongs to a later period. The name Bonifatius—derived from *bonum fatum*, not from *bonum facere* as commonly believed—did not come into use before the middle of the second century. At all events, Ampliatus, husband of Bonifatia and father of Gordianus, may be the son, grandson, or even a later descendant of the man in whose memory the cubiculum was originally built.

Shall we recognize in this man the friend of S. Paul? I do not think the question can as yet be answered with certainty. Further excavations in the galleries radiating from the crypt may disclose fresh particulars, and supply more conclusive evidence.

The discoveries of which a summary description has here been given deserve a place of honor in the comments to Suetonius' "Lives of the Emperors." The exploration of underground Rome must be greeted with pleasure, not only by the pious believers in Christ and his martyrs, but also by agnostic students of classical history. A tombstone, which on one side is inscribed with the records of the victories gained by the imperial legions, on the other with the simple and humble name of a Christian who has given his life for his faith, is a monument worthy the consideration of all thoughtful men. Christian archæology has an intimate and indissoluble connection with classical studies, and there is no discovery referring to the first century of Christianity which does not throw new and often unexpected light on general history, art, and science. Those made at Torre Marancia in 1875 illustrate the history of Rome and the Campagna, after the fall of the empire. In the niche where the episcopal chair was placed,— behind the high altar, in the middle of the apse,—a rough hand has sketched the figure of a priest, dressed in a casula, in the act of preaching from his seat. This sketch reminds us of Gregory the Great, when in this very cemetery of Nereus and Achilleus, in this very apse, he read one of his homilies from this episcopal chair, deploring to the panic-stricken congregation the state of the city, the queen of the world, desolated by famine, by pestilence, and by the Lombards, who at that very moment were burning and plundering the villas and farms of the surrounding Campagna. 345

CEMETERY AD CATACUMBAS.[163] The cemetery near the church of S. Sebastiano was originally called in an indefinite way *cimiterium ad catacumbas*. The etymology of the name is uncertain. De Rossi suggests the roots *cata*, a Græco-Latin preposition of the decadence, signifying "near," and *cumba*, a resting-place. The word would therefore mean *apud accubitoria*, "near the resting-places," an allusion to the many tombs which surrounded the old crypt above and below ground. This crypt dates from apostolic times, or, at all events, from a period much earlier than the martyrdom of Sebastian, the Christian officer whose name it now bears.

The great interest of the cemetery is derived from the shelter which the bodies of the apostles are said to have had in its recesses during the fiercest times of persecution. The temporary transferment of the remains of SS. Peter and Paul, from their graves on the Via Cornelia and the Via Ostiensis, to the catacombs, is not a mere tradition. It is described by Pope Damasus in a metric inscription published by de Rossi,[164] and by Pope Gregory in an epistle to the empress Constantina, no. 30 of book iv. A curious entry in the calendar called *Bucherianum*, from its first editor, seems to point to a double transferment. The entry is dated June 29, A. D. 258:— 346

Tertio Kalendas Julias, Tusco et Basso consulibus, Petri in Vaticano, Pauli in via Ostiensis—utriusque in Catacumbas.

Since, in early calendars, the date is only appended in case of transferment of remains, archæologists have suggested the theory that the bodies of the apostles may possibly have found shelter in the catacombs of the Appian Way a second time, during the persecution of Valerian (A. D. 258). Marchi asserts that the evidences of a double concealment are still to be found in the frescoes of the crypt, some of which belong to the first, others to the third, century; but this hardly seems to be the case. I lowered myself into the hiding-place on February 23 of the present year, and, after careful examination, have come to the conclusion that its paintings are by one hand and of one epoch, the epoch of Damasus. However, whether they were laid there once or twice, its temporary connection with the apostles made the "locus ad catacumbas" one of the great suburban sanctuaries. The cubiculum, called Platonia, was decorated by Damasus with marble incrustations. According to the Acts of S. Sebastian (January 20) he expressed the wish to be buried "ad catacumbas, at the entrance of the crypt, near the memorial of the apostles." These events were represented in the frescoes of the old portico of S. Peter's, destroyed in 1606-1607 by Paul V. One of them 347 showed the bodies of the apostles, bandaged like mummies, being lowered into the place of concealment; the other, Lucina and Cornelius bringing back the bodies to their original graves in the Via Cornelia and the Via Ostiensis.

A remarkable monument was discovered in the crypt four years ago. It is a marble bust, or rather the fragment of a bust, of the Redeemer, with locks of hair descending on each shoulder,[165] a work of the fourth century.

It is well known that the oldest representations of the Redeemer are purely ideal. He appears as a young man, with no beard, his hair arranged in the Roman style, wearing a short tunic, and showing the amiable countenance of the Good Shepherd. I give here a characteristic specimen of this type, a statue of the first quarter of the third century, now in the Lateran Museum.[166] Whether performing one of the miracles which prove his divinity, or teaching the new doctrine to the disciples, the type never varies. It is evident that the Christian painters or sculptors of the first three centuries, in drawing or modelling the head of Jesus, had no intention of making a likeness, but only a conventional type, noble and classic, and suggestive of the eternal youth of the Word. A new tendency appears in Christian art towards the middle of the fourth century, the attempt to reproduce the genuine portrait of Christ, or what was regarded as such by the Orientals. The change was a consequence of the peace and freedom given to the Church, and of the cessation of that overbearing contempt in which the Gentiles had held a religion which they believed to be that of the vile followers of a crucified Jew. It 348 had been considered prudent, at the outset, to present the Redeemer to the neophytes, who were not yet entirely free from pagan ideas, in a type which was familiar and pleasing to the Roman eye, rather than with the characteristics of a despised race. The triumph of the Church made these precautions unnecessary, and then arose the desire of exhibiting a truer portraiture of Christ. The first addition to the conventional type was that of the beard, and probably of the hair parted in the middle.

Ancient writers have left but little information about the personal appearance of the Saviour; and the vagueness of their accounts proves the absence of a type which was universally recognized as authentic. Many documents concerning this subject must be rejected as forgeries of a later age. Such is the pretended letter of Lentulus, governor of Judæa, to the Senate, describing the appearance of Jesus. In the same way we should regard the images attributed to Nicodemus and Luke, and those called *acheiropitæ* (not painted by human hands), like the famous one of the chapel of the Sancta Sanctorum,[167] the first historical mention of

The portrait head of Jesus in the Sancta Sanctorum

which dates from A. D. 752, when Pope Stephen II. carried it in a procession from the Lateran to S. Maria Maggiore, to obtain divine protection against Aistulphus. Garrucci questions whether it may not be that of Camulianus, described by Gregory of Nyssa; or a copy of the image alleged to have been sent by the Saviour himself to Abgar, king of Edessa,[168] with an autograph letter. Must we consider these and other portraits, like the "Volto Santo" in the Vatican, as fanciful as the old youthful Roman type of the Good Shepherd? There can be no doubt that in some provinces of the East, like Palestine, Syria, and Phœnicia, the oral traditions about the personal appearance of the Saviour were kept for many generations. It is also probable that the tradition was confirmed by some work of art, like the celebrated group of Paneas (Bâniäs). With regard to this, Eusebius says that the woman with the issue of blood, grateful to the Saviour for her cure (Mark v., 25-34), caused a statue, representing Him in the act of performing the miracle, to be set up in front of her house; that it still existed when he wrote, and was held in great veneration throughout Palestine and the whole East. Sozomenos adds that Julian the Apostate substituted his own statue for it, but that the imperial image was struck by lightning. This excited the wrath of the pagans to such an extent that they destroyed the group of Christ and the Woman, which Julian had caused to be removed. Cassiodorus, Rufinus, Kedrenos, and Malala, assert that the head was saved from destruction. It has been suggested that the group did not represent the woman at the feet of the Saviour, but a conquered province kneeling before the Roman emperor and addressing him as her Saviour (ΣΩΤΗΡΙ). But this explanation seems more ingenious than probable, because it implies that Christians, Eusebius included, had mistaken the portrait of a Roman conqueror for that of Christ, which would have been so different in type, dress, and attitude. At all events, the belief that the group of Bâniäs was a genuine likeness was general in the fourth century. Eusebius contributed to make it known in the Western world; and to this diffusion we probably owe the second type of the Saviour's physiognomy, the bearded face, the large impressive eyes, the hair parted in the middle, and falling in locks on the shoulders.[169]

To this type belongs the bust discovered four years ago in the "locus ad catacumbas." According to an ingenious hypothesis of Bottari, adopted by de Rossi, the Paneas group is represented on the Lateran sarcophagus, engraved by Roller in the second volume of his "Catacombs," plate 58.

THE CEMETERY OF CYRIACA. This, the principal cemetery of the Via Tiburtina, was excavated in the hill above the basilica of S. Lorenzo fuori le Mura. It is the one with which I have had most to do, because the building of the new Camposanto, together with the sinking of the foundations of the new tombs, has been the occasion of frequent discoveries. One of the characteristic features of Cyriaca's cemetery is the large number of military inscriptions from the prætorian camp which were used to close the graves, the name of the deceased Christian being engraved on the blank side of the slab. On December 23, 1876, a landslide of considerable extent took place along the southern face of the rock in which the catacombs are excavated, in consequence of which many loculi, arcosolia, and painted cubicula were laid open. I happened to witness the accident, and was able to direct the exploration of the graves. Among the objects discovered, I remember a pair of silver earrings, a necklace of gold and emeralds, sixteen inches long, clay objects of various kinds, gladiatorial and theatrical lamps, and nine Christian tombstones. One of them was engraved on the back of a slab from the prætorian camp, containing the roster of one hundred and fifty soldiers from the twelfth and fourteenth city cohorts (*cohortes urbanæ*). Each individual has his prænomen, nomen, and cognomen, carefully indicated, together with the names of his father, tribe, and country. The men are grouped in companies, which are indicated by the name of their captains, such as the "company of Marcellus" or the "company of Tranquillinus," with the consular date of the year in which Marcellus and Tranquillinus were in command of that company. Another part of the same roster, engraved on a slab of the same marble and size, and containing many more names, was found a century and a half ago in the same place, and removed to the Vatican Museum.

352

Landslip in the Cemetery of Cyriaca.

One of the tombs, discovered during the following January, seems to have belonged to a lady of rank. A gold necklace and a pair of opal earrings were found in the earth which filled the grave. Relatives or friends of the occupants of the cubiculum had written on the plaster words of affection and devotion, such as "Gaianus, live in Christ with Procula;" "Semplicius, live in Christ."

It is to be regretted that, in order to make room for the daily victims of death, the municipality of Rome should be obliged to turn out of their graves the faithful of the third and fourth centuries who were buried in the neighborhood of S. Lorenzo. In 1876 I witnessed the discovery of a section of the old cemetery at the foot of the hill of Cyriaca. The tombs were mostly sarcophagi, with reliefs, the subjects of which are taken from the Bible. One of them, carved in the rude but pathetic style of the fifth century, represents the crossing of the Red Sea, and the Egyptian hosts, led by Pharaoh, following closely on the Jews. The waves are closing over the persecutors, just as the last of the fugitives emerges safely on the land. The "column of fire" is

Inscription from the tombstone of a dentist.

represented, according to the Vitruvian rules, with base and capital; and the costumes of the warriors of the Nile are those of Roman *gregarii*, or privates, under Constantine. Another sarcophagus shows the Virgin Mary, with the infant Saviour in her arms, receiving the offering of the Eastern kings. A third represents a sort of pageant of court dignitaries of one of the Valentinians. Besides these and many other pieces of sculpture seventy-two inscriptions or fragments of inscriptions were dug up, mostly from the pavement of a ruined chapel, one of the seven by which the basilica of S. Lorenzo was surrounded in ancient times.

353

Another

Inscription from the grave of Alexander, a dentist.

inscription, discovered in 1864, deserves attention on account of the instruments which are engraved upon it. It is a fragment from the tomb of a dentist named Victorinus, or Celerinus, with the representation of the instruments he used in extracting teeth. Such representations are by no means rare on

Surgeon's instruments; relief on a tombstone.

gravestones. The other two specimens reproduced here are also from the catacombs. Alexander was a dentist; the unknown owner of the other slab was a general surgeon, yet the symbol of dentistry occupies the prominent place in his display of tools. In my experience of Roman or Latin excavations, in which thousands of tombs have been brought to light, I have hardly ever met with a skull the teeth of which showed symptoms of decay, or evidence of having been operated upon by a professional hand. Specimens of filling are even more rare than those of gold plating. Of this latter process we have now a beautiful sample in a skull discovered in the excavations of Faleria, and exhibited in the Faliscan Museum at the Villa

354

Giulia, outside the Porta del Popolo. The gold socket or plating of three molar teeth is still in excellent condition. And here I may recall the ancient law, mentioned by Cicero (De Leg. ii. 24), which made it illegal to bury a body with gold, except such as had been used in fastening the teeth.

THE CEMETERY AD DUAS LAUROS (of SS. Peter and Marcellinus).[170] To the left of the second milestone of the Via Labicana there was an imperial villa, named *ad Duas Lauros* (the two laurels), where the empress Helena was buried by Constantine, and Valentinian III. was murdered when playing with other youths, in 455. Adjoining the tomb of the empress, which was described in chapter iv., pp. 197 sq., were two cemeteries,—one above ground, belonging to the "Equites Singulares," or body guards; the other, below. The latter was the largest of the Via Labicana, and was known in early Church annals under the same name as the imperial villa. In 1880-82 a third and deeper network of galleries was excavated for the sake of extracting the pozzolana, the beds of which support the tufa and the catacombs excavated in it. Some damage was done to the tombs, but the Italian proverb *Non tutto il male viene per nuocere* proved true once more on this occasion. The excavation of the catacombs, which is generally a difficult and costly work, and sometimes impossible, when the owner of the ground above them objects to this form of trespassing on his estate, here became an easy matter, the earth being simply thrown into the sandpits from the catacombs above. The discoveries made on this occasion, added to the descriptions and drawings left by former explorers, give us a thorough knowledge of these labyrinths. The impression which they make at first is rather poor; but this is due chiefly to the ravages committed by early explorers.

The inscriptions are few and not particularly interesting, excepting one, which was discovered in 1873, and is written in excellent style: "Aurelius Theophilus, a citizen of Carrhæ, a man of pure mind and great innocence, at the age of twenty-three has rendered his soul to God, his body to the earth." His native city, the Haran, or Charan of the Bible, where Abraham lived, is known in Church annals as one of the strongholds of paganism in Mesopotamia. When Julian the Apostate led the Roman armies against the Persians, in 362, he halted for some time at Carrhæ, to perform impious and cruel sacrifices in the sanctuary of Luno. A description of the crime is given by Theodoretus in Book III. ch. xxvi. At that time Carrhæ, in spite of its devotion to the old religion, had a bishop named Vitus, who died in 381, and was succeeded by Protogenes. According to Theodoretus, he succeeded in "cultivating that wild field which had been covered with idolatrous thorns." Aurelius Theophilus was probably a contemporary of these events, as the inscription on his tombstone belongs undoubtedly to the end of the fourth century. There are also a few inscriptions scratched on plaster, by pilgrims who visited the three historical crypts of Marcellinus and Peter, Gorgonius, and Tiburtius. To save devout visitors the trouble and danger of crossing the labyrinths, each of these crypts was made accessible directly from the ground above by means of a staircase. The *graffiti* are found mostly on the sides or at the foot of these staircases, or else on the door-posts of the crypts themselves.

The historical and religious associations of this catacomb are summed up and illustrated in a beautiful picture representing the Saviour with S. Paul on his right and S. Peter on his left: and, on a line below, the four martyrs who were buried in the cemetery, Gorgonius, Peter, Marcellinus, and Tiburtius, pointing with their right hands to the Divine Lamb on the mountain. The heads of the two apostles are particularly fine, and the shape of their beards most characteristic. This well-known fresco, preserved in cubiculum no. 25 of Bosio's plan, was discovered in 1851 by de Rossi, in a curious manner. Having obtained from padre Marchi permission to carry the excavations towards the cubiculum, and finding that the work proceeded too slowly for his impatience, he crept on his hands and feet for fifty yards along the narrow gap between the ceiling of the galleries and the earth with which they were filled, and reached the cubiculum nearly suffocated. Here, by means of a skylight which was not obstructed by rubbish, he found that the place was used as a deposit for carrion, as the half-putrefied carcass of a bull was lying under the famous fresco.

Many cubiculi were painted by one artist, whose power of invention was rather restricted. He has but two subjects: the story of Jonah, and the Symbolic Supper. Of this last there are four representations, all reproduced from the same pattern, of which I give an example. A family consisting of father, mother, and children, are sitting around a table, upon which the ιχθυς or fish is served; the banquet is presided over by two mystic figures, Irene or Peace on the left, Agape or Love on the right. The head of the family addresses Peace with these words: "Irene, da calda!" and Love, "Agape, misce mi!" The last words are easily understood: "Give me to drink," the verb *mescere* being still used in the same sense in Tuscany, where a wine-shop is sometimes called a *mescita di vino*. The meaning of the word *calda* is not certain. There is no doubt, as Bötticher says, that the ancients had something to correspond to our tea: but the *calda* seems to have been more than an infusion; apparently it was a mixture of hot water, wine, and drugs, that is, a sort of punch, which was drunk mostly in winter.[171] The names written in charcoal above the principal inscriptions in this illustration are those of Pomponio Leto and his academicians.[172]

Another artist distinguished himself in these catacombs, not from skill in design and color, but from the beautiful subjects chosen by him for the decoration of the walls and ceilings of three cubiculi,—compositions which may be called "The Gospel Illustrated." They have been admirably described and reproduced by photographs and in outline by monsignore Joseph Wilpert, in his book referred to in the note on page 354. The intuition of this learned man in detecting paintings which have been effaced by age, dampness, and smoke is fully appreciated by students of Christian archæology: but on this occasion he accomplished a real *tour de force*. When, on December 19, I entered the cubiculum no. 54, in which the paintings are, and he began to point out to me outlines of figures and objects, I thought he was laboring under an optical delusion; I could see nothing beyond a blackened and mouldy plaster surface. My eyes, however, soon became initiated to the new experience, and able to read the lines of this curious palimpsest. The dark spots soon grew into shape, and lovely groups, inspired by the purest Christian symbolism, appeared on the walls. There are thirteen pictures, representing the following-named subjects: the annunciation, the three magi following the star (which is shaped like the monogram   ), their adoration at Bethlehem, the baptism of our Lord, the last judgment, the healing of the blind, the crippled, and the woman with the issue of blood, the woman of Samaria, the Good Shepherd (twice), the Orantes (twice).

The catacombs of SS. Peter and Marcellinus have another attraction for students. Poor as they are in epitaphs and works of art, they contain hundreds of names of celebrated humanists, archæologists, and artists who explored these depths in the fifteenth and sixteenth centuries, and made record of their visits. When one walks between two lines of graves, in the almost oppressive stillness of the cemetery, with no other company than one's thoughts, the names of Pomponius Letus and his academicians, of Bosio, Panvinio, Avanzini, Severano, Marangoni, Marchi, and d'Agincourt, written in bold letters, give the lonely wanderer the impression of meeting living and dear friends; and one wonders at the great love which these pioneers of "humanism" must have had for antiquities, to have spent days and days, and to have held their conferences and banquets, in places like these.

In chapter i., page 10, of "Ancient Rome," I mentioned Pomponio's Academy, and its visits to the crypts of Callixtus. Since the publication of my book, the subject has been investigated again and illustrated by Giacomo Lombroso[173] and de Rossi.[174] It appears that after the trial which the Academicians underwent at the time of Paul II., and their unexpected liberation from the Castle of S. Angelo, they decided to turn over a new leaf. From a fraternity which was pagan in manners and instincts, which had made itself conspicuous by the use of profane language, and by the celebration of profane meetings over the tombs of the martyrs, they became the "Societas literatorum S. Victoris et sociorum in Esquiliis," a literary society under the patronage of S. Victor and his companion saints, namely, Fortunatus and Genesius. Their *pontifex maximus* became a president; their *sacerdos* a priest, whose duty it was to say mass on certain anniversaries. The most important celebration fell, as before, on April 21, the birthday of Rome. We have a description by an eye-witness, Jacopo Volaterrano, of that which took place in 1483: "On the Esquiline,[175] near the house of Pomponius, the society of literary men has celebrated the birthday of Rome. Divine service was performed by Peter Demetrius of Lucca; Paul Marsus delivered the oration. The dinner was served in the hall adjoining the chapel of S. Salvatore de Cornutis," etc. In 1501, after the death of Pomponius, the anniversary meetings were held on the Capitol; the solemn mass was sung in the church of the Aracœli, while the banquet took place in the Palazzo dei Conservatori. The convivial feast of 1501 was not a success. Burckhardt describes it as *satis feriale et sine bono vino* (commonplace and with no good wine).

Was the conversion of the Academicians a sincere one? We believe it was not; they manifested under Sixtus V. the same feelings which had brought them to justice under Paul II.

In the calendars of the Church of Rome only one name is registered on April 21, that of Pope Victor. His alleged companions, Fortunatus and Genesius, were singled out of old, disused calendars of the church of Africa, unknown to the Latins. Why did the academicians select such enigmatic and obscure protectors? The reason is evident. Genesius was chosen because his name suggested an allusion to the *genesis* (*natalis*) or birthday of Rome; Victor and Fortunatus, likewise, were considered names of good omen, with a suggestion of the Victory and Fortune who presided over the destinies of ancient Rome.

Under the protection of these alleged saints, Pomponius and his friends worshipped, and celebrated the birthday of Rome, and the goddesses connected with the city.[176]

This state of things did not wholly escape the attention of contemporary observers. One of them, Raffaele Volaterrano, expressly says: "Pomponius Lætus worshipped Romulus and kept the birthday of Rome; the beginning of a campaign against religion (*initium abolendæ fidei*)."

The Roman academy found the means of keeping faithful to its traditions, and to the spirit of its institutions, in spite of the reform of its statutes. Victor, Fortunatus, Genesius, in whose honor divine service was performed on April 20, did not represent to the initiated the saints of the Church, but the fortunes of ancient Rome, its founder, the *Palilæ*. Still, we are not yet able to discover whether all this was done simply out of love and admiration for the ancient world, under the influence of the Renaissance of classical studies; or from hatred and contempt of Christian faith: *initium abolendæ fidei*.

THE END.

INSCRIPTION COMMEMORATING THE

LUDI SÆCULARES

CELEBRATED IN THE YEAR 17, B. C.

TEXT AS EDITED BY MOMMSEN

(See Chapter II., pp. 73-82)

INDEX.

For the names of individual arches, basilicas, catacombs, churches, forums, palaces, piazzas, statues, streets, temples, tombs, and villas, see the headings, *Arch, Basilica, Catacombs, Churches*, etc.

374

FOOTNOTES:

[1]   The relations between the Empire, the Christians, and the Jews have been
discussed by really numberless writers, beginning with the Fathers of the
Church. I have consulted, among the moderns: Mangold: *De ecclesia primæva
pro cæsaribus et magistratibus romanis preces fundente.* Bonn, 1881.—Bittner:
De Græcorum et Romanorum deque Judæorum et christianorum sacris jejuniis.

Posen, 1846.—Weiss: *Die römischen Kaiser in ihrem Verhältnisse zu Juden und Christen.* Wien, 1882.—Mourant Brock: *Rome, Pagan and Papal.* London, Hodder & Co. 1883.—Backhouse and Taylor: *History of the primitive Church.* (Italian edition.) Rome, Loescher, 1890.—Greppo: *Trois mémoires relatifs à l'histoire ecclésiastique.*—Döllinger: *Christenthum und Kirche.*—Champagny (Comte de): *Les Antonins,* vol. i.—Gaston Boissier: *La fin du paganisme,* etc., 2 vols. Paris, Hachette, 1891.—Giovanni Marangoni: *Delle cose gentilesche trasportate ad uso delle chiese.* Roma, Pagliarini, 1744.—Mosheim: *De rebus Christianis ante Constantinum.*—Carlo Fea: *Dissertazione sulle rovine di Roma,* in Winckelmann's *Storia delle arti.* Roma, Pagliarini, 1783, vol. iii.—Louis Duchesne: *Le liber pontificalis.* Paris, Thorin, 1886-1892.—G.B. de Rossi: *Bullettino di archeologia cristiana.* Roma, Salviucci, 1863-1891.

[2] See de Rossi: *Bullettino di archeologia cristiana,* 1888-1889, p. 15; 1890, p. 97.—Edmond Le Blant: *Comptes rendus de l'Acad. des Inscript.,* 1888, p. 113. —Arthur Frothingham: *American Journal of Archæology,* June, 1888, p. 214. —R. Lanciani: *Gli horti Aciliorum sul Pincio,* in the *Bullettino della commissione archeologica,* 1891, p. 132; *Underground Christian Rome,* in the *Atlantic Monthly,* July, 1891.

[3] See Ersilia Lovatelli: *Il Monte Pincio,* in the *Miscellanea archeologica,* p. 211. —Rodolfo Lanciani: *Su gli orti degli Acili sul Pincio,* in the *Bullettino di corrispondenza archeologica,* 1868, p. 132.

[4] A description of the beautiful villa of Herodes, adjoining the Catacombs of Prætextatus, will be found in chapter vi. pp. 287 sqq.

[5] A *consul suffectus* was one elected as a substitute in case of the death or retirement of one of the regular consuls.

[6] Lampridius, in *Sev. Alex.,* c. 43.

[7] In chapter v., p. 122, of *Ancient Rome,* I have attributed these *graffiti* to the second half of the first century; but after a careful examination of the structure of the wall, on the plaster of which they are scratched, I am convinced that they must have been written towards the end of the second century.

[8] Orelli, 4024, *Digest L.,* iv. 18, 7.

[9] See Ulpian: *De officio Procons.,* i. 3.

[10] Lampridius, *Heliog.,* 3.

[11] See Greppo: *Mémoire sur les laraires de l'empereur Alexandre Sevère.*

[12] The name of the villa was *Cassiacum;* its memory has lasted to the present age. See the memoir of Luigi Biraghi, *S. Agostino a Cassago di Brianza.* Milano, 1854.

[13] See *Bullettino di archeologia cristiana,* 1865, p. 50.

[14] It contains the words PETRO LILLVTI PAVLO. They are surely genuine and ancient. I examined them in company with Mommsen, Jordan, and de Rossi,

and they attributed them to the beginning of the third century of our era. The best suggestion regarding their origin is that they belong to a person, probably Christian, who used the name Petrus as *gentilitium*, and Paulus as *cognomen*, and who was the son of Lillutus, however barbaric this last name may sound.

[15] See de Rossi: *Bullettino di archeologia cristiana*, 1863, p. 49.—Rohault de Fleury: *L'arc de triomphe de Constantin*, in the *Révue archéologique*, Sept. 1863, p. 250.—W. Henzen: *Bullettino dell' Instituto*, 1863, p. 183.

[16] See Bibliography, p. 1. The title of the book may be translated thus: *On the pagan and profane objects transferred to churches for their use and adornment*.

[17] The two busts of S. Peter and S. Paul, described in Cancellieri's book, *Memorie storiche delle sacre teste dei santi apostoli Pietro e Paolo*, Roma, Ferretti, 1852 (second edition), were stolen by the French revolutionists in 1799.

[18] See *Corpus Inscriptionum Latinarum*, part VI., No. 351.

[19] In the Byzantine period this church and the adjoining monastery were called *casa Barbara patricia*. They are now comprised within the cloisters of S. Antonio all' Esquilino, on the left side of S. Maria Maggiore.

[20] These incrustations, and the basilica to which they belong, have been illustrated by Ciampini: *Vetera monumenta*, vol. i. plates xxii.-xxiv.—D'Agincourt: *Histoire de l'art, Peinture*, pl. xiii. 3.—Minutoli: *Ueber die Anfertigung und die Nutzanwendung der färbigen Gläser bei den Alten*, pl. iv.—De Rossi: *La basilica di Giunio Basso*, in the *Bullettino di archeologia cristiana*, 1871, p. 46.

[21] See Andrea Amoroso: *Le basiliche cristiane di Parenzo*. Parenzo, Coana, 1891. —Mommsen: *Corpus Inscriptionum Latinarum*, vol. v. part i. nos. 365-367.

[22] See Lovatelli: *I labirinti e il loro simbolismo nell' età di mezzo*, in the *Nuova Antologia*, 16 Agosto, 1890.—Arné: *Carrelages émaillés du moyen âge.*— Eugène Müntz: *Etudes iconographiques et archéologiques sur le moyen âge*.

[23] See Pietro Pericoli: *Lo spedale di S. Maria della Consolazione*. Imola Galeati, p. 64.

[24] Published in two volumes with the title: *Indicazione delle immagini di Maria, collocate sulle mura esterne di Roma*. Ferretti, 1853.

[25] The inscription, after all, was very mild in comparison with the violent formula imposed upon Alexander VII. It read: "In memory of the absolution given by Clement VIII. to Henry IV. of France and Navarre, September 17, 1595."

[26] The amphora corresponds to 26.26 litres; the metreta to 39.39 litres; the modius to 8.75 litres. The pound, divided into twelve ounces, corresponds to 327.45 grammes, a little more than 11-1/2 English ounces.

[27] See *Antichi pesi inscritti del museo capitolino*, in the *Bullettino della commissione archeologica comunale di Roma*, 1884, p. 61, pls. vi., vii.

[28] See de Rossi: *Bullettino di archeologia cristiana*, 1864, p. 57.

[29] See *Acta purgationis Cæciliani*, post Optati opp. ed Dupin, p. 168.

[30] *Confess.* vi. 2.

[31] See Gaetano Marini: *Iscrizioni doliari*, p. 114, n. 279.—Giuseppe Gatti: *La lex horreorum*, in the *Bullettino della commissione archeologica comunale di Roma*, 1885, p. 110.

[32] The place was called *in tribus fatis*, from the three statues of sibyls described by Pliny, *H.N.* xxxiv. See *Goth.* i. 25.

[33] "Sank into the great flower, that is adorned
With leaves so many, and thence reascended
To where its love abideth evermore."

Longfellow's Translation.

[34] On the almanacs (*Notitia, Curiosum*), containing catalogues and statistics of Roman buildings in the fourth century, see Mommsen: *Chronograph von 354*, etc., in the *Abhandlungen der Sächsischen Gesellschaft der Wissenschaften*, vols. ii. 549; iii. 269; viii. 694.—Preller: *Die Regionen der Stadt Rom*. Jena: Hochhausen, 1846.—Jordan: *Topographie der Stadt Rom*. Berlin: Weidmann, ii., pp. 1 & 178.—Richter: *Topographie der Stadt Rom*, 1889, p. 5; id.: *Hermes*, xx., p. 91.—De Rossi: *Piante iconografiche e prospettiche di Roma anteriori al sec. XVI*. Roma: Salviucci, 1879.—Guido: *Il testo siriaco della descrizione di Roma*, etc., in the *Bullettino Comunale*, 1884, p. 218; and 1891, p. 61.—Lanciani: *Ricerche sulle XIV regioni urbane*, in the *Bullettino comunale*, 1890, p. 115.

[35] *Inscript.* 139, i.

[36] The fac-simile here presented is from the *Corpus Inscriptionum Latinarum*, vi. 820.

[37] The sale of skins of victims sacrificed at Athens in the year 334 B. C., in state sacrifices only, brought a revenue of 5,500 drachmas.

[38] See Henzen, *Bullettino dell' Instituto*, 1863, p. 58.—Mommsen: *Corpus Inscriptionum Latinarum*, vol. i. no. 1503.

[39] See Cicero: *De Divinatione*, ii. 59, 123.—Preller: *Die Regionen*, p. 133.—Nibby: *Roma Ant.*, ii. p. 334.—Beckner: *Topogr.*, p. 539.—Cavedoni: *Bull. dell' Inst.* 1856, p. 102.—Visconti: *Bullettino Comunale*, 1887, p. 154, 156.—Middleton: *The Remains of Ancient Rome*, ed. 1892, vol. ii. p. 233.

[40] Concerning this celebrated monument, see Tambroni and Poletti: *Giornale arcadico*, vol. xviii., 1823, p. 371-400.—Gell: *Rome and its Vicinity*, i. p. 219.—Klausen: *Æneas*, ii. p. 1083.—Canina: *Via Appia*, i. p. 209-232.—Mommsen: *Corpus Inscriptionum Latinarum*, vol. i. p. 207, no. 807.

[41] Pliny, *N. H.*, x. 29, 41.

[42] A copy of this celebrated picture, dating from the second century B. C., has been found in a tomb on the Esquiline. It was published in facsimile and

illustrated by Visconti in the *Bullettino Comunale*, 1889, p. 340, tav. xi.-xii.

[43] See the *Annali dell' Instituto*, 1854, p. 28.

[44] The convent and its garden occupy the sites of the house of Augustus, the temples of Vesta and Apollo, the Greek and Latin libraries, and the Portico of the Danaids, described in *Ancient Rome*, ch. v., p. 109. The estate has been owned successively by the Mattei, Spada, and Ronconi families, and by Charles Mills. Its finest ornament is a portico built by the Matteis in the sindexteenth century from the designs of Raffaellino del Colle. This pupil of Raphael was also the painter of the exquisite frescoes representing Venus and Cupid, Jupiter and Antiope, Hermaphrodite and Salmace, and other subjects engraved by Marcantonio and Agostino Veneziano. These frescoes, greatly injured by age and neglect, were restored in 1824, by Camuccini, at the expense of Mr. Charles Mills.

[45] See Lanciani: *L' itinerario di Einsiedlen*, in the *Monumenti antichi pubblicati dalla Accademia dei Lincei*. 1891.

[46] This inscription is of such exceptional interest that it is given, as edited by Mommsen, at the close of this volume.

[47] *Codex Vatic*. 7,721, f. 67.

[48] See Rycquius: *De Capitolio romano*. Leyden, 1669.—Bunsen: *Beschreibung der Stadt Rom*, iii. A, p. 14.—Hirt: *Der capitolinische Jupitertempel*, in the *Abhandlungen der Berliner Akademie*, 1813.—Dureau de la Malle: *Mémoire sur la position de la roche tarpeienne*, in the *Mémoires de l'Academie des Inscriptions*, 1819.—Niebuhr: *Römische Geschichte*, i. 5,588.—Mommsen: *Bullettino dell' Instituto*, 1845, p. 119.—Lanciani: *Il tempio di Giove Ottimo Massimo*, in the *Bullettino comunale*, 1875, p. 165, tav. xvi.—Jordan: *Osservazioni sul tempio di Giove Capitolino*. Lettera al sig. cav. R. Lanciani, Roma, 1876.—Hülsen: *Osservazioni sull' architettura del tempio di Giove Capitolino*, in the *Mittheilungen des deutschen archäologischen Instituts, römische Abtheilung*, 1888, p. 150.—Audollent: *Dessin inédit d'un fronton du temple de Jupiter Capitolin*, in the *Mélanges de l'Ecole française*, 1889, Juin.

[49] See *Bullettino Comunale*, 1886, p. 403; 1887, p. 14, 124, 251; 1888, p. 138. —Mommsen: *Zeitschrift für Numismatik*, xv. p. 207-219.

[50] The same illustration has been selected by Middleton: *The Remains of Ancient Rome*, vol. i. p. 363.—The reliefs of the pediment are also well shown in a sketch by Pierre Jacques, dated 1576, and published by Audollent in the *Mélanges*, 1889, planche ii.

[51] See Clemente Cardinati: *Diplomi imperiali di privilegi*. Velletri, 1835.—Joseph Arneth: *Zwölf römische Militärdiplome*, Wien, 1843.—Mommsen: *Bullettino dell' Instituto*, 1845, p. 119; *Annali dell' Instituto*, 1858, p. 198; *Corpus Inscriptionum Latinarum*, vol. iii. part ii. p. 843.—Léon Rénier: *Récueil des diplomes militaires*, première livraison, Paris, 1876.

[52] *Die Flotte einer ägyptischen Königin aus dem siebzehnten Jahrhundert.*

[53] See Flavius Josephus, *Ant. Ind.*, xviii. 4.

[54] See Morel: *Révue Archéologique*, 1868.—De Rossi: *Bullettino di archeologia cristiana*, 1868.

[55] See Parker's *Forum Romanum*, London, 1876, plates xxiii. and xxiv.

[56] It has since been published by Middleton himself in his *Remains of Ancient Rome*, vol. i. p. 275, fig. 35, from a heliogravure of the original.

[57] In the *Cod. Vat.*, 3,439, f. 46.

[58] See Dressel: *Bullettino dell' Instituto*, 1881, p. 38.—Lanciani: *Bullettino Comunale*, 1881, p. 4.—Visconti: *Un simulacro di Semo Sancus*, Roma, 1881.—Preller: *Römische Mythologie*, p. 637.

[59] *Apolog.* 26.

[60] In volume index. of the *Spicilegium romanum*, pp. 384-468.

[61] Baldwin Brown: *From Schola to Cathedral*, p. 1. Edinburgh, Douglas, 1886.

[62] See de Rossi: *Bullettino di archeologia cristiana*, 1867, p. 46; *Corpus Inscriptionum Latinarum*, vi. no. 1454.—Spalletti: *Tavola ospitale trovata in Roma sull' Aventino.* Roma, Salomoni, 1777 (p. 34).—Lanciani: *The Atlantic Monthly*, July, 1891.—Armellini: *Chiese*, first edition, p. 500.

[63] 2 Timothy, iv. 21.

[64] Gaspare Celio: *Memoria dei nomi degli artefici*, p. 81. Napoli, Bonino, 1638.

[65] See Duchesne: *Liber pontificalis*, vol. i. pp. 132, 133.—De Era: *Storia di S. Pudenziana*, two MSS. volumes in the library of S. Bernardo alle Terme.—Bartolini: *Sopra l'antichissimo altare di legno della basilica lateranense.* Roma, 1852.—De Rossi: *Bullettino di archeologia cristiana*, 1867, p. 49; *Musaici delle chiese di Roma.*—Pellegrini: *Scavi nelle terme di Novato*, in the *Bullettino dell' Instituto*, 1870, p. 161.

[66] See Lorenzo Fortunati: *Relazione degli scavi e scoperte fatte lungo la via Latina.* Roma, 1859.

[67] Baldwin Brown: *ubi supra*, p. 17.

[68] Dionysii: *Vaticanæ basilicæ cryptarum monumenta*, pl. xxvii.—De Rossi: *Inscriptiones Chrisilanæ urbis Romæ*, ii. p. 56, 350, 411.—Duchesne: *Liber pontificalis*, i. cxxii.

[69] See Eugene Müntz: *Ricerche intorno ai lavori archeologici di Giacomo Grimaldi.* Firenze, 1881.—The best autograph work of Grimaldi, dedicated to Paul V. in 1618, belongs to the Barberini library, and is marked xxxiv. 50.

[70] The author of *Le Latran, dans le moyen âge.*

[71] S. Pietro Montorio, rebuilt towards 1472, by Ferdinand IV. and Isabella of Spain, from the designs of Baccio Pontelli, stands on the site of an older church.

[72] *Chiese di Roma*, 1st edition, p. 520.

[73]   "Collocate e poste una appresso all' altra con diligenza e cura esatta."

[74]   Francesco Maria Torrigio: *Le sacre grotte vaticane*, p. 64. Roma, 1639.

[75]   *Le liber pontificalis: Texte, introduction et commentaire par l'abbé L. Duchesne.* Paris, Thorin, 1886-1892.

[76]   The letters LINVS might be the termination of a longer name, like [ANUL]LINVS or [MARCEL]LINVS.

[77]   See Lampridius: *Heliog*, 23.

[78]   See p. 345 sq.

[79]   *Liber Pontificalis*, Silvester, xvi. p. 176.

[80]   Pietro Mallio says that they came from the Temple of Apollo in Troy. This statement, however absurd, confirms the opinion that the tradition about Solomon's Temple is of modern origin. It seems that Constantine's canopy was borne by only sindex columns, and that the other sindex were added at the time of Gregory III.

[81]   Venuti: *Ragionamento sopra la pina di bronzo*, etc., in the *Codex Vaticanus* 9024.—Gayet Lacour: *La pigna du Vatican*, in the *Mélanges de l'Ecole française*, 1881, p. 312.—Lanciani: *Il Pantheon e le terme di Agrippa*, in the *Notizie degli scavi*, 1882.—De Rossi: *Inscriptiones christianæ urbis Romæ*, vol. ii., 428-430.—Gori: *Archivio storico artistico*, 1881, p. 230.

[82]   *Numismata summorum pontificum templi vaticani fabricam indicantia*, by Philippus Bonanni. Rome, 1696.

[83]   See *Bullettino di archeologia cristiana*, 1867, p. 33, sq.—*Idem*, 1883, p. 90.

[84]   De Rossi: *Inscriptiones christianæ*, ii. p. 428-430.—Febeo: *De identitate cathedræ S. Petri*, Rome, 1666.—Cancellieri: *De secretariis*, p. 1245.

[85]   But Sindextus V. (+ 1590) did not complete the lantern surmounting the dome, upon which the gilded cross was placed November 18, 1593.

[86]   Vincenzo Briccolani: *Descrizione della basilica vaticana*, third ed. Roma, 1816. —Pietro Ercole Visconti: *Metrologia vaticana*. Roma, 1828.

[87]   The baldacchino raised with questionable taste above the ciborium of Arnolfo di Cambio, a pupil of Nicolò Pisano (A. D. 1285), rests on four columns of Oriental alabaster, from the quarries of Sannhur, in the district of the Beni Souef, offered to Gregory XVI. by Mohammed Ali, viceroy of Egypt. The pedestals are inlaid with malachite, a present from the emperor Nicholas of Russia.

[88]   *Sulla grandezza e disposizione della primitiva basilica ostiense*. Roma, 1835.

[89]   *Acta apost. apocrif.* p. 1-39. Lipsiæ, 1851.

[90]   See: *Die Grabplatte des h. Paulus: neue Studien über die römischen Apostelgräber*, von H. Grisar, S. I. In the *Römische Quartalschrift*, 1892. Heft. I., II.

[91]   See chapter ii., p. 99.

[92] My map of ancient Rome (scale 1:1000), which has cost me twenty-five years of labor, will be published in forty-sindex sheets measuring 0.90 m. × 0.60 m. each. The first, comprising sheets nos. iii., x., xvii., xxiii., xxx., and xxxvi. (from the gardens of Sallust to the Macellum Magnum on the Cælian), will be ready in May, 1893. The plan is drawn in five colors, referring respectively to the royal, republican, imperial, mediæval and modern epochs.

[93] The basilica of S. Valentine, discovered in 1886, by our archæological commission, is mentioned on p. 120 of the present volume.

[94] See Otto Hirschfeld: *Die kaiserlichen Grabstätten in Rom*, in the *Sitzungsberichte der kgl. Akademie der Wissenschaften*. Berlin, 1866.

[95] Visitors to Rome may form an idea of a [Greek: sebasteion] from that found at Ostia, in 1889, in the barracks of the firemen. I have given an illustrated description of this remarkable discovery in the *Mèlanges de l'Ecole française de Rome*, tome index., 1889, and in the *Notizie degli scavi*, January-April, 1889.

[96] The birthplace of Mithridates the Great, and of the geographer Strabo; it still retains its ancient name.

[97] See Mommsen: *Res gestæ divi Augusti*, 2d edition. Berlin, Weidmann, 1883.

[98] Augustus enrolled his first army in October of the year 41 B. C. He died in August, A. D. 14.

[99] This house is described in *Ancient Rome*, chapter i., p. 17.

[100] *Don Juan*, canto III. eindex.

[101] The other instance was in the excavations of the palace of the Valerii Aradii, near S. Erasmo, on the Cælian, the most successful ever made in Rome.

[102] *La bolla di Maria, moglie di Onorio*. Milan, 1819.

[103] *Dissertazione su d' una antica argenteria, letta nell' accademia archeologica il di 7 gennaio*, 1811.

[104] Garrucci has reproduced them in the *Storia dell' arte cristiana*, vol. ii. pl. 108-111.

[105] Garrucci: *Vetri adornati di figure in oro*.—Swoboda, quoted by De Waal in the *Römische Quartalschrift*, 1888, p. 135.—Armellini: *ibidem*, 1888, p. 130. —De Rossi: *Bullettino di archeologia cristiana*, 1864, p. ——; 1887, p. 130.

[106] *Les tombeaux des papes romains*. Traduction Sabatier. Paris, 1859.

[107] *Roma sotterranea*, i., p. 283.

[108] The hypogæum, discovered in 1617, excavated and pillaged in 1780-81, has, through my exertions, become national property, together with the Columbaria of Hylas.

[109] It contained the graves of Marcellus † 308, Sylvester † 385, Siricius † 396, and Celestinus † 422.

[110] Dyer: *History of Rome*, p. 344.

[111] See the *Anglo-Saxon Chronicle*, edited by J.A. Giles, in Bohn's Antiquarian Library; and the excellent memoir of Domenico Tesoroni, *King Ceadwalla's Tomb in the Ancient Basilica of S. Peter* (Rome, Bertero, 1891), from which I quote almost verbatim.

[112] De Rossi: *Inscriptiones christianæ*, ii. p. 288.

[113] Duchesne: *Lib. pontif.* ii. 258.—Marucchi: *Iscrizioni relative alla storia di Roma dal secolo V al XV*. (p. 74). Roma, 1881.

[114] Barbier de Montault: *Revue archéologique*, xiv. 244.—Frothingham: *American Journal of Archæology*, 1891, p. 44.—De Rossi: *Bullettino di archeologia cristiana*, 1875, p. 29; 1891, p. 91.—Stevenson: *Mostra di Roma, all' esposizione di Torino*, 1884, p. 174.—Rohault de Fleury: *Le latran au moyen âge* (planches 45, 46). Paris, 1877.

[115] *Storia delle arti*, edizione Fea, vol. ii. p. 144.

[116] Zizim died by poisoning, February 24, 1495, during the pontificate of Alexander VI., Borgia.

[117] Published by Müntz, in the *Archivio storico dell' arte*, vol. iv., 1891, p. 366.

[118] The question as to the birthplace of Christopher Columbus seems to have been finally settled in favor of Savona. Unquestionable evidence has been discovered on June 17 of the present year, by the Historical Society at Madrid.

[119] Theodor Sprenger: *Roma Nova*, p. 232. Frankfort, 1660.—Caylus: in vol. xxv. of the *Mémoires de l'Académie des inscriptions et belles lettres*.—Cancellieri: *Il mercato*, p. 42.

[120] *Vita di Benvenuto Cellini* lib. 1, xxxvi.

[121] See chapter iii., p. 67, of *Ancient Rome*

[122] *De titulis in quibus impensæ monumentorum sepulcralium indicatæ sunt.*

[123] See Luigi Grifi: *Sopra la iscrizione antica dell' auriga Scirto*, in the *Accademia archeologica*, 1854, v. xiii.

[124] See the *Corpus inscriptionum latinarum*, vol. vi., part 2, nos. 4327-5886.

[125] See Walch: *Ad Gorii Xenia*, p. 98.—Orelli-Henzen: vol. 2, no. 4789, etc.

[126] *Monumenti inediti dell' Instituto di correspondenza archeologica*, Supplemento, 1891.

[127] *Titus*, 4.

[128] See:—Pietro Sante Bartoli: *Gli antichi sepolcri*. Roma: de Rossi, 1727. —*Corpus inscriptionum latinarum*, vol. vi., part ii., pp. 1073, 1076.—*Villa Pamphylia, ejusque palatium cum suis prospectibus: statuæ, fontes, vivaria*. Romae: fol. max.—Ignazio Ciampi: *Innocenzo X Pamfili e la sua corte*. Roma: Galeati, 1878.

[129] See:—Otto Jahn: *Die Wandgemälde des Columbariums in der Villa Pamfili*, in the *Abhandlungen der bayerischen Akademie*, 1857.—Eugen Petersen: *Sitzungsberichte des Archäologischen Instituts*, Römische Abtheilung, March

18, 1892.

[130] A discovery of the same kind has come within my experience. In 1885, while excavating near the city walls, between the Porta S. Lorenzo and the Porta Maggiore, we found an amphora of great size, containing the corpse of a little child embedded in lime. He had probably died of a contagious disease. The corpse had been reduced to a handful of tiny bones; and the impression of them was so spoiled by dampness and age that it was found impossible to cast the form of the infant.

[131] *Digest*, index., 2, 5, § 3.

[132] See:—*Notizie degli Scavi*, 1884, p. 393.—Henzen: *Bullettino dell' Instituto*, 1885, p. 9.—Stevenson: *idem*, 1885, p. 22.—Geffroy: *Mélanges de l'Ecole française de Rome*, 1885, p. 318, pl. vii-xiii.

[133] See C. Ludovico Visconti: *Il sepolcro del fanciullo Quinto Sulpicio Massimo*. Roma, 1871.—Wilhelm Henzen: *Sepolcri antichi rinvenuti alla porta salaria*, in the *Bullettino dell' Instituto*, 1871, p. 98.—Luigi Ciofi: *Inscriptiones latinæ et græcæ, cum carmine græco extemporali Quinti Sulpicii Maximi*. Roma, 1871.—J. Henry Parker: *Tombs in and near Rome*. Oxford, 1877. (Plate X.)

[134] On the subject of this competition see:—Suetonius: *Domitian*, 4.—Stefano Morcelli: *Sull' Agone Capitolino*. Dissertazione postuma. Milano, 1816.—Joachim Marquardt: *Handbuch der römischen Alterthümer*, iv., 453.

[135] See Cesare Lucchesini: *Esame della questione se i latini avessero veri poeti improvvisatori*. Lucca, 1828.

[136] The bibliography on Herodes Atticus and his villa at the second milestone of the Appian Way is so rich that I can mention but a few of the leading works, besides Visconti's.—Claude Saumaise: *Mémoires sur la vie d'Herodes Atticus*, in *Académie des inscriptions et belles lettres*, xxx. p. 25; *Corpus inscriptionum græcarum*: vol. iii. no. 6280, p. 924.—Wilhelm Dittenberger: *Die Familie des Herodes Atticus*.—Richard Burgess: *Description of the Circus on the Via Appia*. Italian translation, p. 89. Rome, 1829.—Ludovico Bianconi: *Descrizione dei circhi e particolarmente di quello di Caracalla*. Roma, 1786.—Antonio Nibby: *Del circo volgarmente detto di Caracalla*. Roma, 1825.

[137] When Maxentius repaired the Appian Way in 309, one of these commemorative columns was converted into a milestone, the seventh from the Porta Capena. The column was removed in the Middle Ages to the Church of S. Eusebio on the Esquiline, where it was seen and purchased, at the beginning of the last century, by cardinal Alessandro Albani. It now belongs to the Capitoline Museum.

[138] *I comentari di Frontino intorno le acque e gli acquedotti*: Opera premiata dalla r. Accademia dei Lincei col premio reale di lire 10,000. Roma, Salviucci, 1880.

[139] Among the modern writers on the subject are:—Christian Hülsen: *Die Auffindung der römischen Leiche vom Jahre* 1485, in the *Mittheilungen des Instituts für österreichische Geschichtforschung*, Band iv., Heft 3.—J.

Addington Symonds: *History of the Renaissance*, i. 23.—Giovanni Antonio
Riccy: *Dell' antico pago Lemonio*. Roma, 1802 (p. 109).—Gregorovius:
Geschichte der Stadt Rom im Mittelalter, vii., 3, p. 571.—*Corpus
inscriptionum latinarum*, vol. vi., no. 20,634.

Contemporary documents:—Stefano Infessura: *Diario*, edited by Tommasini.
Rome, 1890.—Notarius a Nantiportu: in *Cod. Vatic.*, 6,823, f. 250.—Raffaele
Maffei da Volterra (Volterranus, born 1451, died 1522): *Commentarii rerum
Urbanarum*, column 954 of the Lyons edition, 1552.—Bartolomeo Fonte
(Humanist, born 1445, died 1513): letter to Francesco Sassetto, published by
Janitschek: *Gesells. der Rénaissance*, p. 120.—Letter from Laur Pehem, dated
April 15, 1475, in the *Cod. Munich*, 716 (among the papers collected by
Hartman Schedel).—Copy of a letter from messer Daniele da San Sebastiano to
Giacomo di Maphei, citizen of Verona, in the *Cod. Marciano* (Venice), xiv.
267.—Alexander ab Alexandro (born at Naples, 1461, died in Rome, 1523):
Genialium Dierum, iii. 2.—Fragment of the diary of Antonio di Vaseli (1481-
1486), in the *Archives of the Vatican*, Armar. XV. fasc. 41.—Fragment of the
diary of Corona (first entry Jan. 30, 1481; last July 25, 1492) in the possession
of H.D. Grissel, Esq.—Anonym ap. Mountfaucon, *Diarium Italicum*, xi. 157.

[140]   Sponges are most frequently found in the *cistæ* at Palestrina, which were
nothing else but toilet-boxes. I have had the opportunity of examining the
contents of twelve of them, lately discovered. These include sponges, combs
of various kinds and shapes, hairpins, wooden boxes with movable lids, still
full of excellent powders, cosmetics, and ointments, and other articles of the
mundus muliebris.

[141]   Principal authorities:—Philip de Winghe: *Cod. biblioth. Bruxell.* 17872.—
Panvinius: *De Cæmeteriis Urbis Romæ*. Rome, 1568.—Antonio Bosio: *Roma
sotterranea*; opera postuma. Roma, 1632-34.—Paolo Aringhi: *Roma
subterranea novissima*. Roma, 1651 fol. Cologne, 1659 fol.—M.A. Boldetti:
Osservazioni sopra i cimiteri de' SS. martiri. Roma, Salvioni, 1720.—Giovanni
Bottari: *Sculture e pitture estratte dai cimiteri di Roma*. 3 vol. Roma, 1737-54.
—Filippo Buonarroti: *Vasi antichi di vetro ornati di figure*, etc. Firenze, 1716,
4.—Raoul Rochette: *Le catacombe di Roma*. Milano, 1841.—Giuseppe Marchi:
Monumenti delle arti cristiane primitive. Roma, Puccinelli, 1844.—Raffaele
Garrucci: *Storia dell' arte cristiana*. Roma: 6 vol. fol.; *Vetri ornati di figure in
oro, trovati nei cimiteri dei Cristiani*. Rome, Salviucci, 1858.—Louis Perret:
Les catacombes de Rome, etc. 6 vol. fol. Paris, 1852-1856.—De Rossi: *Roma
sotterranea cristiana*. 3 vol. fol. Roma, Salviucci, 1864; *Inscriptiones
Christianæ Urbis Romæ*. 2 vol. fol. Rome, 1861-1887; *Bullettino di
archeologia cristiana*. Roma, Salviucci, 1863-1891.—Northcote and
Brownlow: *Roma sotterranea*. 2 volumes 8vo, 2d ed. London, Longmans,
1878.—Northcote: *Epitaphs of the Catacombs*. London, Longmans, 1878.—
Henry Parker: *The Catacombs of Rome*. Oxford, Parker, 1877.

[142]   See *Cod. Theodos.* index. 17, 2.

[143]   On the subject of the Jewish colony in Rome, see:—Emmanuel Rodocanachi:

Le saint-siège et les Juifs: le Ghetto a Rome. Paris, Didot, 1891.—A. Bertolotti: *Les Juifs à Rome.* Revue des études juives, 1881, fasc. 4.—Raffaele Garrucci: *Cimiterio degli antichi Ebrei.* Roma, 1862.—Pietro Manfrin: *Gli Ebrei sotto la dominazione romana.* Roma, 1888-1890.—Ettore Natali: *Il Ghetto di Roma.* Roma, 1887.—Perreau: *Education et culture des Israelites en Italie au moyen âge.* Corfou, 1885.

[144] This "poster," painted in red letters, which is now in the Museo Nazionale, Naples, was published by Zangemeister in vol. iv., p. 13, n. 117, of the *Corpus inscriptionum latinarum.*—Prof. Mommsen, in the *Rheinisches Museum,* xindex. (1864), p. 456, contradicts the opinion of de Rossi as regards the religious persuasion of this Fabius Eupor (*Bullettino di archeologia cristiana,* 1864, pp. 70, 92).

[145] See Champagny: *Rome et la Judée,* p. 31, of the first edition.

[146] See Suetonius, *Domitian,* chap. 92; Dion Cassius, lxvii. 13.

[147] See Pliny, *Epistolæ,* x. 67.

[148] See de Rossi: *Bullettino di archeologia cristiana,* 1868, p. 19.

[149] See *Bullettino di archeologia cristiana,* 1867, p. 76.

[150] See *Atti dell' Accademia dei Nuovi Lincei,* sessione 6 maggio, 1860.

[151] *Bullettino di archeologia cristiana,* 1863, p. 75.

[152] ... passim corpora condens
   Plurima sanctorum subter hæc mœnia ponit.

[153] The attention of learned men had been directed towards Christian underground Rome just ten years before this event, by the publication of Panvinio's pamphlet *De cæmeteriis urbis Romæ,* 1566.

[154] *Ad ann. 575;* 130, 226.

[155] See *Bullettino di archeologia cristiana,* 1865, p. 36.

[156] See Fea: *Miscellanea,* vol. i., pp. 238, 245, etc.

[157] It is now in the Vatican Library. A good engraving is to be found in Buonarroti's *Osservazioni sui medaglioni,* p. 497.

[158] *Historiar.,* iii. 65.

[159] *Historiæ,* iii. 65.

[160] The name Ampliatus belongs to servants and freedmen; it was never used by men of rank, whether pagans or Christians.

[161] Baronius *ad Martyr.* 31 October.

[162] See Renan's *St. Paul,* lxvii.

[163] Orazio Marucchi: *Di un ipogeo scoperto nel cimitero di S. Sebastiano.* Roma, 1879; *Un antico busto del Salvatore, etc.,* in the *Mélanges de l'Ecole française,* 1888, p. 403.—Pietro d' Achille: *Il sepolcro di S. Pietro.* Roma, 1867.—Giovanni B. Lugari: *Le catacombe ossia il sepolcro apostolico dell'*

Appia. Roma, 1888.—De Rossi: *Roma sotterranea cristiana*, vol. iii., p. 427; *Il sepolcro degli Uranii cristiani a S. Sebastiano*, in the *Bullettino di archeologia cristiana*, 1886, p. 24.—Pietro Marchi: *Monumenti primitivi delle arti cristiane*, p. 212, tav. xxxindex-xli.

[164] *Inscriptiones Christianæ*, vol. ii. 32, 77.

[165] Represented in plate index. of the *Mélanges de l'Ecole française de Rome*, 1888.

[166] This is also illustrated by Martigny: *Dictionnaire*, 2d ed. p. 586.—Kraus: *Realencyclopädie*, ii. p. 580.—Northcote and Brownlow: *Roma Sotterranea*. London, 1879. (ii. p. 29.)—Roller: *Catacombes*, planche i., xl. n. 2.—Garrucci: *Arte cristiana*, tav. 428, 5.—Duchesne: *Bullettino critique*, Décembre, 1882, p. 288.—De Rossi: *Bullettino comunale*, 1889, p. 131, tav. v., vi.

[167] See:—Giovanni Marangoni: *Istoria dell' oratorio appellato Sancta Sanctorum*. Roma, 1747.—Gaspare Bambi: *Memorie sacre della cappella di Sancta Sanctorum*. Roma, 1775.—Giuseppe Soresini: *Dell' immagine del SS. Salvatore ad Sancta Sanctorum*. Roma, 1675.—Benedetto Millini: *Oratorio di S. Lorenzo ad Sancta Sanctorum*. Roma, 1616.—Raffaele Garrucci: *Storia dell' arte cristiana*, vol. i. p. 408.—Rohault de Fleury: *Le Latran*.

[168] A pious but unfounded tradition identifies this picture of Edessa with the one preserved in Genoa, in the church of S. Bartolomeo degli Armeni.

[169] On the subject of the Paneas group see:—André Peraté: *Note sur le groupe de Paneas*, in *Mélanges de l'Ecole française de Rome*, 1885, p. 302.—Raoul-Rochette: *Discours sur les types imitatifs qui constituent l'art du Christianisme*, 1834.—Bayet: *Recherches pour servir à l'histoire de la peinture en Orient*, p. 29.—Orazio Marucchi: *Di un busto del Salvatore*, etc., in the *Mélanges*, 1888, p. 403.—Eusebius: H.E. VII., 185, edition Teubner, p. 315.—Grimouard de St. Laurent: *Guide de l'art Chrétien*, ii. p. 215.

[170] See:—Bossio: *Roma sotterranea*, p. 591, D.—Bruder: *Die heiligen Martyren Marcellinus und Petrus*. Mainz, 1878.—De Rossi: *Bullettino di archeologia cristiana*. 1882, p. 111.—Wilpert: *Ein Cyclus christologischer Gemälde aus der Katacombe der heiligen Petrus und Marcellinus*. Freiburg, 1891.

[171] See Becker: *Gallus*, p. 4.

[172] See *Ancient Rome*, p. 10.

[173] Giacomo Lombroso: *Gli accademici nelle catacombe*, in the *Archivio della società romana di storia patria*, 1889, p. 219.

[174] *Bullettino di archeologia cristiana*, 1890, p. 81.—See also: de Nollac: *Mélanges de l'Ecole française de Rome*, 1866, p. 165.

[175] The house of Pomponius and the seat of the Academy was not on the Esquiline, but on the Quirinal, on the area of the Baths of Constantine, opposite the gate of the Colonna Gardens. The mistake in the name of the hill must be attributed to Pomponius himself, who had written on the door of the house:— POMPONI · LÆTI · ET · SOCIETATIS · ESCVVILINAI. After the reform of

the statutes, another sign, less classic in style, was put up: SOCIETAS-LITERATORUM-S-VICTORIS-IN-ESQUILIIS.

[176]   The Temple of Fortune in Rome was dedicated on this very day. See Mommsen, in the *Corpus inscriptionum latinarum*, vol. i. p. 392.

Section 1. General Terms of Use and Redistributing Project Gutenberg-tm
electronic works

1.A. By reading or using any part of this Project Gutenberg-tm
electronic work, you indicate that you have read, understand, agree to
and accept all the terms of this license and intellectual property
(trademark/copyright) agreement. If you do not agree to abide by all
the terms of this agreement, you must cease using and return or destroy
all copies of Project Gutenberg-tm electronic works in your possession.
If you paid a fee for obtaining a copy of or access to a Project
Gutenberg-tm electronic work and you do not agree to be bound by the
terms of this agreement, you may obtain a refund from the person or
entity to whom you paid the fee as set forth in paragraph 1.E.8.

1.B. "Project Gutenberg" is a registered trademark. It may only be
used on or associated in any way with an electronic work by people who
agree to be bound by the terms of this agreement. There are a few
things that you can do with most Project Gutenberg-tm electronic works
even without complying with the full terms of this agreement. See
paragraph 1.C below. There are a lot of things you can do with Project
Gutenberg-tm electronic works if you follow the terms of this agreement
and help preserve free future access to Project Gutenberg-tm electronic
works. See paragraph 1.E below.

1.C. The Project Gutenberg Literary Archive Foundation ("the Foundation"
or PGLAF), owns a compilation copyright in the collection of Project
Gutenberg-tm electronic works. Nearly all the individual works in the
collection are in the public domain in the United States. If an
individual work is in the public domain in the United States and you are
located in the United States, we do not claim a right to prevent you from
copying, distributing, performing, displaying or creating derivative
works based on the work as long as all references to Project Gutenberg
are removed. Of course, we hope that you will support the Project
Gutenberg-tm mission of promoting free access to electronic works by
freely sharing Project Gutenberg-tm works in compliance with the terms of
this agreement for keeping the Project Gutenberg-tm name associated with
the work. You can easily comply with the terms of this agreement by
keeping this work in the same format with its attached full Project
Gutenberg-tm License when you share it without charge with others.

1.D. The copyright laws of the place where you are located also govern
what you can do with this work. Copyright laws in most countries are in
a constant state of change. If you are outside the United States, check
the laws of your country in addition to the terms of this agreement
before downloading, copying, displaying, performing, distributing or
creating derivative works based on this work or any other Project
Gutenberg-tm work. The Foundation makes no representations concerning
the copyright status of any work in any country outside the United
States.

1.E. Unless you have removed all references to Project Gutenberg:

1.E.1. The following sentence, with active links to, or other immediate
access to, the full Project Gutenberg-tm License must appear prominently
whenever any copy of a Project Gutenberg-tm work (any work on which the
phrase "Project Gutenberg" appears, or with which the phrase "Project
Gutenberg" is associated) is accessed, displayed, performed, viewed,

copied or distributed:

This eBook is for the use of anyone anywhere at no cost and with
almost no restrictions whatsoever. You may copy it, give it away or
re-use it under the terms of the Project Gutenberg License included
with this eBook or online at www.gutenberg.org

1.E.2. If an individual Project Gutenberg-tm electronic work is derived
from the public domain (does not contain a notice indicating that it is
posted with permission of the copyright holder), the work can be copied
and distributed to anyone in the United States without paying any fees
or charges. If you are redistributing or providing access to a work
with the phrase "Project Gutenberg" associated with or appearing on the
work, you must comply either with the requirements of paragraphs 1.E.1
through 1.E.7 or obtain permission for the use of the work and the
Project Gutenberg-tm trademark as set forth in paragraphs 1.E.8 or
1.E.9.

1.E.3. If an individual Project Gutenberg-tm electronic work is posted
with the permission of the copyright holder, your use and distribution
must comply with both paragraphs 1.E.1 through 1.E.7 and any additional
terms imposed by the copyright holder. Additional terms will be linked
to the Project Gutenberg-tm License for all works posted with the
permission of the copyright holder found at the beginning of this work.

1.E.4. Do not unlink or detach or remove the full Project Gutenberg-tm
License terms from this work, or any files containing a part of this
work or any other work associated with Project Gutenberg-tm.

1.E.5. Do not copy, display, perform, distribute or redistribute this
electronic work, or any part of this electronic work, without
prominently displaying the sentence set forth in paragraph 1.E.1 with
active links or immediate access to the full terms of the Project
Gutenberg-tm License.

1.E.6. You may convert to and distribute this work in any binary,
compressed, marked up, nonproprietary or proprietary form, including any
word processing or hypertext form. However, if you provide access to or
distribute copies of a Project Gutenberg-tm work in a format other than
"Plain Vanilla ASCII" or other format used in the official version
posted on the official Project Gutenberg-tm web site (www.gutenberg.org),
you must, at no additional cost, fee or expense to the user, provide a
copy, a means of exporting a copy, or a means of obtaining a copy upon
request, of the work in its original "Plain Vanilla ASCII" or other
form. Any alternate format must include the full Project Gutenberg-tm
License as specified in paragraph 1.E.1.

1.E.7. Do not charge a fee for access to, viewing, displaying,
performing, copying or distributing any Project Gutenberg-tm works
unless you comply with paragraph 1.E.8 or 1.E.9.

1.E.8. You may charge a reasonable fee for copies of or providing
access to or distributing Project Gutenberg-tm electronic works provided
that

- You pay a royalty fee of 20% of the gross profits you derive from
    the use of Project Gutenberg-tm works calculated using the method
    you already use to calculate your applicable taxes. The fee is

owed to the owner of the Project Gutenberg-tm trademark, but he
has agreed to donate royalties under this paragraph to the
Project Gutenberg Literary Archive Foundation. Royalty payments
must be paid within 60 days following each date on which you
prepare (or are legally required to prepare) your periodic tax
returns. Royalty payments should be clearly marked as such and
sent to the Project Gutenberg Literary Archive Foundation at the
address specified in Section 4, "Information about donations to
the Project Gutenberg Literary Archive Foundation."

- You provide a full refund of any money paid by a user who notifies
  you in writing (or by e-mail) within 30 days of receipt that s/he
  does not agree to the terms of the full Project Gutenberg-tm
  License. You must require such a user to return or
  destroy all copies of the works possessed in a physical medium
  and discontinue all use of and all access to other copies of
  Project Gutenberg-tm works.

- You provide, in accordance with paragraph 1.F.3, a full refund of any
  money paid for a work or a replacement copy, if a defect in the
  electronic work is discovered and reported to you within 90 days
  of receipt of the work.

- You comply with all other terms of this agreement for free
  distribution of Project Gutenberg-tm works.

1.E.9. If you wish to charge a fee or distribute a Project Gutenberg-tm
electronic work or group of works on different terms than are set
forth in this agreement, you must obtain permission in writing from
both the Project Gutenberg Literary Archive Foundation and Michael
Hart, the owner of the Project Gutenberg-tm trademark. Contact the
Foundation as set forth in Section 3 below.

1.F.

1.F.1. Project Gutenberg volunteers and employees expend considerable
effort to identify, do copyright research on, transcribe and proofread
public domain works in creating the Project Gutenberg-tm
collection. Despite these efforts, Project Gutenberg-tm electronic
works, and the medium on which they may be stored, may contain
"Defects," such as, but not limited to, incomplete, inaccurate or
corrupt data, transcription errors, a copyright or other intellectual
property infringement, a defective or damaged disk or other medium, a
computer virus, or computer codes that damage or cannot be read by
your equipment.

1.F.2. LIMITED WARRANTY, DISCLAIMER OF DAMAGES - Except for the "Right
of Replacement or Refund" described in paragraph 1.F.3, the Project
Gutenberg Literary Archive Foundation, the owner of the Project
Gutenberg-tm trademark, and any other party distributing a Project
Gutenberg-tm electronic work under this agreement, disclaim all
liability to you for damages, costs and expenses, including legal
fees. YOU AGREE THAT YOU HAVE NO REMEDIES FOR NEGLIGENCE, STRICT
LIABILITY, BREACH OF WARRANTY OR BREACH OF CONTRACT EXCEPT THOSE
PROVIDED IN PARAGRAPH F3. YOU AGREE THAT THE FOUNDATION, THE
TRADEMARK OWNER, AND ANY DISTRIBUTOR UNDER THIS AGREEMENT WILL NOT BE
LIABLE TO YOU FOR ACTUAL, DIRECT, INDIRECT, CONSEQUENTIAL, PUNITIVE OR
INCIDENTAL DAMAGES EVEN IF YOU GIVE NOTICE OF THE POSSIBILITY OF SUCH

DAMAGE.

1.F.3. LIMITED RIGHT OF REPLACEMENT OR REFUND - If you discover a
defect in this electronic work within 90 days of receiving it, you can
receive a refund of the money (if any) you paid for it by sending a
written explanation to the person you received the work from. If you
received the work on a physical medium, you must return the medium with
your written explanation. The person or entity that provided you with
the defective work may elect to provide a replacement copy in lieu of a
refund. If you received the work electronically, the person or entity
providing it to you may choose to give you a second opportunity to
receive the work electronically in lieu of a refund. If the second copy
is also defective, you may demand a refund in writing without further
opportunities to fix the problem.

1.F.4. Except for the limited right of replacement or refund set forth
in paragraph 1.F.3, this work is provided to you 'AS-IS' WITH NO OTHER
WARRANTIES OF ANY KIND, EXPRESS OR IMPLIED, INCLUDING BUT NOT LIMITED TO
WARRANTIES OF MERCHANTIBILITY OR FITNESS FOR ANY PURPOSE.

1.F.5. Some states do not allow disclaimers of certain implied
warranties or the exclusion or limitation of certain types of damages.
If any disclaimer or limitation set forth in this agreement violates the
law of the state applicable to this agreement, the agreement shall be
interpreted to make the maximum disclaimer or limitation permitted by
the applicable state law. The invalidity or unenforceability of any
provision of this agreement shall not void the remaining provisions.

1.F.6. INDEMNITY - You agree to indemnify and hold the Foundation, the
trademark owner, any agent or employee of the Foundation, anyone
providing copies of Project Gutenberg-tm electronic works in accordance
with this agreement, and any volunteers associated with the production,
promotion and distribution of Project Gutenberg-tm electronic works,
harmless from all liability, costs and expenses, including legal fees,
that arise directly or indirectly from any of the following which you do
or cause to occur: (a) distribution of this or any Project Gutenberg-tm
work, (b) alteration, modification, or additions or deletions to any
Project Gutenberg-tm work, and (c) any Defect you cause.

Section 2. Information about the Mission of Project Gutenberg-tm

Project Gutenberg-tm is synonymous with the free distribution of
electronic works in formats readable by the widest variety of computers
including obsolete, old, middle-aged and new computers. It exists
because of the efforts of hundreds of volunteers and donations from
people in all walks of life.

Volunteers and financial support to provide volunteers with the
assistance they need, is critical to reaching Project Gutenberg-tm's
goals and ensuring that the Project Gutenberg-tm collection will
remain freely available for generations to come. In 2001, the Project
Gutenberg Literary Archive Foundation was created to provide a secure
and permanent future for Project Gutenberg-tm and future generations.
To learn more about the Project Gutenberg Literary Archive Foundation
and how your efforts and donations can help, see Sections 3 and 4
and the Foundation web page at http://www.pglaf.org.

Section 3.   Information about the Project Gutenberg Literary Archive
Foundation

The Project Gutenberg Literary Archive Foundation is a non profit
501(c)(3) educational corporation organized under the laws of the
state of Mississippi and granted tax exempt status by the Internal
Revenue Service. The Foundation's EIN or federal tax identification
number is 64-6221541. Its 501(c)(3) letter is posted at
http://pglaf.org/fundraising. Contributions to the Project Gutenberg
Literary Archive Foundation are tax deductible to the full extent
permitted by U.S. federal laws and your state's laws.

The Foundation's principal office is located at 4557 Melan Dr. S.
Fairbanks, AK, 99712., but its volunteers and employees are scattered
throughout numerous locations. Its business office is located at
809 North 1500 West, Salt Lake City, UT 84116, (801) 596-1887, email
business@pglaf.org. Email contact links and up to date contact
information can be found at the Foundation's web site and official
page at http://pglaf.org

For additional contact information:
     Dr. Gregory B. Newby
     Chief Executive and Director
     gbnewby@pglaf.org

Section 4.   Information about Donations to the Project Gutenberg
Literary Archive Foundation

Project Gutenberg-tm depends upon and cannot survive without wide
spread public support and donations to carry out its mission of
increasing the number of public domain and licensed works that can be
freely distributed in machine readable form accessible by the widest
array of equipment including outdated equipment. Many small donations
($1 to $5,000) are particularly important to maintaining tax exempt
status with the IRS.

The Foundation is committed to complying with the laws regulating
charities and charitable donations in all 50 states of the United
States. Compliance requirements are not uniform and it takes a
considerable effort, much paperwork and many fees to meet and keep up
with these requirements. We do not solicit donations in locations
where we have not received written confirmation of compliance.   To
SEND DONATIONS or determine the status of compliance for any
particular state visit http://pglaf.org

While we cannot and do not solicit contributions from states where we
have not met the solicitation requirements, we know of no prohibition
against accepting unsolicited donations from donors in such states who
approach us with offers to donate.

International donations are gratefully accepted, but we cannot make
any statements concerning tax treatment of donations received from
outside the United States. U.S. laws alone swamp our small staff.

Please check the Project Gutenberg Web pages for current donation
methods and addresses. Donations are accepted in a number of other

ways including checks, online payments and credit card donations.
To donate, please visit: http://pglaf.org/donate

Section 5. General Information About Project Gutenberg-tm electronic
works.

Professor Michael S. Hart is the originator of the Project Gutenberg-tm
concept of a library of electronic works that could be freely shared
with anyone. For thirty years, he produced and distributed Project
Gutenberg-tm eBooks with only a loose network of volunteer support.

Project Gutenberg-tm eBooks are often created from several printed
editions, all of which are confirmed as Public Domain in the U.S.
unless a copyright notice is included. Thus, we do not necessarily
keep eBooks in compliance with any particular paper edition.

Most people start at our Web site which has the main PG search facility:

    http://www.gutenberg.org

This Web site includes information about Project Gutenberg-tm,
including how to make donations to the Project Gutenberg Literary
Archive Foundation, how to help produce our new eBooks, and how to
subscribe to our email newsletter to hear about new eBooks.

www.ingramcontent.com/pod-product-compliance
Lightning Source LLC
Chambersburg PA
CBHW021052030726
47496CB00006B/1807